First World War
and Army of Occupation
War Diary
France, Belgium and Germany

62 DIVISION
Headquarters, Branches and Services
Royal Army Ordnance Corps
Deputy Assistant Director Ordnance Services
8 January 1917 - 31 August 1919

WO95/3074/2

The Naval & Military Press Ltd
www.nmarchive.com
Published in association with The National Archives

Published by

The Naval & Military Press Ltd

Unit 10 Ridgewood Industrial Park,

Uckfield, East Sussex,

TN22 5QE England

Tel: +44 (0) 1825 749494

www.naval-military-press.com

www.nmarchive.com

This diary has been reprinted in facsimile from the original. Any imperfections are inevitably reproduced and the quality may fall short of modern type and cartographic standards.

© **Crown Copyright**
Images reproduced by permission of The National Archives, London, England, 2015.

Contents

Document type	Place/Title	Date From	Date To
Heading	WO95/3074/1		
Heading	62nd Division C.R.E 1917 Jan-1919 Aug		
Heading	War Diary of Headquarters 62nd (W.R) Div R.E From 8th Jan 1917 To 31st Jan 1917 Vol I		
War Diary	Bedford	08/01/1917	08/01/1917
War Diary	Harvre	09/01/1917	10/01/1917
War Diary	Auxi-Le-Chateau	11/01/1917	11/01/1917
War Diary	Frohen-Le-Grand	12/01/1917	21/01/1917
War Diary	Beauval	22/01/1917	22/01/1917
War Diary	Bus-Les-Artois	23/01/1917	29/01/1917
War Diary	Beauval	29/01/1917	31/01/1917
Miscellaneous	Appendix I	19/01/1917	19/01/1917
Miscellaneous	G.176 Appendix 2	22/01/1917	22/01/1917
Miscellaneous	V Corps/GX 8781/18	25/01/1918	25/01/1918
Miscellaneous	Appendix 4	25/01/1917	25/01/1917
Heading	War Diary of Hd Qrs 62nd Div R.E From 1st Feb 1916 To 28th Feb 1917 Volume II		
War Diary	Bus	01/02/1917	07/02/1917
War Diary	Bus Les Artois	07/02/1917	28/02/1917
Operation(al) Order(s)	C.R.E 62nd Divn Order No.2		
Operation(al) Order(s)	C.R.E 62nd Divn Order No.3		
Miscellaneous	Table "A"		
Miscellaneous	C.R.E 62nd Division Amendment to Operation Order No.2	13/02/1917	13/02/1917
Miscellaneous	A Form Messages And Signals		
Operation(al) Order(s)	C.R.E 62nd Division Order No.4	20/02/1917	20/02/1917
Miscellaneous	Appendix 5	10/02/1917	10/02/1917
Operation(al) Order(s)	C.R.E 62nd Division Order No.2		
Operation(al) Order(s)	C.R.E 62nd Division Order No.3		
Miscellaneous	Table "A"		
Operation(al) Order(s)	C.R.E 62nd Division Order No.4	20/02/1917	20/02/1917
Miscellaneous	Amendment To C.R.E 62nd Divn Order No.4	21/02/1917	21/02/1917
Miscellaneous	Appendix 10	24/02/1917	24/02/1917
Miscellaneous	Appendix 11	25/02/1917	25/02/1917
Operation(al) Order(s)	C.R.E 62nd Division Order No.5		
Operation(al) Order(s)	C.R.E 62nd Division Order No.6	26/02/1917	26/02/1917
Miscellaneous	E/3187/7	27/02/1917	27/02/1917
Operation(al) Order(s)	C.R.E 62nd Division Order No.7	27/02/1917	27/02/1917
Heading	War Diary of Hdqrs 62nd Div R.E From 1st March & 31st March 1917 Volume III		
War Diary	Bus-Les-Artois	01/03/1917	03/03/1917
War Diary	Englebelmer	04/03/1917	17/03/1917
War Diary	R.8.b.5.3	18/03/1917	25/03/1917
War Diary	Achiet-Le-Grand	26/03/1917	31/03/1917
Operation(al) Order(s)	C.R.E 62nd Division Order No.8		
Operation(al) Order(s)	C.R.E 62nd Division Order No.9	08/03/1917	08/03/1917
Operation(al) Order(s)	C.R.E 62nd Division Order No.10	16/03/1917	16/03/1917
Operation(al) Order(s)	C.R.E 62nd Division Order No.11	17/03/1917	17/03/1917
Heading	War Diary of Hdqrs 62nd Div R.E From 1st April To 30th April 1917 Volume 4		

War Diary	Achiet-Le-Grand	01/04/1917	09/04/1917
War Diary	Achiet	10/04/1917	12/04/1917
War Diary	Achiet-Le-Grand	13/04/1917	30/04/1917
Operation(al) Order(s)	C.R.E 62nd Division Order No 14	03/04/1917	03/04/1917
Operation(al) Order(s)	C.R.E 62nd Division Order No 15	04/04/1917	04/04/1917
Operation(al) Order(s)	C.R.E 62nd Division Order No 16	07/04/1917	07/04/1917
Operation(al) Order(s)	C.R.E 62nd Division Order No 17	09/04/1917	09/04/1917
Operation(al) Order(s)	C.R.E 62nd Division Order No 18	09/04/1917	09/04/1917
Operation(al) Order(s)	62nd Division Order No 33	09/04/1917	09/04/1917
Operation(al) Order(s)	C.R.E 62nd Division Order No 19	10/04/1917	10/04/1917
Operation(al) Order(s)	C.R.E 62nd Division Order No 20	14/04/1917	14/04/1917
Operation(al) Order(s)	62nd Division Order No 35	10/04/1917	10/04/1917
Heading	R.E Order And Instruction For Attack		
Map	Ecoust-St-Mein		
Miscellaneous	Amendments to C.R.E 62nd Division Order No 20	27/04/1917	27/04/1917
Diagram etc	Diagram		
Operation(al) Order(s)	C.R.E 62nd Division Order No 21	30/04/1917	30/04/1917
Miscellaneous	Amendments to C.R.E 62nd Division Order No 20	28/04/1917	28/04/1917
Miscellaneous	G 948/5		
Miscellaneous	Report On R.E Scheme For Attack On Hindenburg Line	27/04/1917	27/04/1917
Diagram etc	Diagram		
Miscellaneous	Amendment To C.R.E Order No 20	23/04/1917	23/04/1917
Miscellaneous	Amendments to C.R.E. 32nd Division Order No. 20	27/04/1917	27/04/1917
Diagram etc	Diagram		
Miscellaneous	Amendment To C.R.E Division Order No 20	28/04/1917	28/04/1917
Operation(al) Order(s)	C.R.E 62nd Division Order No 21	30/04/1917	30/04/1917
Heading	War Diary of H.Q 62nd Div R.E From May 1st 1917 To May 1917 Vol V		
War Diary	Achiet-Le-Grand	01/05/1917	01/05/1917
War Diary	Ervillers	02/05/1917	04/05/1917
War Diary	Achiet-Le-Grand	05/05/1917	31/05/1917
Miscellaneous	RE/0/5	02/05/1917	02/05/1917
Operation(al) Order(s)	C.R.E 62nd Division Order No 22	05/05/1917	05/05/1917
Map	Map		
Miscellaneous	RE/650/1039	09/05/1917	09/05/1917
Miscellaneous	RE/650/1039/6	10/05/1917	10/05/1917
Heading	War Diary of H.Q 62nd Div R.E From 1st June 1917 To 30th June 1917 Volume VI		
War Diary	Achiet-Le-Grand	01/06/1917	27/06/1917
War Diary	Favrieul	28/06/1917	30/06/1917
Operation(al) Order(s)	C.R.E 62nd Division Order No.23	20/06/1917	20/06/1917
Operation(al) Order(s)	C.R.E 62nd Division Order No.24	22/06/1917	22/06/1917
Heading	War Diary of H.Q 62nd Division R.E From 1st July 1917 To 31st July 1917 Vol VII		
War Diary	Favreuil	01/07/1917	31/07/1917
Heading	War Diary of H.Q 62nd Div. Eng From 1st Aug To 31st Aug 1917 Volume VIII		
War Diary	Favreuil	01/08/1917	31/08/1917
Operation(al) Order(s)	C.R.E 62nd Division Order No 29	03/08/1917	03/08/1917
Operation(al) Order(s)	C.R.E 62nd Division Order No 30	10/08/1917	10/08/1917
Operation(al) Order(s)	C.R.E 62nd Division Order No 31	16/08/1917	16/08/1917
Operation(al) Order(s)	C.R.E 62nd Division Order No 31	24/08/1917	24/08/1917
Heading	War Diary of HQ 62nd Div Engineers From Sept 1st 1917 To Sept 30th 1917 Volume VIII		
War Diary	Favreuil	01/09/1917	30/09/1917

Operation(al) Order(s)	C.R.E 62nd Division Order No.33	02/09/1917	02/09/1917
Operation(al) Order(s)	C.R.E 62nd Division Order No.34	09/09/1917	09/09/1917
Operation(al) Order(s)	C.R.E 62nd Division Order No.35	17/09/1917	17/09/1917
Operation(al) Order(s)	C.R.E 62nd Division Order No.36	23/09/1919	23/09/1919
Operation(al) Order(s)	C.R.E 62nd Division Order No.37	27/09/1917	27/09/1917
Heading	War Diary of Hdqrs 62nd Div Engineers From 1st Oct 1917 To 31st Oct 1917 Volume IX		
War Diary	Favreuil	01/10/1917	12/10/1917
War Diary	Haplincourt	13/10/1917	31/10/1917
Operation(al) Order(s)	C.R.E 62nd Division Order No.38	03/10/1917	03/10/1917
Operation(al) Order(s)	C.R.E 62nd Division Order No.39	08/10/1917	08/10/1917
Miscellaneous	Move Table To Go With C.R.E Order No 39		
Miscellaneous	C.R.E 62nd Division Provisional Order	27/10/1917	27/10/1917
Heading	War Diary of H.Q 62nd Div. Eng. 1st Nov To 30th Nov 1917 Vol XI		
War Diary	Haplincourt	01/11/1917	20/11/1917
War Diary	Neuville	20/11/1917	29/11/1917
War Diary	Havrincourt	29/11/1917	30/11/1917
Miscellaneous	Appendix 49	14/11/1917	14/11/1917
Miscellaneous	Table Of Labour And Transport To Accompany IV Corps No 15/5 G	13/11/1917	13/11/1917
Operation(al) Order(s)	C.R.E 62nd Division Order No 40	14/11/1917	14/11/1917
Operation(al) Order(s)	C.R.E 62nd Division Order No 41		
Operation(al) Order(s)	C.R.E 62nd Division Order No 42	19/11/1917	19/11/1917
Miscellaneous	RE/2241/2	20/11/1917	20/11/1917
Operation(al) Order(s)	C.R.E 62nd Division Order No 43	21/11/1917	21/11/1917
Miscellaneous	A Form Messages And Signals		
Operation(al) Order(s)	C.R.E 62nd Division Order No 44	22/11/1917	22/11/1917
Operation(al) Order(s)	C.R.E 62nd Division Order No 45	22/11/1917	22/11/1917
Miscellaneous	Amendment To C.R.E 62nd Division Order 45	23/11/1917	23/11/1917
Operation(al) Order(s)	C.R.E 62nd Division Order No. 46	23/11/1917	23/11/1917
Operation(al) Order(s)	C.R.E 62nd Division Order No. 47	25/11/1917	25/11/1917
Operation(al) Order(s)	C.R.E 62nd Division Order No. 48	28/11/1917	28/11/1917
Heading	War Diary December 1917 Headquarters 62nd (W.R) Divisional R.E		
War Diary	Havrincourt	01/12/1917	07/12/1917
War Diary	Mingoval	07/12/1917	11/12/1917
War Diary	Le Beovriere	12/12/1917	18/12/1917
War Diary	Mingoval	19/12/1917	31/12/1917
Operation(al) Order(s)	C.R.E 62nd Division Order No.49		
Miscellaneous	Table 'A' To Accompany C.R.E 62nd Division Order No.49		
Miscellaneous	March Table "B" of Transport To Accompany C.R.E Order No.49		
Operation(al) Order(s)	C.R.E 62nd Division Order No 30	04/12/1917	04/12/1917
Miscellaneous	March Table To Accompany C.R.E 62nd Division Order 50		
Heading	Headquarters 62nd Divnl Engineers		
War Diary	Mingoval	01/01/1918	31/01/1918
War Diary	Poptsmouth Camp	22/01/1918	31/01/1918
Heading	H.Q 62nd Divnl R.E War Diary February 1918 Vol XIV		
War Diary	Portsmouth Camp	01/02/1918	28/02/1918
Heading	War Diary C.R.E 62nd Division March 1918		
Heading	Headquarters of 62nd Divisional R.E From March 1st 1918 To March 31st 1918 Original Vol XV		

Type	Description	Start	End
War Diary	Roclincourt	01/03/1918	31/03/1918
Heading	62nd Divisional Engineers War Diary C.R.E 62nd Division April 1918		
Heading	War Diary of Headquarters 62nd (W.R) Divnl R.E From April 1st 1918 To April 30th 1918 Volume 16		
War Diary	Souastre to Pas	01/04/1918	01/04/1918
War Diary	Pas	01/04/1918	07/04/1918
War Diary	Pas-Henu	07/04/1918	07/04/1918
War Diary	Hanu	08/04/1918	21/04/1918
Operation(al) Order(s)	62nd Divnl R.E Order No 60	06/04/1918	06/04/1918
Operation(al) Order(s)	62nd Divisional R.E Operation Order No.61	21/04/1918	21/04/1918
Heading	War Diary of H.Q 62nd Divisional R.E From May 1st 1918 To May 31st 1918 Volume XVII		
War Diary	Pas	01/05/1918	17/05/1918
War Diary	Pas-Henu	17/05/1918	17/05/1918
War Diary	Henu	18/05/1918	31/05/1918
Miscellaneous	Amendment To 62nd Divnl R.E Order No 62	14/05/1918	14/05/1918
Operation(al) Order(s)	62nd Divisional R.E Order No 62	14/05/1918	14/05/1918
Miscellaneous	Location List		
Heading	War Diary of Headquarters 62nd Divnl R.E From June 1st 1918 To June 30th 1918 Vol XVIII		
War Diary	Henu	01/06/1918	25/06/1918
War Diary	Henu-Pas	25/06/1918	25/06/1918
War Diary	Pas	26/06/1918	30/06/1918
Operation(al) Order(s)	62nd Divisional Engineers Order No 64	23/06/1918	23/06/1918
Miscellaneous	Locations of 62nd Divisional R.E and Pioneers on Completion of Relief		
Miscellaneous			
Heading	Divl Engineers 62nd Division C.R.E 62nd Division July 1918		
War Diary	Pas	01/07/1918	16/07/1918
War Diary	Tours	17/07/1918	18/07/1918
War Diary	St Imoges	19/07/1918	20/07/1918
War Diary	Chamury	21/07/1918	25/07/1918
War Diary	Nanteuil	26/07/1918	29/07/1918
War Diary	Hautvillers	30/07/1918	31/07/1918
Heading	War Diary of H.Q 62nd Divisional R.E From August 1st 1918 To August 31st 1918 Volume XX		
War Diary	Bisseuil	04/08/1918	04/08/1918
War Diary	Pas	15/08/1918	15/08/1918
War Diary	Authie	19/08/1918	19/08/1918
War Diary	Grenas	20/08/1918	20/08/1918
War Diary	Bavincourt	21/08/1918	21/08/1918
War Diary	Doullens	22/08/1918	22/08/1918
War Diary	Pas	23/08/1918	23/08/1918
War Diary	La Brazeque	24/08/1918	24/08/1918
War Diary	Les Quesnoy Farm	25/08/1918	31/08/1918
Heading	War Diary of Headquarters 62nd Divisional R.E From Sept 1st 1918 Sept 30th 1918 Vol XXI		
War Diary	Gomiecourt	01/09/1918	10/09/1918
War Diary	Maricourt Wood	11/09/1918	26/09/1918
War Diary	J.35.c.0.0	27/09/1918	27/09/1918
War Diary	Hermies	28/09/1918	28/09/1918
War Diary	Flesquieres	23/09/1918	30/09/1918
Heading	War Diary of Headquarters 62nd Divisional R.E From October 1st 1918 To October 31st 1918 Vol XXII		

War Diary	Flesquieres	01/10/1918	09/10/1918
War Diary	Mesnieres	10/10/1918	11/10/1918
War Diary	Estourmel	12/10/1918	17/10/1918
War Diary	Bevillers	18/10/1918	30/10/1918
War Diary	Solesmes	31/10/1918	31/10/1918
Heading	War Diary of Headquarters 62nd Divisional R.E From November 1st 1918 To November 30th 1918 Vol XXIII		
War Diary	Solesmes	01/11/1918	01/11/1918
War Diary	Escarmain	03/11/1918	04/11/1918
War Diary	Ruesnes	05/11/1918	05/11/1918
War Diary	Frasnoy	06/11/1918	07/11/1918
War Diary	Le Trechon	08/11/1918	09/11/1918
War Diary	Neuf Mesnil	10/11/1918	10/11/1918
War Diary	Maubeuge	11/11/1918	15/11/1918
War Diary	Colleret	16/11/1918	17/11/1918
War Diary	Ham Sur Heure	18/11/1918	20/11/1918
War Diary	Acoz	21/11/1918	21/11/1918
War Diary	Mettit	22/10/1918	23/10/1918
War Diary	Denee	24/11/1918	24/11/1918
War Diary	Yvoir	25/11/1918	25/11/1918
War Diary	Ciney	26/11/1918	26/11/1918
War Diary	Lignion	27/11/1918	30/11/1918
Heading	Report On Work Of 62nd Div R.E From March To Nov 1918		
Miscellaneous	Report By C.R.E 62nd Division Of Engineer Work Of 62nd Divl R.E During Operation Period March 1918 To Nov 11th 1918		
Miscellaneous	Public Record Office		
Heading	War Diary of Headquarters 62nd Divisional R.E From December 1st 1918 To December 31st 1918 Vol XXIV		
War Diary	Legnion	01/12/1918	09/12/1918
War Diary	Barvaux	10/12/1918	31/12/1918
Heading	War Diary of Hdqrs 62nd Divisional R.E From January 1st 1919 To January 31st 1919 Vol XXV		
War Diary	Schleiden	01/01/1919	31/01/1919
Heading	War Diary of H.Q 62nd Divisional R.E From February 1st 1919 To February 28th 1919 Vol XXVI		
War Diary	Schleiden	01/02/1919	28/02/1919
Heading	War Diary of H.Q Highland Divisional R.E From March 1st 1919 To March 31st 1919 Vol XXVII		
War Diary	Schleiden	01/03/1919	12/03/1919
War Diary	Duren	13/03/1919	31/03/1919
Heading	War Diary H.Q Highland Div R.E Vol XXIX May 1919		
War Diary	Keuzau	01/05/1919	24/05/1919
Heading	War Diary of C.R.E Highland Division From 1.5.19 To 30.5.19 (Volume XXX)		
War Diary	Kreuzau	01/06/1919	30/06/1919
Heading	War Diary of Headquarters R.E From July 1st To July 31st Vol XXXI		
War Diary	Kreuzau	01/07/1919	31/07/1919
Heading	War Diary of Highland Division Engineers From Aug 1st 1919 To Aug 31st 1919		
War Diary	Kreuzau	01/08/1919	09/08/1919
War Diary	Duren	09/08/1919	09/08/1919
War Diary	Charleroi	10/08/1919	10/08/1919

War Diary	Tournai	10/08/1919	10/08/1919
War Diary	Lille	10/08/1919	10/08/1919
War Diary	Bethune	10/08/1919	10/08/1919
War Diary	Calais	11/08/1919	11/08/1919
War Diary	Folkestone	11/08/1919	11/08/1919
War Diary	Clipstone	12/08/1919	31/08/1919

w095/3074/1/5900m

62ND DIVISION

C. R. E.
~~JAN 1917 DEC 1918~~

1917 JAN — 1919 AUG

Confidential   _Original_

WAR DIARY

of

Headquarters 62nd (W.R.) Div. R.E.

from

8th Jan 1917 to 31st Jan 1917.

Army Form C. 2118.

WAR DIARY
or
INTELLIGENCE SUMMARY.
(Erase heading not required.)

HdQrs 82nd Inf Bde

Instructions regarding War Diaries and Intelligence Summaries are contained in F. S. Regs., Part II. and the Staff Manual respectively. Title pages will be prepared in manuscript.

Place	Date	Hour	Summary of Events and Information	Remarks and references to Appendices
BEDFORD	8/1/15		Entrained for Ovenees at 8.0 a.m.	
			Arrived SOUTHAMPTON 1-35 p.m.	
			Embarked and sailed for HAVRE 7 p.m. MR	
HAVRE	9/1/15		Docked at HAVRE 2.30 p.m. after very rough crossing. No casualties to men & animals. Reached HAVRE REST CAMP (Docks Rest Camp) at 7 p.m. MR	
HAVRE	10/1/15		Entrained for up-country at 8.0 a.m. Train stopped at 10·35 a.m.	
AUXI-LE-CHATEAU	11/1/15		Arrived at AUXI-LE-CHATEAU at 1·0 p.m. and detrained. Marched to FROHEN-LE-GRAND (5 miles) and went into billets.	
FROHEN LE GRAND	12/1/15		Nil MR	
"	13/1/15		Information received that the 8rd Division will be attacked 1·19th. 32nd Division for instruction MR	
	14/1/15		Nil MR	
	15/1/15		Nil MR	
	16/1/15		Nil MR	

WAR DIARY
INTELLIGENCE SUMMARY

Army Form C. 2118.

HdQrs 62nd Div R.E.

Place	Date	Hour	Summary of Events and Information	Remarks and references to Appendices
FRONCHEN-COURT	17/1/17		Instructions received to detail four officers & 16 N.C.Os to be attached to 19th Division for a period of 11 days instruction commencing 20.1.17	
-BEAND	18/1/17		Nil	
	19/1/17		Orders received to move to BEAUVAL Area on 22nd Jan 1917 Div Op Order	
	20/1/17		Orders received cancelling move of 31. W.R Field Coy to BEAUVAL Area on 22/1/17. The unit to proceed instead to AUTHUILE on 21/1/17 to come out and work under the I Corps RE	
	21/1/17		Orders received to move from BEAUVAL to BUS-LES-ARTOIS on 23rd Jan 1917. Div Operation Order No 2.	
BEAUVAL	22/1/17		HdQrs 62nd Div R.E moved to BEAUVAL by road route. Instructions received that 1/3 W.R Field Coy is to proceed to MAILLY WOOD EAST on 23/1/17 & not to BUS-LES-ARTOIS and temporary attached	
BUS-LES-ARTOIS	23/1/17		HdQrs 62nd Div R.E moved by road route to BUS-LES-ARTOIS. Instructions received that Field Coys are to be allotted for work as follows:— 1 Field Coy to 32nd Division (1/3 W.R. Riding)	

Army Form C. 2118.

WAR DIARY
or
INTELLIGENCE SUMMARY.
(Erase heading not required.)

HdQrs 141st D of Rs

Place	Date	Hour	Summary of Events and Information	Remarks and references to Appendices
Bus-les-Artois	23/1/17 contd		1 Field Coy to 19th Division (2/3 W.R.Field Coy) 1 Field Coy to V Corps (3/1 W.R.Field Coy)	Appendix 2
	24/1/17		Nil	
	25/1/17		Instructions received that 3/1 W.R.Field Coy will be employed for work under 32nd Division & not attached to work for V Corps. Orders issued to 3/1 W.R.Field Coy to move to Bus-les-Artois on 27/1/17.	Appendix 3
	26/1/17		Reports on arrangements made re working of Field Coys and to 2nd Div. Instructions received that 3/1 W.R.Field Coy are at present at Mailly Wood East on 27/1/17 and not to Bus-les-Artois on temporary contract. 1 Section however to stay at Bus-les-Artois for work in 62nd Division area.	Appendix 4
	27/1/17		Nil	
	28/1/17		Nil	
	29/1/17		Information received that a further section of 3/1 W.R.Field Coy is to be withdrawn from 32nd Division at Varennes for work in 62nd Divisional School. Section to move 30/1/17. Instructions issued that the following items are to be placed under	

Army Form C. 2118.

WAR DIARY
or
INTELLIGENCE SUMMARY.
(Erase heading not required.)

H.Qrs 62nd Div R.E.

Instructions regarding War Diaries and Intelligence
Summaries are contained in F. S. Regs., Part II.
and the Staff Manual respectively. Title pages
will be prepared in manuscript.

Place	Date	Hour	Summary of Events and Information	Remarks and references to Appendices
BEAUVAL	29/1/17		C.R.E. Rode Div as regards roads and material required for im- provements of Roads.	
"			BUS LOUVENCOURT VAUCHELLES THIEVRES & FAMECHON	
"	30/1/17		nil	
"	31/1/17		nil	

R. Williams
Lieut.-Colonel, R.E.
C.R.E. 62nd (W.R.) DIVISION

G. 1/38   APPENDIX B. /.

From Headquarters, 62nd Division.

C. R. E.
   62nd Division.

---

1.   The 3/1st Field Company R.E. will march tp AUTHIE on the 21st January via DOULLENS and ORVILLE.

2.   A Billetting party of 1 officer and 2 N.C.Os will proceed to AUTHIE on the 20th inst. The officer will report to 19th Division H.Q. at COUIN for instruction regarding billets.

3.   This Field Company will be employed in the construction of a system of trenches consisting of three lines in the vicinity of AUTHIE.

4.   The O.C. Field Company will report at V Corps Headquarters at ACHEUX on the 21st instant for instructions. Work will commence on January 22nd.

3.   ACKNOWLEDGE.

                                          W. G. Charles Major, for
                                                   Lieut.Colonel,
                           General Staff, 62nd Division.

19.1.17.

Copies to 62nd Divn "Q")
         187th Inf.Bde) For information.
         V Corps   )

176.
G. XXX.   Appendix. 2.

C. R. E.   From 62nd Div. G.

62nd Division.

On arrival of the 62nd Division in V Corps area the Field Companies R.E. will be allotted for work as follows

    1 Field Company R.E.   - to 32nd Division.

    1   do   - to 19th Division.

    1   do   - to C.E. V Corps, for work on the YELLOW LINE.

Please arrange direct with the C. R. E's 32nd and 19th Divns and C.E. V Corps, and report arrangements made to this office.

                                          A. HORE-RUTHVEN Lt.Col,
                              General Staff, 62nd Division.

22. 1. 17.

G.279. V Corps /GX 8781/18 APPENDIX 3.
24th Jan 1917.

From V Corps

32nd Division.
62nd Division.
C.E. (for information).

The Field Coy of 62nd Division, on completion of the work on the Training Ground at AUTHIE, will be attached for work to the 32nd Division, and not work under C.E., V Corps on YELLOW LINE Necessary arrangements to be made between Divisions concerned.

(Sd) --- Capt,
for B.G., G.S. V Corps.

C.R.E. 62nd Division.
"Q" 62nd Division.)
187th Inf Bde.) For Information.
32nd Division.)

Please arrange direct with the C.R.E. 32nd Division regarding work to be done and billets to which the 3/1st Field Coy will move. It will probably be possible to billet the 3/1st Field Coy in the 32nd Divisional area, but failing this there is room for it near BUS (in huts).

The 3/1st Field Coy should move from AUTHIE on the 26th or 27th January.

Please inform this office of arrangements you decide.

W. G. Charles Major,
General Staff, 62nd Division.

25.1.17.

62nd Division "G".

Appendix 4.
From CRE 62nd Div.

In reply to your G. 176 - 22. 1. 17, I have to report that the Field Companies of this Division are now attached for work to the 19th and 32nd Divisions as under :-

2/3 W.R. FIELD COY (MAJOR WALTHEW) - In hut billets at COIGNEUX. Attached for instruction to the 82nd and 94th Field Coys of the 19th Division, whose Headquarters are at BAYENCOURT and COURCELLES respectively. It has been arranged for 2 Sections of 2/3 (W.R) Field Coy to work with 82nd Coy and 2 Sections with 94th Coy in front line.

1/3 W.R. FIELD COY (MAJOR COLLEY).- In hut billets at MAILLY. Undergoing instruction with the 206th and 219th Field Coys of the 32nd Division, whose Headquarters are at MAILLY and on the BEAUSART-MAILLY road respectively. 2 Sections of the 1/3 W.R. Field Coy are attached to 206th Coy and 2 Sections to 219th Coy for work in the line.

All section officers and a proportion of senior N.C.Os were conducted round the most advanced system of trenches last night (24th/25th). 2 Sections go into the line this afternoon with each of their affiliated companies for work until midnight. They are to be employed at first on U framing of 2 main communication trenches.

3/1 W.R. FIELD COY (MAJOR SEAMAN) - As reported to-day this Unit will leave AUTHIE early on the 27th inst and thence go into Billets at BUS.

3 sections will be employed on back area work in the vicinity of BERTRANCOURT under the C.R.E. 32nd Division from the 29th inst inclusive, the reamining section being retained for work under C.R.E. 62nd Division.

It is hoped to be arrange later for sections of this Unit to be put under instruction in front line by changing them with those of the 1/3rd Field Coy.

R.A. GILLAM Lieut.Colonel R.E
C. R. E. 62nd Division.

25.1.17.

Original

Vol 2

Confidential

WAR DIARY
of
Hd Qrs 42nd Div. R.E.

From 1st Feb 1916 to 28th Feb 1917

Volume II

Army Form C. 2118.

WAR DIARY
or
INTELLIGENCE SUMMARY.

(Erase heading not required.)

Instructions regarding War Diaries and Intelligence Summaries are contained in F.S. Regs., Part II. and the Staff Manual respectively. Title pages will be prepared in manuscript.

Place	Date	Hour	Summary of Events and Information	Remarks and references to Appendices
BUS.	1/2/17		Designation of the Field Coys of the 62nd (W.R) Div Ret changed as follows:- Hdqrs 62nd Div	
			Old Designation — New Designation	
			1/3 W.R. Field Coy — 457th (W.R) Field Coy	
			2/3 W.R. Field Coy — 460th (W.R) Field Coy	
			3/1 W.R. Field Coy — 461st (W.R) Field Coy	
			Authority W.O.L. of Engineers /7611 (A.G.7) dated 5/1/17	
	2/2/17		2nd Lt E.J. TRUBSHAW 460th (W.R) Field Coy R.E. killed in action. WH	
	3/2/17		Nil.	
	4/2/17		Nil.	
	5/2/17		Information received that 62nd Div is to take over the line from 32nd Div on or about 12/2/17.	
	6/2/17		C.R.E. visited front line trench system of 32nd Division with G.S.O.1 62nd Div & C.R.E. 32nd Div	
	7/2/17		1 Officer (2nd Lt HAMMOND 457th (W.R) Field Co) and 8 Sappers detailed to assist the G.O.C R.A 62nd Div in estimating materials for and enhancing all R.E. Work required by 62nd Div Artillery in the	

WAR DIARY or INTELLIGENCE SUMMARY

Army Form C. 2118.

Place	Date	Hour	Summary of Events and Information	Remarks and references to Appendices
Bus le ARTOIS	7.2.17	contd.	the front line, 28 men to be Detailed by R.A. to be under orders of the R.E. Officer and at his disposal for construction work.	Hd Qrs 6th Div R.E.
	8.2.17		Instructions received from C.R.E. II Corps that owing to transport difficulties all stocks of R.E. material are very much depleted & must be economised accordingly.	
			Div. Operation Order No 3 received. The 6th Division will relieve 32nd Division commencing 12th Feb 1917. C.R.E. 6th Div to arrange relief with C.R.E. 32nd Div. 20 officers & reliefs of Field Companies. Orders received for Major E.J. Matthew & Major H.W. Seaman to attend a course in Field Engineering at LE PARCQ on 13th Feb. Protest forwarded.	
	9.12.17		Instructions rcd. that a camp for Div. Hd Qrs 6th Div. must be constructed at FOREVILLE.	
	10.12.17		C.R.E. visited front line, trench system with C.R.E. 32nd Div. Orders for relief of Field Coys 32nd Div. by Field Coys 32nd Div. issued.	Appendix 5
	11.12.9		Div Operation Order No 5 rcd. G.O.C. 6th Div. will assume command of the line from R.1.B.3.C. to K.29.C.61 at 9 am on 15th Feb.	

WAR DIARY or INTELLIGENCE SUMMARY

Army Form C. 2118.

HdQrs 63rd Divl R.E.

Place	Date	Hour	Summary of Events and Information	Remarks and references to Appendices
Bus la Artes	11.2.17		contd. Information received that Caplain Stephenson may be attached instead of Major for service at 1st Farce on 13th inst. Capt H.W. WEBSTER and Capt K.N.C. DERRIS attached accordingly. C.R.E. 63rd Divl Operation Order No 2 issued relating to move of Field Coys on relief of Field Coys of 32nd Divl.	
				Appendix 6
			C.R.E. 63rd Divl Operation Order No 3 issued directing routes to be taken over by Field Coys & work to be carried out in the various offln. taking over the No 4 Section of 461st D.R. Field Co. moved to Forceville for work on the No 4 Section of Divl Hdqrs camps.	Appendix 7
	12.2.17		460th (W.R) Field Coy moved from Couzeaux (M.td Divl Area) to Liver Camp BEAUSART. (2nd Divl Area.)	
	13.2.17		No 2 Section 461st D.R. Field Coy moved from Bus to MAILY WOOD EAST. No 3 Section 461st D.R. Field Coy moved from VAUCHELLES to MAILY WOOD EAST. C.R.E. Operation Order No 2 amended. moving of 460th & 461st D.R. Field Coys & postponed to 17th Feb.	
	14.2.17		C.R.E. attended a conference at I Corps. Hd Qrs	

WAR DIARY
or
INTELLIGENCE SUMMARY.
(Erase heading not required.)

Army Form C. 2118.

Place	Date	Hour	Summary of Events and Information	Remarks and references to Appendices
Bus les Artois	14.2.17	contd.	CRE 62nd Div took over BEAUSART and AVELUY VILLERS Dumps from HdQts 62nd Div R.E.	
	15.2.17		CRE 32nd Div.	
			CRE 63rd Div. took over duties as CRE of the sector of line extending from R.2.a.1.9 to K.29.c.6.1. from CRE 3rd Div. at 9am this date.	
			CRE visited front line trenches with OC's 461st & 460th Field Coy.	
	16.2.17		Adjutant visited CE IE Lab. re the selection of site for a new Div R.E. Dump. Site suggested at Q.13 B.1.9. approved.	
			Orders issued to 460 B(2h) Field Coy to move to MAILLY CHATEAU 17/2/17.	
	17.2.17		460th (2L) Field Coy moved to MAILLY CHATEAU	
	18.2.17		Nil.	
	19.2.17		CRE visited front line to reconnoitre for advance Brigade Battle H.d Qts.	
	20.2.17		Div Operation Order No 10 received. 7th Division to take over section of line from L.31.c.2.6. to K.29.c.3.1. Arrangement for relief of Field Coys to be made by C.R.E's concerned.	
			CRE Order No 4 issued re relief by 7th Div.	Appendix 8
	21.2.17		Amendment to CRE Order No 4 issued	Appendix 9

WAR DIARY or INTELLIGENCE SUMMARY.

Army Form C. 2118.

Place	Date	Hour	Summary of Events and Information	Remarks and references to Appendices
Bus les Artois	22.2.17		Nil	HdQrs. 62nd Div 7th Corps
	23.2.17		Handed over R.E. work in sector L31.c.2.5 - K29.c.3.1 to C.R.E. 7th Division. Conference of O.C. Units. New Divisional R.E. Dump opened at MAILLY Q.13.b. C.R.E. visited front line.	
	24.2.17		Major WALTHEW (OC 1/10 Field Coy) and SEAMAN 1/1st Field Coy left to attend R.E. School of Instruction at 5th ARMY C.R.E. Information received that every officer to have ordered along whole of Corps front. (see Div Operation Order No 12.) Orders issued to O.C. 457th Field Coy to Push his work in readiness to move VILLENAUXE at very short notice. Orders received from C.R.E. V Corps to commence work on relaying of BEAUCOURT - PUISIEUX road. 2 Sections 461st Field Coy detailed for this work with working party of 1 Battn Infantry.	
	26.2.17		Orders received from 62nd Div to detail a section R.E. to proceed to WOOD T WERK L32.D.7.7. Orders moved to O.C. 457th Field Coy to detail a section for this duty. Orders received from V Corps through 62nd Div for a reconnaissance to be made of Rly siding in BEAUREGARD DOVE COTE 261st Field Coy detailed to carry out reconnaissance carried out.	Volume 11

Army Form C. 2118.

WAR DIARY
or
INTELLIGENCE SUMMARY.
(Erase heading not required.)

Instructions regarding War Diaries and Intelligence Summaries are contained in F. S. Regs., Part II. and the Staff Manual respectively. Title pages will be prepared in manuscript.

Place	Date	Hour	Summary of Events and Information	Remarks and references to Appendices
			HdQrs 2nd Division R.E.	
Bus le Artois	24/7/16		6 . " Dn Operation Order 16 received. Shew Divisional front now runs L30910 to R28. Central Thou. from BEAUREGARD DOVECOTE – WURST WERK – LZAC tembel C.R.E. Order No 5. issued stating one section 460" (483)Field Coy to move forward in to line under the orders of the E.O.C. 185th Infantry Brigade. C.R.E. went to front line to inspect work in trenches on BEAUCOURT – PUISIEUX road. Order received from C.R.E. later for reconnaissance of the road of road from HAMEL Q23d & BAILLESCOURT FARM R3a. O.C. 463rd Field Coy instructed to have this reconnaissance carried out. 2nd Lt. J. S. McEWEN wounded in leg whilst carrying out reconnaissance of BEAUREGARD WATER SUPPLY. Going to inspection of forming found of BEAUCOURT – PUISIEUX road – distribution of cabins on road to attend by C.R.E.'s Order. No. 6. One section of mill Field Coy being lifted off for work on this road.	Appendix 12 Appendix 13

T2134. Wt. W708—776. 50000. 4/15. Sir J. C. & S.

Army Form C. 2118.

WAR DIARY
or
INTELLIGENCE SUMMARY.
(Erase heading not required.)

Place	Date	Hour	Summary of Events and Information	Remarks and references to Appendices
Bus-Les-ARTOIS	27/2/17		Holds 2nd Div Ref. Instructions issued from C.E. C.O. to report on Forward Roads and tools available for work thereon.	Appendix 14.
	28/2/17		C.R.E. Order No 7 issued detailing work on roads. C.E.T. and Adjutant met representatives of 56th & 2nd Div by 31 Manchesters & 5 Yorks Pioneer Battns and conferred orders issued 27/2/17. Allocated to 2nd Div for repair maintained via HAMEL - BEAUCOURT - MIRAUMONT Road. STATION ROAD and BEAUCOURT - PUISIEUX Road. Instructions received that all traffic on above roads (except horse wagons with R.E. material) will be closed from 6 am to noon daily. Orders issued to units to work from 6am to 3pm accordingly. Steam actual work to be carried out on all roads daily.	Appendix 15.

R.P.Wilson
Lieut-Colonel R.E.
C.R.E. 63rd (R.N.) DIVISION

Secret. Appendix I

C.R.E. 62nd Divn   Order No 2.   Copy No 2.

~~O.C. 457th Field Coy.~~
O.C. 460th Field Coy.
~~O.C. 461st Field Coy.~~
62nd Division G (for information)

1. The 62nd Division will relieve the 32nd Division in the right sector of V Corps front commencing on February 12th 1917.

2. With reference to the preliminary move orders issued on the 10th inst in connection with the above relief the moves of Field Coys of the 62nd Division will be carried out in accordance with the following tabular detail :-

No	Date	Unit	From	To	Remarks
1.	Feb 12th	460th (W.R) Fd Coy.R.E.	COIGNEUX	LIVRE CAMP MAILLY.	Take over Billets from the 218th Field Co R.E.
2.	Feb 12th	No 4 Section 461st (W.R) Fd Coy.R.E.	MAILLY	FORCEVILLE.	For work on building Divisional H.Q.
3.	Feb 13th	No 3 Section 461st (W.R) Fd Coy R.E.	VAUCHELLES		To rejoin H.Q. of Company.
4.	Feb 13th	No 2 Section 461st (W.R) Fd Coy R.E.	BUS	MAILLY	To rejoin H.Q. of Company.
5.	Feb 15th	460th (W.R) Fd Coy R.E.	LIVRE CAMP MAILLY	MAILLY CHATEAU.	Take over Billets from 219th Field Co R.E.
6.	Feb 15th	461st (W.R) Fd Coy R.E.	MAILLY WOOD EAST	LIVRE CAMP MAILLY.	

Billeting parties will be sent on in advance to take over Billets in the case of 1, 2, 5 & 6 above.

3. 457th (W.R) Field Coy will remain in the camp at present occupied by it in MAILLY WOOD EAST.

4. Headquarters, 62nd Divisional R.E. will remain at BUS.

Copy No 1 - 457th Field Co.
       2 - 460th Field Co
       3 - 461st Field Co
       4 - Retained
       5 - 62nd Division "G"

R.L.Gillam
Lieut.Colonel R.E.
C.R.E. 62nd Division.

(Appendix I. pom)

C. R. E. 62nd Division   Order No 3.   Copy No ..2..

~~O.C. 457th Field Co R.E.~~
O.C. 460th Field Co R.E.
~~O.C. 461st Field Co R.E.~~
"G" ~~62nd Division~~ — For information.

The following are the arrangements for the employment of the Field Companies R.E. in the front line and back areas when the Division goes into the line on the 12th February 1917.

1. DISTRIBUTION. 460th (W.R) Field Coy and 457th (W.R) Field Coy will be allotted for the purpose of front line work to the sectors held by their respective affiliated Brigades, viz - 460th Field Coy with the 185th Brigade in the right sector and 457th Field Coy with the 186th Brigade in the left sector.

Each of these two Field Companies will, in accordance with the general principles to be observed in the case of Field Coys allotted to definite sections of Brigades in the line, have 3 sections working every night on forward work in the front line and 1 section working by day in the back area or employed on work the conditions of which will admit of its being carried out in the daytime.

The 461st (W.R) Field Coy, whose affiliated Brigade will not be in the line, will be disposed for work as follows - 2 sections on front line work on left sector to be specially detailed, two sections on back area work.

2. The attached tabular statement (Table A) gives the distribution of the Field Companies for work when the Division goes into the line, and supersedes previous preliminary orders which have been issued on the subject.

Copy No 1 - 457th Field Co
      2 - 460th Field Co
      3 - 461st Field Co
      4 - "G" 62nd Division
      5 - Retained.

                                        Lieut.Colonel R.E.
                                        C. R. E. 62nd Division.

-1-

(Appendix to (cm))

TABLE "A".

UNIT	Nature of Work	Working Parties & Hutting Parties required.	Remarks.
460th (W.R) Field Co R.E.	FRONT LINE. 3 Sections on Communication trenches - TANK ALLEY - STATION ALLEY - WALKER AVENUE - and probably an intermediate communication trench. Also a lateral trench to connect head of STATION ALLEY with either WAGGON ROAD or WALKER AVENUE. 1 Section on Brigade Battle Headquarters, dugouts, etc.	Working parties as required will be demanded in due course.	By night. Detailed distribution to be arranged after consultation with Brigadiers.
457th (W.R) Field Co R.E.	FRONT LINE. 3 Sections on Communication trenches - CRATER LANE, CAKE TRENCH and extension of latter back towards WATLING STREET. 1 Section on Divisional Battle H.Q., dugouts, etc	As above. do do	As above do do
461st (W.R) Field Co R.E.	FRONT LINE. 1 Section on SIXTH AVENUE. 1 Section on TOURNAI TRENCH. BACK AREA. 1 Section (No 4) to FORCEVILLE (on 12 Feby) for building Divnl Headquarters. 1 Section to be employed on Building Brigade H.Qrs at MAILLY & other work to be detailed.	As above. As above. 1 Hutting Squad of 30 O.R. to be attached to Fd Coy for work at FORCEVILLE. 1 Hutting Squad of 30 O.R. to be attached for work.	As shown. By night as above. By Day. Move orders in this connection have been issued separately

Appendix No 2

Operation
C.R.E. 62nd Division. Amendment to ~~Move~~ Order No 2.   Copy No 1.

O.C. 460th Field Co.
~~O.C. 461st Field Co.~~
~~"G" 62nd Division.~~)
~~A.P.M. 62nd Division.~~) ~~For information.~~

With reference to the Table of moves contained in the above order, the 219th Field Coy R.E. will not vacate the billets at MAILLY CHATEAU until the 17th February.

The following postponement of moves is therefore necessitated

460th (W.R) Field Co from LIVRE CAMP to MAILLY CHATEAU on the 17th February instead of the 15th.

461st (W.R) Field Co from MAILLY WOOD EAST to LIVRE CAMP on the 17th February instead of the 15th.

ACKNOWLEDGE.

Lieut. Colonel R.E.
C. R. E. 62nd Division.

13. 2. 17.

Copy No 1 - 460th Field Co.
       2. - 461st Field Co
       3. - "G" 62nd Division.
       4.   A.P.M. 62nd Divn.

"A" Form. Army Form C. 2121.
MESSAGES AND SIGNALS.

Prefix	Code	m.	Words	Charge	This message is on a/c of:	Recd. at .... m.
Office of Origin and Service Instructions.			Sent At .... m.	3	..........Service.	Date ....
			To			From ....
			By		(Signature of "Franking Officer.")	By ....

TO 460¹ Field Coy. R.E.

Sender's Number.	Day of Month	In reply to Number	
R.E.A.29	16.2.17		AAA

In accordance with orders received from C.E. I Corps 460¹ Field Coy will move into MAILLY CHATEAU to-morrow 17¹ inst aaa 95² Field Coy will remain in present billets aaa Acknowledge aaa Addressed 460² Field Coy R.E. repeated 95² Field Coy R.E.

From CRE 62nd Divn.
Place
Time

(Z) Signature of Addressor

SECRET.　　APPENDIX N.4　　　　　　　　　Copy No ..2..

C. R. E. 62nd Division.　　Order No 4.　　　20. 2. 17.

1. The 7th Division will take over that portion of the line now held by the 62nd Division from L.31.c.2.6. to K.29.c.3.1., both exclusive, and the reliefs will be carried out on the nights of the 21st/22nd and 22/23rd February.

The relief will be completed by 10 a.m. on 23rd February.

2. The Field Companies of 62nd Division will hand over work on communication trenches, etc, to Field Companies of 7th Division as stated hereunder

		From	To
WALKER AVENUE	460th (W.R)	Field Coy	54th Field Coy
CRATER LANE	457th	do	54th do
CAKE TRENCH	457th	do	95th do
SIXTH AVENUE	461st	do	95th do
DRESSING STATION) at SUCHERIE.)	457th	do	528th (Durham) Field Coy.

The above handing over will be completed by 10 a.m. on 23rd February.

The Field Coys of the 62nd Division will be responsible for carrying on work on the above communication trenches on the night 22/23rd February, subject to working parties being available.

3. The R.E. Officer i/c of work for 62nd Divnl R.A. (Lieut Hammond 457th Field Coy) will hand over all work on R.A. positions in the area to be taken over by 7th Division (as defined in 1 above) to the corresponding R.E. Officer in the 7th Division (name to be notified later) to whom he will afford all information regarding the work under execution for R.A. in the area in question.

4. Os.C. Field Companies of the 62nd Division will furnish by 1 p.m. on February 21st for communication to C.R.E. 7th Division, a list of all works upon which their Units have been employed together with the detailed information regarding the state of progress of communication trenches called for by C.R.E. 62nd Division No RE/257/355 of 20. 2. 17.

5. On completion of relief the boundary between the 7th and 62nd Divisions will run from L.31.c.2.6. through Q.6.a.5.o., North of LEAVE AVENUE, South of cross roads BEAUMONT HAMEL and along the Southern Side of BEAUMONT HAMEL-AUCHONVILLERS Road.

-2-

6. On completion of the relief the Field Companies of the 62nd Division will remain in their present billets as under

        457th (W.R) Field Coy R.E. - P.18.b.2.8.
        460th   do   Q.13.b.o.8.
        461st   do   P. 18.central.

7. 62nd Divisional R.E. Headquarters at BUS.

R.A. Cullam
Lieut.Colonel R.E.
C. R. E. 62nd Division.

20. 2. 17.

To 457th Field Co - Copy No 1.
    460th   do   - do   2.
    461st   do   - do   3.
    C.R.E. 7th Divn - do   4. For information.
    62nd Divn "G"   - do   5. For information.
    Retained   - do   6.
    War Diary   - do   7 & 8.

SECRET.

RE/257.

O.C. 457th Field Co
O.C. 460th Field Co.
O.C. 461st Field Co.
C.R.E. 32nd Division.)
"G" 62nd Division.) For information.

The Field Companies of the 62nd Division will relieve those of the 32nd Division as under when the 62nd Division goes into the line.

457th (W.R) Field Co will relieve the 218th Field Coy on work on ~~BARXXXX~~ CRATER LANE and will take over work on CAKE TRENCH from the 206th Field Coy and the 461st W.R. Field Coy on the night of 12-13th February, leaving a party to continue work on STATION ALLEY on the night of the 12-13th February prior to handing this over to the 460th W.R. Field Coy on the night of the 13-14th February.

460th W.R. Field Co will relieve the 219th Field Coy on work at WALKER AVENUE and will take over the work at STATION ALLEY from the 457th Field Coy on the night of the 13/14th February

461st Field Coy will continue to work on SIXTH AVENUE as heretofore and will detail a party to carry forward the excavation of TOURNAI Trench which commences at WHITE CITY until it is prolonged to meet SIXTH AVENUE at K.34d.4.4.

In future the general system which will be adopted as far as possible by each Unit will be to detail 3 Sections for night work in the line with 1 setion back, but this may of course require to be varied from time to time.

Further detailed instructions for the employment of the Units on the work will be issued at an early date.

ACKNOWLEDGE.

Sd R.A. Gillam
Lieut.Colonel R.E.
C.R.E. 62nd Division.

10.2.17.

C. R. E. 62nd Division Order No 2.   Copy No ....

O.C. 457th Field Co.
O.C. 460th Field Co.
O.C. 461st Field Co.
"G" 62nd Division - For information.

----

1. The 62nd Division will relieve the 32nd Division in the right sector of V Corps front commencing on February 12th 1917.

2. With reference to the preliminary move orders issued on the 10th inst in connection with the above relief the moves of Field Companies of the 62nd Division will be acrried out in accordance with the following tabular detail.:-

No	Date	Unit	From	To	Remarks
1.	Feb 12th	460th (W.R) Fd Coy R.E.	COIGNEUX	LIVRE CAMP MAILLY	Take over Billets from the 218th Field Co.R.E.
2.	Feb 12th	No 4 Section 461st (W.R) Field Co R.E.	MAILLY	FORCEVILLE	For work on building Divisional H.Q.
3.	Feb 13th	No 3 Section 461st (W.R) Field Co R.E.	VAUCHELLES	MAILLY	To rejoin H.Q. of Company.
4.	Feb 13th	No 2 Section 461st Field Co R.E.	BUS	MAILLY	To rejoin H.Q. of Company.
5.	Feb 15th	460th (W.R) Field Co R.E.	LIVRE CAMP MAILLY	MAILLY CHATEAU	Take over Billets from 219th Field Co.R.E.
6.	Feb 16th	461st (W.R) Field Co R.E.	MAILLY WOOD EAST.	LIVRE CAMP MAILLY.	

Billetting parties will be sent on in advance to take over Billets in the case of 1.2. 5 & 6 above.

3. 457th Field Coy will remain in the camp at present occupied by it in MAILLY WOOD EAST.

4. Headquarters 62nd Divisional R.E. will remain at BUS.

(Sd) R.A.Gillam Lt.Colonel R.E.
C.R.E. 62nd Division.

Copy No 1 - 457th Field Co
        2 - 460th Field Co
        3 - 461st Field Co
        4.- Retained.
        5.- "G" 62nd Divn.

C.R.E. 62nd Division.   Order No 3.   Copy No ...

Appendix 7

O.C. 457th Field Co.R.E.
O.C. 460th Field Co R.E.
O.C. 461st Field Co R.E.
"G". 62nd Division - For information.

The following are the arrangements for the employment of Field Companies R.E. in the front line and back areas when the Division goes into the line on the 12th February 1917.

1. DISTRIBUTION.   460th (W.R) Field Co and 457th (W.R) Field Co will be allotted for the purpose of front line work to the sectors held by their respective affiliated Brigades, viz - 460th Field Coy with the 185th Brigade in the right sector and 457th Field Co with the 186th Brigade in the left sector.

Each of these two Field Companies will, in accordance with the general principles to be observed in the case of Field Coys allotted to definite sections of Brigades in the line, have 3 sections working every night on forward work in the front line and 1 section working by day in the back area or employed on work the conditions of which will admit of its being carried out in the daytime.

The 461st (W.R) Field Coy, whose affiliated Brigade will not be in the line, will be disposed for work as follows - 2 sections on front line work on left sector to be specially detailed, two sections on back area work.

2. The attached tabular statement (Table A) gives the distribution of the Field Companies for work when the Division goes into the line, and supersedes previous preliminary orders which have been issued on the subject.

R. A. Gillam   Lieut.Colonel R.E.
C.R.E. 62nd Division.

Copy No 1 - 457th Field Co.
       2 - 460th do
       3.- 461st do
       4 - "G" 62nd Divn.
       5.- Retained.

TABLE "A"

UNIT	Nature of work.	Working Parties & Hutting Parties required.	Remarks.
460th (W.R) Field Coy R.E.	FRONT LINE. 3 sections on Communitcation trenceges - TANK ALLEY - STATION ALLEY -WALKER AVENUE and probably an intermediate communication trench. Also a lateral trench to connect head of station alley with either WAGGON ROAD or WALKER AVENUE. 1 Section on Bde Battle H.Q., dug-outs etc.	Working parties as required will be demanded in due course.	By night. Detailed distribution to be arranged after consultation with Brigadiers.
457th (W.R) Field Coy R.E.	FRONT LINE. 3 sections on Communication trenchs - CRATER LANE? CAKE TRENCH and extension of latter back towards WATLING STREET. 1 section on Divnl Battle H.Q., dug-outs etc.	as above. do	as above do
461st)W.R) Field Coy R.E.	FRONT LINE. 1 Section on SIXTH AVENUE. 1 Section on TOURNAI TRENCH. BACK AREA. 1 Section (No 4) to FORCEVILLE(on 12 Feb) for Bidling Divnl H.Q. 1 Section to be employed on building Bde H.Q. at MAILLY & other work to be detailed.	 do do 1 Hutting Squad of 30 O.R. to be attached to Fd Coy for work at FORCEVILLE. 1 Hutting Squad of 30 O.R. to be attached for work.	 By night as above. By day. Move orders in this connection have been issued separately.

SECRET.   Copy No. 8.

Appendix 8.

C.R.E. 62nd Division.   Order No 4.   20. 2. 17.

---

1. The 7th Division will take over that portion of the line now held by the 62nd Division from L.31.c.2.6. to K.29.c.3.1., both exclusive, and the reliefs will be carried out on the nights of the 21st/22nd and 22/23rd February.

The relief will be completed by 10 a.m. on 23rd February.

2. The Field Companies of 62nd Division will hand over work on communication trenches etc, to Field Companies of 7th Division as stated hereunder

	From	To
WALKER AVENUE	460th(W.R) Field Co	54th Field Co.
CRATER LANE	457th do	54th do
CAKE TRENCH	457th do	95th do
SIXTH AVENUE	461st do	95th do
DRESSING STATION) AT SUCHERIE)	457th do	528th (Durham) Field Coy.

The above handing over will be completed by 10 a.m. 23rd Feby.

The Field Coys of the 62nd Division will be responsible for carrying on work on the above communication trenches on the night 22/23rd February, subject to working parties being available.

3. The R.E. Officer i/c work for 62nd Divnl R.A. (Lieut Hammond, 457th Field Coy) will hand over all work on R.A. positions in the area to be taken over by 7th Division (name to be notified later) to whom he will afford all information regarding the work under execution for R.A. in the area in question.

4. Os.C. Field Companies of the 62nd Division will furnish by 1 p.m. on February 21st for communication to C.R.E. 7th Division, a list of all works upon which their Units have been employed together with the detailed information regarding the state of progress of communication trenches called for by C.R.E. 62nd Division No RE/257/355 of 20.2.17.

5. On completion of relief the boundary between the 7th and 62nd Divisions will run from L.31.c.2.6. through Q.6.a.5.o., North of LEAVE AVENUE, South of cross roads BEAUMONT HAMEL - AUCHONVILLERS Road.

over

6. On completion of the relief the Field Companies of the 62nd Division will remain in their present billets as under

        457th (W.R) Field Coy R.E.   - P.18.b.2.8.
        460th   do   Q.13.b.o.8.
        461st   do   P. 18.central.

7. 62nd Divisional R.E. Headquarters at BUS.

                        (Sd) R.A. Gillam   Lieut.Colonel
                                                         R.E.
                        C.R.E. 62nd Division.

20. 2. 17.

To 457th Field Co - Copy No 1.
   460th   do   do   2.
   461st   do   do   3.
   C.R.E. 7th Divn   do   4. For information
   62nd Divn "G"   do   5.   do
   Retained   do   6.
   War Diary   do   7 & 8.

Copy No ...8......

Amendment to C. R. E. 62nd Divn Order No 4.

With reference to C.R.E. Order No 4 dated 20. 2. 17 the instructions contained in para 3 will be considered to be in abeyance for the present. Lieut Hammond will continue to be in charge of the work for the Divisional R.A. for the same front as heretofore, until he receives further orders on this subject.

            R.A. Gillam Lieut.Col R.E
            C. R. E. 62nd Division.

21. 2. 17.

Copy No 1. - 457th Field Coy & for communication to Lt Hammond.
    2. - 460th Field Coy
    3. - 461st Field Coy
    4. - C.R.E. 7th Divn (For information)
    5. - "G" 62nd Divn.   do
    6. - Retained.
    7 & 8. War Diary.

457th Field Coy R.E.

R.E. 69. 24.2.17.

Be prepared to move your Company at short notice aaa Work to be continued in accordance with existing arrangements pending receipt of further orders aaa Men working forward should carry full equipment and a small party should be left in Camp to load wagons etc if necessary.

                                               C.R.E. 62nd Division.

457th Field Coy R.E.

R.E. 71. 24. 2. 17.

Reference my R.E. 69 Company must be held in readiness to move at any hour after 6 a.m. to-morrow 25th inst aaa Only the working party for STATION ALLEY and forward Duckboard track will be sent out to work and this party will go out fully equipped in readiness to join Unit should you be required to move forward aaa No working parties other than that for STATION ALLEY and duck-board track will be sent out on the work to-morrow.

                                               C.R.E. 62nd Division.

Appendix 11

C. R. E.

G. 245   25th.

Please detail one section R.E. to proceed as early as possible to WUNDT-WERK L.32.b.6t6. to report to Officer commanding there.

            62nd Division.

457th Field Coy R.E.

R.E.81. 25. 2. 17. ---

detail one section to move forward immediately to WUNDT-WERK L.32.b.5.8. and there report for work to Officer Commanding Battalion at that point aaa Tools to be carried approximately one pick or shovel per man with a ~~proportion~~ proportion of light tools to be detailed by you aaa Pack mules will be taken aaa This section must go forward this evening and you should therefore detail the one which was left in Camp to-day aaa It is understood that a certain quantity of material is available at the above point for work on repairing dug-outs etc aaa Section will proceed fully armed and equipped aaa Two days rations to be carried on if possible aaa remaining section will continue work to-morrow as for to-day and press forward duck board tracks with all speed.

            C.R.E. 62nd Division.

SECRET.   Copy No. 8

                    C.R.E., 62nd Division, Order No. 5.
                    ───────────────────────────────────

Ref. Map SERRE 1/10,000
     sheet 57D 1/40,000.

1.   The following reliefs will take place to-day and will be
        completed by 6 a.m. 27.2.17.

2.   185th Infantry Brigade will relieve the 190th Infantry
        Brigade (63rd Division) about the line L.30.a.1.0. to L.28.central

3.   <u>Brigade Headquarters, 185th Infantry Brigade will be in the
        SUNKEN ROAD about R.3.c.central.</u>

4.   O.C. 460th Field Coy R.E. will detail one section to go
        forward in to the line with the 185th Infantry Brigade. This
        section will come under the orders of the G.O.C. 185th Infantry
        Brigade.

5.   O.C. 460th Field Co R.E. will report at once to Headquarters
        185th Infantry Brigade for detailed instructions as to the move
        of this section.   The name of the officer in charge of the
        section detailed will be reported to Headquarters, 62nd Divnl R.E.
        by wire.

6.   The 186th Infantry Brigade will relieve the 187th Infantry
        Brigade from about the line BEAUREGARD DOVECOTE – HORST-WERK
        to L.28.c.central, the 7th Division taking over the remainder of
        the line now being held by the 187th Infantry Brigade.

7.   <u>Brigade Headquarters 186th Infantry Brigade will be established
        at about L.31.c.central.</u>

8.   The section of the 457th Field Co R.E. already in the line
        will come under orders of the G.O.C. 186th Infantry Brigade on
        completion of the relief of the 187th Infantry Brigade, at 6 a.m.
        27. 2. 17. The Officer i/c of this section will report to 186th
        Infantry Brigade Headquarters at the point indicated in para 7
        as soon after that hour as possible.

-2-

9. The section of the 457th Field Co R.E. at present in the line will not be relieved without reference to Headquarters 62nd Divisional R.E. and in any case must not be relieved before 28. 2. 17.

10. ACKNOWLEDGE.

              Lieut.Colonel R.E.
            C. R. E. 62nd Division.

```
Copy No 1  to  62nd Division "G"
        2  -   461st Field Co
        3.     457th Field Co
        4      460th Field Co
        5      185th Infantry Bde.
        6      186th Infantry Bde.
        7-9    File.
```

Copy No ....

G.R.E. 62nd Division Order No 6.

From the 27th inst inclusive, and onwards until further orders, the Field Companies of the 62nd Division will be employed as under.

1. 457th FIELD COY R.E.

1 Section in front line, as already detailed, for work under orders of G.O.C. 186th Infantry Brigade.

The Officer in charge of this section will report daily for information of G.R.E. what work he is carrying out and any recommendations he has to make for the useful employment of R.E. in the front line under present conditions.

1 Section only of the 457th Field Coy will continue to be employed on STATION ALLEY duckboard track which will be pushed forward as quickly as possible. A working party of 100 men has been ordered to report at 9.30 a.m. 27.2.17 at GREEN DUMP for work with this section.

The Section of 457th Field Coy hitherto employed on improving STATION ALLEY will be withdrawn.

<u>Two Sections 457th Field Co will be detailed forthwith for work on BEAUCOURT-PUISIEUX Road commencing morning of 27th inst.</u>

Lieut Best with a few men of suitable trades will in accordance with previous instructions carry on with work on BEAUMONTHAMEL water supply which must be considered very urgent.

2. 460th FIELD COY R.E.

1 Section in front line, as already detailed, for work under orders of G.O.C. 185th Infantry Brigade.

The Officer in charge of this section will carry out instructions and furnish report as required in (1) above.

The two sections employed at present on TANK ALLEY on work on dug-outs at the Tank will be withdrawn forthwith.

460th Field Coy (contd)

> Three sections of the 460th Field Co will be detailed for work on the BEAUCOURT-PUISIEUX Road commencing morning of the 27th inst.

3. 461st FIELD COY R.E.

One section under Lieut Collins will continue to work on the hutment Camp at FORCEVILLE pending the issue of further orders on this subject.

The Section which has been employed under Lieut McEwen on making 63nd Divisional R.E. Dump on STATION ROAD will be withdrawn forthwith.

> Three sections will be detailed for work on the BEAUCOURT PUSIEUX Road commencing morning of the 27th inst.

4. In effect all available personnel of Field Companies not required for other work especially detailed above will be employed in conjunction with Infantry working parties on repairing and re-making BEAUCOURT-PUSIEUX Road and any other roads that may in future be ordered, such roads being very urgently required to be rendered practicable for the passage of Artillery and other transport.

5. All sections for work on Roads will parade at their Billets at 7 a.m. and march to the site of the work (at R. 7.b.8.1.) via GREEN DUMP where the Infantry Working parties will rendezvous at 9.30 a.m.   Haversack rations will be carried.

All R.E. Sections and working parties employed on this work will be under the orders of Lieut Paul, 461st Field Coy who will be responsible for all arrangements in connection with this work and for having the Infantry Working Parties met at the rendezvous and conducted to the site of the work.

6. Field Companies will place all available Company Transport at the disposal of the work on Roads - firstly for conveying sleepers from ACHEUXVILLERS DUMP to the site and then for carting timber, bricks etc available in the vicinity of the work to the site.

7. Application has been made for as many G.S. Wagons as possible to be allotted for road work and it is hoped that a number of these

will soon be made available.

8. Of the three Brigade Mining Sections now available one will work with the section of the 457th Field Coy which is laying STATION ALLEY duckboard Track forthwith. The 2 other Brigade Mining sections will work on the BEAUCOURT-PUISIEUX road.

O.C. 457th Field Coy will arrange for these sections to be detailed accordingly.

9. ACKNOWLEDGE.

(signed)
Lieut.-Colonel R.E.
C.R.E. 62nd Division.

26. 2. 17.

Copy No 1 - 457th Field Co
 2 - 460th Field Co
 3. - 461st Field Co
 4 - "G" 62nd Division)
 5. - "Q" 62nd Division) For information
 6-9 Retained.

E/3187/7

C.R.E. 62nd Division
C.R.E. 7th Division.
C.R.E. 11th Division

The following arrangements are made for work in the following roads.

    (a) HAMEL - BEAUCOURT - MIRAUMONT.

    (b) Station Q.18.b. towards BEAUMONT HAMEL.

    (c) BEAUCOURT R.7.d. to PUSIEUX ROAD.

Lieut.Col. Gillam C.R.E. 62nd Division will have the general supervision of this work and will issue subsidiary orders.

Troops available.

    86th Field Coy 11th Division at Q.18.a.

    East Yorks Pioneer Battalion, 11th Divn billetted between HAMEL and BEAUCOURT

    Two Companies Manchester Pioneer Bn 7th Division.

    Field Companies (less detachments) 62nd Divn.

    1 Bn Infantry 62nd Division.

Materials available.

    Bricks from ruined houses.

    Logs obtainable in vicinity of work.

    Sleepers from AUCHONVILLERS Station.

There is no immediate prospect of any road metal being available.

Transport available.

Pontoon and G.S. Wagons of Field Companies and Pioneer Bns and such other transport as can be arranged divisionally. G.S. Wagons which should be demanded from C.E. V Corps and will be supplied as far as possible.

At present 10 G.S. Wagons will report at HAMEL at 8.30 a.m. and 30 at AUCHONVILLERS Station at 8.30 a.m. daily.

Work should be arranged in reliefs.

                                        R.D. Petrie B.G.
                                       C.E. V Corps.

27. 2. 17.

SECRET.

C.R.E. 62nd Division Order No 7.
----

1. In accordance with instructions received from Chief Engineer V Corps the following Units and detachments have been placed under orders of the C.R.E. 62nd Division for work on forward roads.

        86th Field Co R.E. 11th Division at Q.18.a.
        East Yorks Pioneer Bn, 11th Division.
        2 Companies, Manchester Pioneer Bn 7th Divn.
        Field Coys (less detachments) 62nd Divn.
        1 Battalion Infantry 62nd Divn.

2. DISTRIBUTION OF WORKING PARTIES. The above Units will be distributed for work in accordance with the following detail from 28th Feb inclusive.

The 86th Field Coy R.E. 11th Division, will carry out all necessary repairs to the HAMEL-BEAUCOURT Road from Hamel to its junction with STATION ROAD at Q.18.b.5.7. The Northern Half of this road being in the worst condition will receive first attention.

The East Yorks Pioneer Bn, 11 th Division will carry out and be responsible for the repairs and renewals to the HAMEL-MIRAUMONT Road for that portion extending from the Road junction at Q.18.b.6.7. to MIRAUMONT. The portion Q.18.b.6.7. to R.8.a.4.3. will be dealt with first commencing from Q.18.b.6.7.

Two companies of the Manchester Pioneer Bn will execute the repairs to STATION ROAD from Q.18.b. towards BEAUMONT HAMEL commencing with the Eastern portion of same.

Field Companies of the 62nd Division with 1 Battalion 62nd Divn will carry out the work on renewing the BEAUCOURT- PUISIEUX Road.

3. MATERIALS AVAILABLE.

(a) Bricks from ruined houses at HAMEL, BEAUCOURT Railway Station and BEAUCOURT. These will be used in lieu of Road metal their being no immediate prospect of the latter being available.

(b) Sleepers from AUCHONVILLERS STATION. Arrangements are being made for transport of these to convenient sites in the vicinity of the work. In the first instance Dumps for sleepers will be made at Q.18.b.6.7. and R.7.b.8.1. O.c. 460th Field Coy will arrange for the feeding and control of these Dumps and for issues from same to Units as concerned.

(C) Logs. A quantity of these are already dumped at the eastern side of the road from HAMEL to Q.18.b.6.7. ready to be utilised for the purpose of repairing this road.

(d) Derelict timber is available in some quantities to the west of BEAUCOURT-PUSIEUX Road, which will be found useful for repair purposes.

4. TRANSPORT. 10 G.S. Wagons will report at HAMEL at 8.30 a.m. and 30 at AUCHONVILLERS at 8.30 a.m. daily from the 28th inst inclusive. O.C. 86th Field Coy R.E. will be responsible for having the 10 wagons met at HAMEL. 5 of these will remain at his disposal and 5 will be at the disposal of the East Yorks Pioneer Battn, 11th Divn. for transporting bricks and other material as required.

The 30 G.S. Wagons reporting at AUCHONVILLERS will be utilised under he direction of O.C. 460th Field Coy for conveying sleepers to sites above mentioned.

Units will arrange to bring with them all available regimental transport for use on the work.

5. WORK. Work will be carried out in reliefs. Os.C. Units will report the probable working strength of their Units and the arrangements for working in reliefs.

6. The officers Commanding the following Units will report to the C.R.E. 62nd Division at point Q.18.b.6.7. at 9.30 a.m. 28th inst.
        86th Field Coy R.E.
        East Yorks Regt.
        2 Coys Manchester Pioneer Bn.

Orders in this connection for Field Coys and Infantry Bns 62nd Division have been issued separately.

7. ACKNOWLEDGE.

                       R.A. Gillam Lieut.Col,R.E.
                         C.R.E. 62nd Divn.

27.2.17

ORIGINAL

Vol 3

CONFIDENTIAL

WAR DIARY
of
Hdqrs 2nd Div RE

From 1st March to 31st March 1919

Volume II

WAR DIARY or INTELLIGENCE SUMMARY

Army Form C. 2118.

Place	Date	Hour	Summary of Events and Information	Remarks and references to Appendices
Bus-les-ARTOIS	1/3/17		CRE moved forward to MAILLY-MAILLET. HdQrs with 110th Field Coy in odr t/w main Forward Roads. Instructions ret from X=n Div that work on STATION ALLEY continues back my be shortened. All bet in course of erection at Div HdQrs Camp FORCEVILLE to be completed. Data on the same in Ren 6 2 1/2. Instructions red that all traffic on forward Roads in the registered Rhown between 8:0 am + 2:0 pm + not as previously ordered. Hd Qrs 110th O in RE	
	2/3/17		CRE keep at work on Roads all day. Orders recd that X=n Div is to relieve ACM 2 Div. Petit at an early date. CRE visited MIRAUMONT to reconnoiter roads	
	3/3/17	3/3/17	CRE attended conference at Div HQ. In accordance with verbal instructions issued by Cor X Corps, Adjutant reconnoitred for site of new Div RE Dump at BEAUCOURT STATION Q18 b 6.7 sheet BEAUCOURT. HdQs X=n Div RE moved to ENGLEBELMER	
ENGLEBELMER	4/3/17		CRE regnid at HQ at the station	

WAR DIARY
or
INTELLIGENCE SUMMARY.
(Erase heading not required.)

Army Form C. 2118.

Place	Date	Hour	Summary of Events and Information	Remarks and references to Appendices
ENGLEBELMER	5.3.17		H.Q. 62nd Div Art	
	6.3.17		Orders received from 62nd Div with regard to Dumps of R.E. Stores to be formed for forthcoming operations.	
			Attached C.R.E. Order No. 8 issued with reference to disposition and dump of Field Bgde during attack on ACHIET LE PETIT	
			457ᵗʰ & 460ᵗʰ Field Bgdes started for their operation	Appendix 16
	7.3.17		C.R.E. worked in preparation at MIRAUMONT.	
	8.3.17		Conference of Bgde Majors 155ᵗʰ & 183ᵗʰ Inf Bgdes. G.S.O.2. O.C. 457ᵗʰ & 460ᵗʰ Field Bgdes held at R.E. H.Q. Distribution of R.E. in forthcoming offensive is considered	
			Operation Order No. 8 cancelled & Operation Order No. 9 issued	
			Two schemes of 457ᵗʰ & 460ᵗʰ Field Bgr Stand at disposal of 155ᵗʰ & 183ᵗʰ Inf Brigades for offensive	Appendix 17
	9.3.17		Nil	
	10.3.17		R.E. Stores commenced to arrive by rail at new Div Dump BEAUCOURT.	
			C.R.E. made visit in Bazun valley.	

WAR DIARY or INTELLIGENCE SUMMARY

Army Form C. 2118.

(Erase heading not required.)

Place	Date	Hour	Summary of Events and Information	Remarks and references to Appendices
ENGLEBELMER	11/3/17		Nil	
	12/3/17		Nil	
	13/3/17		Rebel received that enemy have evacuated ACHIET-LE-PETIT, not confirmed. Orders rcvd from II Corps to carry out reconnaissance of MIRAUMONT STATION YARDS, MIRAUMONT – PUISIEUX and MIRAUMONT – ACHIET-LE-PETIT roads. Rebels forwarded same night.	Hd Qrs rcvd Div Ref
	14/3/17		Orders rcvd from II Corps that work on roads in Div Area i.e BEAUCOURT and the undertaken by Road Board and that it is to take a work met forward roads. Work on Road from BEAUCOURT to MIRAUMONT probable ahead in accordance with orders of II Corps of 13/3/17. Instructions rcvd from II Corps that work on BEAUCOURT – PUISIEUX may start when road is completed up to point in which work has commenced.	
	15/4/17		Instructions rcvd that Road Board are to assume control of BEAUCOURT – PUISIEUX rgt to BOIS D'HOLLANDE R8285	

WAR DIARY
or
INTELLIGENCE SUMMARY.

(Erase heading not required.)

Army Form C. 2118.

Instructions regarding War Diaries and Intelligence Summaries are contained in F. S. Regs., Part II. and the Staff Manual respectively. Title pages will be prepared in manuscript.

Place	Date	Hour	Summary of Events and Information	Remarks and references to Appendices
ENGLEBELMER	16/3/17		Div Order No 25 recd ordering attack on ACHIET-LE-PETIT.	
			C.R.E Order No 10 issued ordering roads of No 6 Field Coy to be placed at disposal of G.O.C. 186th Infantry Bde to enable them to perform.	Appendix 18
			About 20 kilos cancelled later in the day.	
	17/3/17		Div Order No 26 recd giving second instructions for Attack on ACHIET-LE-PETIT.	Appendix 19
			C.R.E order No 11 issued	
			Patrol recd that enemy had vacated BAPAUME	
R.S.R.s-3	18/3/17		R.E. H.Q. and the Field Coys moved to forward positions as under:-	
			R.E. H.Q. R.S.R.s-3. 401st Field Coy R.S.R.s-3 405th Field Coy R 7 R 7 7.	
			466th Field Coy R 8 a 7 3.	
			Work on forward roads extended to ♦♦♦♦♦♦ ACHIET-LE-PETIT	
	19/3/17		C.R.E order No 12 issued ordering work on above roads.	
			Nil.	
	20/3/17		Road from MIRAUMONT to ACHIET-LE-PETIT was traversable for horse transport.	
	21/3/17		Nil	
	22/3/17		Nil	

WAR DIARY
or
INTELLIGENCE SUMMARY.

Army Form C. 2118.

Place	Date	Hour	Summary of Events and Information	Remarks and references to Appendices
R.S.G.S.	23/5/17		Instructions received from G.O.C. Div. G. that G.O.C. 185th Inf. Byde. is to be responsible for work on roads. The field Coys to be employed on more technical R.E. Work.	14 d.9Cs ord Dui RE
	24/5/17		C.R.E. Order No 13 issued allotting area of RS 140 + new feeder Rly & ACHIET-LE-GRAND	
	25/5/17		C.R.E. proceeded with Divisional Commander, G.S.O.I and O.C. 416th Field Coy to select a defensive line running from H.4.c central to the S.E. of ERVILLERS. Work commenced on defensive line	
ACHIET-LE-GRAND	26/5/17		R.E. H.Q. moved to ACHIET-LE-GRAND	
	27/5/17		Nil	
	28/5/17		Nil	
	29/5/17		Nil	
	30/5/17		Nil	
	31/5/17		Nil	

R.S. Livingstone
C.R.E. 62nd Division

SECRET.

Copy No ..... 2 ......

G. R. R. 62nd Division Order No 8.

1. The 185th and 186th Infantry Brigades have been selected to capture ACHIET-LE-PETIT on or about the 14th March and preparations for the attack should be pushed forward as rapidly as possible.

2. The objectives to be gained and the line to be consolidated by each Brigade are

    185th INFANTRY BRIGADE.

        Road running from G 15 d 1 3.5 to G 8 c 7 2

    186th INFANTRY BRIGADE.

        Road running from G 8 c 7 2 to G 7 a 3 7

3. Assaulting troops will be formed up on tapes on the line G 19 d 1 0 and L 17 a 0 1.

    The frontage of Brigades will be allotted as follows

        Right Brigade (185th Infantry Brigade) from the railway line G 19 d 1 0 to the road at L 23 b 6 4 (exclusive).

        Left Infantry Brigade from L 23 b 6 4 to L 17 a 0 1.

        Each Brigade on a front of two Battalions.

4. The 456th Field Coy R.E. with the mining section of the 185th Infantry Brigade will construct three strong points at the following approximate positions:-

    (1) G 14 d 8.5 2.5
    (2) G 14 d 3 6
    (3) G 14 a 9 4.5

The 457th Field Coy R.E. with the Mining Section of the 186th Infantry Brigade will construct three Strong Points at the following approximate positions:-

    (4) G 8 c 4 0.5
    (5) G 7 d 3.5 2
    (6) LH 12 c 7 7.5

5. These strong points will each be constructed for a garrison of one platoon and will be wired all round. They will be commenced as soon as practicable after the objective has been gained, and will be strengthened the following night.

1.

6. A section R.E. will be detailed to construct each strong point and will have as a working party the platoon which will ultimately garrison the strong point when constructed. O.C. Field Coys will arrange with the Brigades concerned for any carrying parties required.

7. All working parties will be withdrawn from the strong points before daylight.

8. The 457th Field Coy R.E. (less 1 section) and 460th Field Coy R.E. (less 1 section) will remain under the orders of the C.R.E. 62nd Division. 1 Section of each of the above Field Coys will be placed under the orders of the G.O.C. 186th and 185th Infantry Brigades respectively for purposes of consolidation.

OsC. 457th and 460th Field Coys will arrange direct with the Brigades concerned as to the disposition and employment of the sections attached to Brigades for consolidation purposes in accordance with the above instructions.

9. The position of Os.C. 457th and 460th Field Coys will be with their respective Brigade Headquarters during the operations.

10. A forward Divisional R.E. Dump is in course of formation at BEAUCOURT STATION Q.18.b.7.5.

A joint Field Coy Dump will be established for use by Field Coys concerned at R.4.a.5.5. west of MIRAUMONT. Os.C. 457th and 460th Field Companies will take early steps to stock this dump from the forward Divisional Dump at BEAUCOURT STATION.

11. Os.C. 457th and 460th Field Coys will arrange with 186th and 185th Infantry Brigades respectively the position of forward R.E. Dumps and will obtain the necessary carrying parties to stock these Dumps from the Brigades concerned.

The positions of these forward dumps will be reported to C.R.E. at a very early date.

12. The following approximate list of stores and tools should be stocked at the Field Coy Dump.

Sandbags (Small Quantity only).	Plain Wire
Picks.	Screw Pickets
Shovels	Crowbars
Barbed wire	Bill Hooks or Hand axes
French wire	Duckwalks (a few)
	Timber (small quantity for dug-out work).

Arrangements should be made to commence the transportation of stores to forward dumps as soon as sites are determined.

13. Further orders as to places and times of assembly of the 457th and 460th Field Coys and orders for the 461st Field Coy R.E. will be issued at a later date.

                                                Lieut.Colonel R.E.
                              C. R. E. 62nd Division.

Copy No 1 -   457th Field Co.
          2   460th Field Co
          3 -   461st Field Co   For information
          4.   62nd Division "G"   do
          5 & 6 War Diary
          7   Retained.

SECRET.   Copy No ...6...

C. R. E. 62nd Division Order No 9.

C.R.E. 62nd Division Order No 8 dated 7.3.17. is hereby cancelled and the following substituted.

1. The 185th and 186th Infantry Brigades have been selected to capture ACHIET-LE-PETIT on or about the 14th March and preparations for the attack should be pushed forward as rapidly as possible.

2. The objectives to be gained and the line to be consolidated by each Brigade are

    185th INFANTRY BRIGADE.

      Road running from G 15 d 1 3.5 to G 8 c 7 2

    186th INFANTRY BRIGADE.

      Road running from G 8 c 7 2 to G 7 a 3 7

3. Assaulting troops will be formed up on tapes on the line G 19 d 1 0 and L 17 a 0 1.

  The frontage of Brigades will be allotted as follows

    Right Brigade (185th Infantry Brigade) from the railway line

      G 19 d 1 0 to the road at L 23 b 6 4 (exclusive).

    Left Infantry Brigade from L 23 b 6 4 0 to L 17 a 0 1.

    Each Brigade on a front of two Battalions.

457th Field Coy and 460th Field Coy will each detail an Officer to assist the 186th and 185th Brigades respectively in taping out these lines.

4. Two sections of the 457th Field Coy and two sections of the 460th Field Coy will be placed at the disposal of the 186th and 185th Brigades respectively for these operations, to be employed on the construction of Strong Points and for purposes of consolidation.

The names of the Subaltern Officers to command these sections will be reported to C.R.E. and the Brigades concerned forthwith.

5. O's.C. 457th and 460th Field Coys will arrange direct with the Brigades concerned as to the detailed position disposition and employment of the 2 sections placed at the disposal of their respective Brigades, and will report to C.R.E. the arrangements made.

6. The position of Os.C. Field Coys will be with their respective Brigade Headquarters during the operations.

7. A forward Divisional R.E. Dump is in course of formation at BEAUCOURT STATION Q.18 b 7 8.

O.C. Field Companies will arrange with their respective Brigades as to the positions of forward R.E. Dumps and will report to C.R.E. in due course the positions seelected.

A list giving the approximate total quantity of tools and stores required to stock forward R.E. Dumps (both Brigade and Field Coy) will be furnished to the C.R.E. by Os.C. Field Coys as soon as possible.

                                                    Lieut.Colonel R.E.
                                            C. R. E. 62nd Division.

8. 3. 17.

```
Copy No 1 -   457th Field Coy
        2     460th Field Coy
        3     461st Field Coy    For information
        4     62nd Division "G"       do
        5 & 6 War Diary
        7     Retained.
```

SECRET.   Copy No. ..4....

C. R. E. 62nd Division Order No 10.
----

16. 3. 17.

Ref:- ACHIET.Rd.5 Map 1/10,000.

1.   62nd Division Order No 23 of 15.3.17 is cancelled and the following substituted.

2.   The 62nd Division will attack ACHIET-LE-PETIT on the morning of the 17th inst from a South Easterly direction.
      186th Infantry Brigade, 54th and 208th Machine Gun Companies will carry out the attack.
      One Battalion 185th Infantry Brigade will move to a position W of MIRAUMONT, and will be at the disposal of the G.O.C. 186th Infantry Brigade.
      Zero hour will be at dawn, the exact hour to be notified later.

3.   The boundaries of the frontage for attack will be :-

      RIGHT BOUNDARY.
      The SUNKEN ROAD from G.15.c.5.9 to G.7.d.9.7.

      LEFT BOUNDARY.
      A line from G.14.d.3.3. to Junction of Trench with roadway at G.14.c.7.9. - Road Junction G.14.a.5.0. to Road Junction G.14.a.0.6.- Road Junction G.7.d.3.1.

4.   OBJECTIVES.

      1st Objective will be:- Roadway from G.14.c.2.7. to G.14.a.5.0.

      2nd Objective Roadway from G.7.d.9.7. to G.7.d.3.1.

5.   METHOD OF ATTACK.

      One Battalion will carry out the attack on the 1st Objective and will be responsible for :-

      (a) Forming a defensive flank on the line of SUNKEN ROAD on their right flank.
      (b) Blocking all trenches and roadways on their left flank as a temporary measure.
      (c) Pushing out strong bombing patrols to clear that portion of the village and such trenches South of the line, Road Junction G.14.c.3.8. - Junction of RESURRECTION TRENCH with Roadway at L.13.c.5.6.

      The 2nd Battalion will be formed up at zero hour in rear of the 1st and move forward at the same time.
      A pause of 10 minutes will be made in the barrage about 200 yards beyond the first objective. This will allow the leading waves of the 2nd Battalion to close up to the barrage and pass through the 1st Battn and move on to the final objective.

      Units will find their own mopping up parties.

      The leading waves will be formed up on tapes on a line parallel to and 300 yards South of the trench in G.15.c.5.2. to G.14.d.2.3.

      Each assaulting Battalion will advance on a two Company frontage, each Company adopting the formations laid down in S.S. 144, Plate B.

5. Strong Officer patrols will be sent forward from the Battalion holding the centre section of the line to establish blocks in RESURRECTION and ARWIN TRENCHES at L.11.d.2.0. and L.11.d.6.0.

6. The attack will be supported by a Sweitching Artillery Barrage which will move through the village in front of the troops, and by a Standing Barrage between BIHUCOURT Line and the SUNKEN ROAD in G.7.d., G.8.c, G.14.b, and G.15.c.

   Detailed Artillery Plan will be issued later.

7. Consolidation on the objectives and on the Right flank of the attack will consist of strong points at intervals. A Lewis Gun or Machine Gun will form part of the garrison of each point.

8. ONE SECTION, 457th FIELD COY R.E. IS PLACED AT THE DISPOSAL OF THE G.O.C. 186th INFANTRY BRIGADE TO ASSIST IN THE CONSOLIDATION OF THE POSITION.

9. O.C. 457th Field Coy R.E. will report at once to G.O.C. 186th Infantry Brigade to ascertain his detailed requirements as to the manner in which the above R.E. Section is to be employed for consolidation purposes.

10. O.C. 457th Field Coy R.E. will report to C.R.E. the name of the Officer in Command of the Section detailed for this work.

11. Headquarters C. R. E. at ENGLEBELMER.
    Divisional H.Q. "O" from 3 p.m. 16th inst will be at Q.12.c.3.1.
    H.Q. 186th Infantry Bde at R.4.a.2.1.

12. ACKNOWLEDGE.

                                            Lieut.Colonel R.E.
                                          C. R. E. 62nd Division.

Copy No 1 - O.C. 457th Field Co.
       2 - O.C. 460th Field Co.)
       3.   O.C. 461st Field Co) For information.
       4 & 5   War Diary.
       6.   Retained.

SECRET.   Copy No. 4

C.R.E. 62nd Division Order No 11.

REF: ACHIET Ed. 5. Map 1/10,000.

1. On the morning of the 18th instant the 62nd Division will attack and occupy the COMMUNICATION TRENCH between SUNKEN ROAD at G.15.c.6.8. and STEP TRENCH at G.14.d.2.3.
    Zero hour will be 4.30 a.m.

2. One Battalion 186th Infantry Brigade and the 34th Machine Gun Coy will carry out the operation.

3. The forming up line will be taped out on a line parallel to and 300 yards South of the COMMUNICATION TRENCH to be attacked.

4. ONE SECTION, 457th FIELD COY R.E. IS PLACED AT THE DISPOSAL OF THE G.O.C. 186th INFANTRY BRIGADE TO ASSIST IN THE CONSOLIDATION OF THE POSITION.
    Carrying parties will be arranged detailed by G.O.C. 186th Brigade to carry up R.E. material for this purpose.

5. Consolidation of the objectives will consist of strong points at intervals. A Lewis Gun or Machine Gun will form part of the garrison of each strong point.

6½. O.C. 457th Field Co will report at once to G.O.C. 186th Infantry Brigade to ascertain his detailed requirements as to the manner in which the above R.E. Section is to be employed for consolidation purposes.

7. O.C. 457th Field Co will report to C.R.E. the name of the Officer in Command of the Section detailed for this work.

8. ACKNOWLEDGE.

                                              [signature]
                                              Lieut. Colonel R.E.
                                              C.R.E. 62nd Division.

17. 3. 17.

Copy No 1 - O.C. 457th Field Co.
       2   O.C. 460th Field Co)
       3   O.C. 461st Field Co) For your information.
       4 & 5 War Diary
       6   Retained.

CONFIDENTIAL

WAR DIARY

of

1st Cdn Div. C.E.

From 1st April to 30th April 1917

VOLUME 4

Army Form C. 2118.

WAR DIARY
or
INTELLIGENCE SUMMARY.
(Erase heading not required.)

Instructions regarding War Diaries and Intelligence Summaries are contained in F.S. Regs., Part II. and the Staff Manual respectively. Title pages will be prepared in manuscript.

Place	Date	Hour	Summary of Events and Information	Remarks and references to Appendices
ACHIET-LE-GRAND			Hd Qr 1st Div R.E.	
	1/4/17		Div Order No 29 issued. 185th Inf Bde to relieve 7th Div on 3rd April after noon	
	2/4/17		Nil	
	3/4/17		Received Div Order No 30. Relief of 7th Div to be completed by 8.0 am. 3rd April. C.R.E Order No 14 issued warning 160th Field Coy to move to ERVILLERS at an early date.	November 20
	4/4/17		C.R.E Order No 15 issued. Relief of 7th Div by 62nd Div & details of moves of units.	November 21
	5/4/17		Nil	
	6/4/17		All roads west of ERVILLERS - BEHAGNIES road taken over by CORPS ROAD OFFICER. Work commenced on ERVILLERS - MORY Road.	
	7/4/17		C.R.E Order No 16 issued & instructions of 2nd Line of Defence 481st Field Coy to reinforce the work. Instructions issued to collect 2 sections R.E. to meet 4th Cav Div in event of an advance. 440th Field Coy ordered to collect 2 sections to meet 5th Cav Div in the event of the advance on ERVILLERS - MORY & MORY road.	November 22
	8/10/17		Div. Order No 31 issued. Instructions for attack on HINDENBURG Line.	
	9/4/17		R.E Order No 17 issued. Instructions for attack on HINDENBURG Line. Div Order No 32 issued. C.R.E Order No 18 issued clearing roads. ECOUST Road.	November 23

Army Form C. 2118.

WAR DIARY
or
INTELLIGENCE SUMMARY.
(Erase heading not required.)

Instructions regarding War Diaries and Intelligence Summaries are contained in F.S. Regs, Part II. and the Staff Manual respectively. Title pages will be prepared in manuscript.

HdQrs G-r Dn R.E.

Place	Date	Hour	Summary of Events and Information	Remarks and references to Appendices
ACHIET			Action to be taken in case of a retirement by enemy	
			Div Order 33 received attaching attack on HINDENBURG LINE on 10/4/17	September 24
			Copies sent to Units	September 24
	10.4.17		Div Order No 34 received. Attack postponed. Copies of return to Units	
			ADjt attended conference at Div HQ at 5pm in absence of C.R.E.	
		4-45pm	Div Operation Order No 35 received. Attack on HINDENBURG line to take place 11/4/17	
		9.0pm	C.R.E. Order No 19 issued. Starting employment + distribution of units for the attack	
			2 sections of 460th Field Coy placed at disposal of 6th Can. div withdrawn	November 26
	11.4.17	1 am	In the event of an advance by 62nd Div. C.R.E. 7th Div will carry out scheme at FREMICOURT - ST LEDGER and ST LEDGER - VRAUCOURT road. (Wire from CE I Corps)	
			Information recd that 186th + 137th Inf Bgde. will relieve 185th Inf Bgde in line	
	12.4.17		by morning 13/4/17	
		4.0pm	Information recd that it is anticipated that enemy has retired 151st to act on	
			Advance Guard in case of necessity. I Section of 463 Field Coy allotted	
			to act as with Advance Guard	
	13.4.17		G-r Div Order No 36 received. Attack abbreviated in Div Order No 33 to take	

T2134. Wt. W708-776. 50000. 4/15. Sir J. C. & S.

Army Form C. 2118.

WAR DIARY
or
INTELLIGENCE SUMMARY.
(Erase heading not required.)

H.Q.O/s 1st + 2nd Div R.E

Place	Date	Hour	Summary of Events and Information	Remarks and references to Appendices
ACHIET LES	13.4.17	con'td	Place as soon as went in sufficiently cut.	
GRAND			C.R.E. Orders No 20 issued detailing disposition of Field Coys.	November 23
	14.4.17		12 Bangalore Torpedoes sent against enemy wire night 13/14 + 9 successfully exploded making gaps from 4 to 8 yds wide in front-line wire.	
	15.4.17		Enemy counter-attacked Coys. on right + left with an initial success. Fifth Army form our defences not strong enough. Front line + N.E. of ECOUST + LONGATTE to be wired. 2 sections 460's Field Coy detailed to wire ECOUST + LONGATTE. 2 Sections 460 to Field/62 to continue wiring of front line. 2 section L'HOMME MORT - VRAUCOURT LINE. to continue wiring of L'HOMME MORT - VRAUCOURT LINE.	
	16.4.17		C.R.E. went over 2nd line of defence with C.E. IV Corps.	
	17.4.17		N.I.	
	18.4.17		N.I.	
	19.4.17		Wiring of front line completed. To be strengthened by Infantry in hand.	
	20.4.17		Defences of ECOUST + LONGATTE completed. To be strengthened by Infantry in their zone.	
	21.4.17		C.R.E. went over MORY with C.E. IV Corps re water supply.	

WAR DIARY or INTELLIGENCE SUMMARY

Army Form C. 2118.

Place	Date	Hour	Summary of Events and Information	Remarks and references to Appendices
ACHIET-LE-GRAND	21.4.17		HdQrs and DHQ RE	
	22.4.17		Nil	
	23.4.17		Information received that only 1 section R.E. need stand by for anything just in connection with	
			enemy move for cavalry.	
			C.R.E. Order No 20 issued detailing disposition of R.E. in attack on	
			HINDENBURG LINE	Appendix 20
	24.4.17		C.R.E 6.2nd Div. met C.R.E 2nd AUSTRALIAN DIV. and decided on allocation	
			on L'HOMME MORT - VRAUCOURT LINE of roads to be constructed was tarred	
			out by both Divisions.	
	25.4.17		Conference with O.C. Field Coys held at 10.30 am & another with G.S.O.1	
			Brigade Majors & O.C. Field Coys at 3.30pm to discuss action of R.E in	
			attack on Hindenburg Line.	
	26.4.17		C.E Fifth Army called to find out disposition of R.E. in forthcoming operations	
	27.4.17		C.R.E. Corps visited 2nd line of defence with O.C 261st Field Coy as C.R.E	
			was unable to keep appointment.	
			Report on employment of R.E. in forthcoming Operations sent D.C.E. & Corps.	

Army Form C. 2118.

WAR DIARY
or
INTELLIGENCE SUMMARY.
(Erase heading not required.)

Instructions regarding War Diaries and Intelligence Summaries are contained in F. S. Regs., Part II. and the Staff Manual respectively. Title pages will be prepared in manuscript.

Place	Date	Hour	Summary of Events and Information	Remarks and references to Appendices
ACHIET-LE-GRAND	22.4.17	contd	Amendments to C.R.E. Order No 20 of 23.4.17 cancelled & fresh amendments issued	Appendix 29
	28.4.17		Visit from C.E. Fifth Army. Further amendment to C.R.E. Order No 20 issued	Appendix 30
	29.4.17		Nil	
	30.4.17		C.R.E. visited Hindenburg Line with C.E. I Corps. C.R.E. Order No 2 issued detailing work on defence of HENDECOURT in the event of its being captured.	Appendix 31

R.P.Wilson Lt Col R.E.
CRE 62nd Divn

Copy No ..6....

C. R. E. 62nd Division Order No 14.

3. 4. 17.

1.   The 460th Field Coy will be prepared to move to ERVILLERS at short notice.

O.C. 460th Field Coy will get into touch with the Field Coy of the 7th Division at present billetted in ERVILLERS with a view to taking over that Company's billets when the 7th Division comes out of the line.

2.   One section 460th Field Coy is placed at the disposal of 185th Infantry Brigade forthwith for front line work.

3.   O.C. 460th Field Coy will submit to C.R.E. without delay his requirements in Barbed wire and other material and will arrange in communication with 185th Infantry Brigade for a forward Field Coy dump to be established at a suitable place.

R.F. Gillиве
Lieut. Colonel R.E.
C. R. E. 62nd Division.

Copy No 1. 460th Field Co.
       2. 461st Field Co.)
       3. 457th Field Co.)
       4. 185th Brigade.) For information.
       5. 62nd Divn G.   )
       6 & 7 War Diary
       8 Retained.

Appendix 21
Copy No. 10.

C.R.E 62nd. DIVISION ORDER NO. 15.

1. The 62nd. Division will take over the line from the 7th Division on the 4th/5th instant.

2. The 185th Infantry Brigade and 1 Battalion 186th Infantry Brigade will relieve the 22nd. Infantry Brigade and 1 Battalion 20th Infantry Brigade in the line on the 4th instant and the night of the 4th/5th instant.

3. The relief of the 7th Division by the 62nd. Division will be completed by 8 a.m. on the 5th instant.

4. 460th Field Company R.E. will move to ERVILLERS on the 4th instant.

   1 Section 460th Field Coy will be at the disposal of G.O.C. 185th. Infantry Brigade from the night of the 4th/5th April inclusive for work in the line.

   1 Section 460th Field Coy will be responsible for the R.E. supervision of work on the MORY - ERVILLERS Road for which the 2/7th Duke of Wellington's Regt (located at MORY) has been allotted from the 5th instant inclusive.

   Further instructions for work to be carried out by the 460th Field Coy will be issued later.

5. 457th. Field Coy R.E. will move to SAPIGNIES on the 6th instant.

   461st. Field Coy R.E. will hold two Sections in readiness to move to ERVILLERS on the 6th instant.

4.4.17.

Lieut.Col.R.E.
C.R.E. 62nd. Division.

Copy No. 1. 461st. Field Coy. R.E.
         2. 457th. Field Coy.
         3. 460th. Field Coy.
         4. 185th. Infantry Brigade.
         5. 186th. Infantry Brigade.
         6. 187th. Infantry Brigade.
         7. 62nd. Division "Q"
         8. 62nd. Division "G"
         9. 62nd. Divl. Signals.
   10 & 11. Retained. (War Diary).
        12. Retained. (File).

SECRET.   Copy No ......

Appendix 22

C. R. E. 62nd Division Order No 16.

7. 4. 17.

1.   A second line will be prepared for defence on the VAULX-VRAUCOURT - ST LEGER Road or East of the above Road.

   (a)   The 62nd Division will be responsible for the V Corps Road Boundary (about B.24.b.1.4) to the Road junction about L'HOMME MORT inclusive.

   (b)   7th Division is responsible from L'HOMME to SENSEE.

A Battalion of the 186th Brigade ERVILLERS will be prepared to occupy this line in case of necessity. In addition the 208th M.G. Coy MORY will be prepared to occupy the M.G. positions which have been selected.

2.   The 208th and 213th M.G. Coys now billetted in MORY have been placed at the disposal of C.R.E. 62nd Division from the 9th inst inclusive for work of preparing the above line of defence under R.E. supervision as detailed in para 3 below.

3.   O.C. 461st Field Coy R.E. will superintend and be responsible for the execution of the work on this defensive line and will detail 2 sections each under an Officer to provide the necessary technical supervision and R.E. assistance.

4.   O.C. 461st Field Coy will arrange for the supply of all R.E. material and the 208th and 213th M.G. Coys will each provide up to 6. G.S. limbers per day for transport of same from R.E. Dump to site.

5.   The two M.G. Coys named above will work under the immediate direction of O.C. 461st Field Coy who will communicate all detailed instructions direct to the M.G. Coys concerned.

6.   The general line of defence to be adopted will be sited immediately along the East of the VAULX-VRAUCOURT - St LEGER Road and will be prepared on the general lines indicated verbally on the ground this morning.

1.

7. O.C. 461st Field Coy will in conjunction with the Corps M.G. Officer and the Os.C. 208th and 213th M.G. Coys reconnoitre the line to-morrow the 8th inst for M.G. Emplacements.

8. O.C. 461st Field Coy will submit to the C.R.E. as early as possible his proposals for carrying out the work and the following requirements should be observed in making his detailed arrangements.

- (a) The exact positions of the M.G. emplacements having been decided upon, the preparation of same will be commenced forthwith.

- (b) The whole front will be wired and the wiring will proceed concurrently with the construction of the M.G. Emplacements.

- (c) Small works will then be prepared to be held in close connection with the M.G. Emplacements which work should be so laid out as to be capable of being eventually connected up into a continuous line of trenches should it be considered necessary to do so later on.

    NOTE: These small works might be traced whilst the wiring and work on M.G. emplacements is being carried out.
    A plan shewing the exact positions of all the works will also be furnished in due course.

9. O.C. 461st Field Coy will decide as to how much of the line can be worked on by day and what parts it is advisable to carry out by night.

One R.E Officer and section of the two above detailed will always be on the work by day and by night.

10. ACKNOWLEDGE.

(sD) R. A. GILLAM
Lieut.Colonel R.E.
C. R. E. 62nd Division.

Copy No 1 - 461st Field Co.
     2.- 208th M.G. Coy
     3   213th M.G. Coy
     4   62nd Division G - for information
     5   Retained.
  6 & 7   War Diary.

SECRET.   Copy No 5

G. R. S.   62nd Division Order No 17.
            ----

                                                  9. 4. 17.

REF: Maps 51.B.S.W. 1/20,000 & 57.C.N.W. 1/20,000

1.   The 62nd Division will attack the HINDENBURG LINE in conjunction
with the 4th Australian Division on a date and at an hour to be
notified later.
       The 4th Australian Division will be attacking simultaneously on
our Right (East of BULLECOURT). The 51st Division will hold the line
on our left from the SENSEE RIVER, but will not attack.
       The 7th Division will be in Reserve with its leading Brigade in
the valley N.W. of MORY at Zero plus 1 hour.
       The Third Army will be operating against the HINDENBURG LINE about
HENIN SUR COJEUL --- NEUVILLE VITASSE, and active demonstrations will
be made by the Fourth Army on the HINDENBURG LINE to the South.

2.   The boundaries of the 62nd Division attack will be :-

RIGHT BOUNDARY :-   The line U.27.d.8.5. - U.27.b.7.5. - U.xx22.c.3.7.
- to the cross roads at U.22.b.2.9.
       The Left of the Australian Division will advance parallel to
this road approximately along a line running through U.28. central
U.22.d. central.
LEFT BOUNDARY :-   The line from U.20.a.9.6. to cross roads at
U.15.a.9.8.
       The 185th Infantry Brigade will attack on the Right and the
187th Infantry Brigade will attack on the Left.

       The boundary between Brigades will be a line through the road
junction at U.20.d.9.4. - junction with trench at roadway in
U.21.a.4.1. - U. 16.a.0.0.

3.   OBJECTIVES.

       1st Objective -   German trench from U.21.d.3.2. to U.20.a.9.5.
                         and German trench from U.21.d.5.5. to U.14.d.3.0.

       2nd Objective.-   Line of roadway from U.22.b.2.9. to U.15.c.6.5.
                         - German trench U.15.d.9.5. - U.15.a.8.5.

       3rd Objective.-   A line running from U.12.c.7.7. - U.11.b.9.0. -
                         U.U.d.2.4. - U.15.a.4.4.

       The advance from the 1st Objective to the 2nd Objective will
commence at Zero plus 1 hour.
       The advance from the 2nd Objective to the 3rd Objective will
commence at Zero plus 2 hours and 20 minutes.

4.   FORMING UP LINE.

       A line, to be taped, parallel to and about 500 yards from the front
trench of the 1st Objective. On X/Y night G.O.C. 185th Infantry Bde
will ensure that our line of posts is established within 500 yards
of the German front line, at not less than 100 yards interval, to
cover the forming up of the attacking troops. The forming up will be made under
cover of the posts of the 185th Infantry Brigade. Forming up will be
completed by Zero minus 1 hour.
       The posts of the 185th Infantry Brigade East of a line through
U.20.a.8.9. - U.19.d.5.7. will be withdrawn at Zero plus 1 hour.
Posts West of this line will remain in position.

-1-

-2-

5. The village of BULLECOURT will not be attacked in the first instance but will be pinched out. The Right flank of the 186th Infantry Bde will therefore rest on the line of the road U.27.a.9.3. and U.21.d.5.6. a special body of troops being told off to establish a strong point at the cross roads at U.27.b.2.9. and to deal with the German trench running from U.27.b.1.7. to U.21.d.3.3. which will have been specially bombarded by the Artillery before the assault takes place and during the advance.

6. Each objective will be consolidated as soon as gained. At least 2 strong points will be made by each Brigade on about the line of the 2nd objective.
A Senior Officer will be detailed by each Brigade to take Command of each Objective when gained.

7. 185th Infantry Brigade will be in Divisional Reserve in the low ground West of ST.LEGER.

8. ASSEMBLY AREAS.
The dividing line between the Assembly Areas of the attacking troops will be the general line U.20.d.9.4. - U.26.c.2.5. - B.17.a.9.7. - B.20.b.7.5.
Detailed orders for move into assembly areas will be issued later.

9. O.C. Field Coys will each detail two sections to be placed at the disposal of their affiliated Infantry Brigade to assist in the consolidation of the positions. These sections will in no case be sent forward until objectives are securely in our hands.
Headquarters and the remaining two sections of each Field Coy will be in Divisional Reserve.
O.C. Units will get into touch at once with the Infantry Brigades concerned with regard to the locations and employment of their two sections during the attack.
The Sections detailed to Brigades and the names of the Officers in Command will be reported to C.R.E.

10. O.C. Units will forward a list of R.E. Stores and material which they may require as early as possible to Adjutant, 62nd Divnl R.E. and must report the position of their forward R.E.Dump without delay.
Units will be responsible for the stocking of their forward Dumps from the Divisional R.E. Dump.
Screw Pickets and Barbed wire may be drawn from the old German Dump at G.6.b.1.9. i/c of O.C. 457th Field Coy. O.C. 457th Field Coy will arrange to issue accordingly.
Loading parties will be sent with transport.

11. MAPS. Special Map 1/10,000 ECOUST-ST MEIN will be carried.

12. REPORT CENTRES:
Report centres will be as follows :-
Divisional Report Centre ACHIET LE GRAND.
Forward Report Centre B.17.a.8.7.
185th Infantry Brigade   ERVILLERS
186th Infantry Brigade)
187th Infantry Brigade) B.17.a.8.7.

13. ACKNOWLEDGE.

R.A.Cullen
Lieut.Colonel R.E.
C.R.E. 62nd Division.

Copy No 1 - 457th Field Co
     2   460th Field Co
     3   461st Field Co
     4   62nd Division G - for information
     5 & 6 War Diary
     7   Retained.

Copy No 5

Appendix 24

C.R.E. 62nd Divn Order No 18.

9. 4. 17.

Reference Maps 51.B.S.E. 1/20,000
57.c.N.W. 1/20,000.

1. The Operations ordered in 62nd Division Order No 31 and detailed in C.R.E. 62nd Divn Order No 17 of this date are postponed, but all arrangements will be made to carry out the attack at short notice when the wire has been sufficiently cut and the trenches adequately bombarded.

2. In the meantime, in the event of the enemy evacuating their positions on account of the attack of the Third Army, the following preparations will be made; all concerned will be prepared to put them into operation at any hour after 4 p.m. to-day on receipt of orders to that effect.
(a) A bombardment will be made as for the attack ordered in 62nd Divn Order No 31 up to and including 1st Objective only, (slight alterations have been made in the timing of the barrage — These will be shown on a barrage table to be issued shortly). Under cover of this 5 strong patrols from each of the Battalions of the 185th Brigade holding the line on the front to be attacked, will be sent forward close under the barrage and will endeavour to occupy the line of the 1st objective. These patrols will be strongly supported without delay if they succeed in their mission.
(b) Should these troops find the 1st objective unoccupied by the enemy, they will push forward as part of an Advanced Guard to the 3rd Objective as defined in 62nd Divn Order No 31.

3. The composition of the Advanced Guard will be as follows :-

Commander :- Brigadier General V.H. de Falbe, C.M.G., D.S.O.
Regiment Corps Cavalry (Glasgow Yeomanry).
1 Brigade R.F.A.
1 Section R.E.
Signal Section 185th Inf. Bde.
212 M.G. Coy.
Infantry Battalions of 185th Inf.Bde.
1 Bearer sub-division Field Ambulance.

4. The Section R.E. detailed above will be found by the 460th Field Coy R.E. O.C. 460th Field Coy will report forthwith to the G.O.C. Advanced Guard,(Brigadier-General V.H. de Falbe, C.M.G. D.S.O.) and to the C.R.E. 62nd Division, the name of the officer in command of the section detailed.

5. The Staff of the 185th Inf. Bde. will form the staffs of the Advanced Guard.

6. 186th and 187th Brigades will be prepared to move, in order as above, in support of the Advanced Guard.

Units will take with them only the baggage supplies and stores as laid down in War Establishments and as far as existing transport permits.

7. ACKNOWLEDGE

Lieut.Colonel R.E.
C.R.E. 62nd Division.

Copies to
1. 460th Field Co.
2. 457th Field Co
3. 461st Field Co.
4 62nd Division G.
5. Retained.
6 & 7 War Diary.

SECRET.

62nd. DIVISION ORDER NO. 33.

Appendix 25

9.4.17.

Ref:- Maps 51.B.S.W. (1/20,000)
      57.C.N.W. (1/20,000)

1. 1st. Army and 3rs. Army have gained the bulk of their objectives. The Cavalry Corps have been ordered to move forward.

2. Unless it is discovered during the night that the enemy have evacuated the HINDENBURG LINE on our front, the 185th Infantry Brigade, in conjunction with the 4th Australian Division, will push forward strong patrols under a barrage, as ordered in Divn Order No. 32. para 2 (A), on the morning of the 10th April.

   Zero hour will be 4.30 a.m.

   The 4th Australian Division attack will be supported by Tanks.

   The objective of the 4th Australian Division will be RIENCOURT and the clearing of BULLECOURT as far as its Western outskirts.

   The 185th Infantry Brigade will push 1 Battalion into BULLECOURT from the South West as soon as the operations by the 4th Australian Division make this possible, and, supported by Tanks will clear and occupy the HINDENBURG LINE Westwards as far as O.20.b.

3. If we succeed in occupying the HINDENBURG LINE, THE Advanced Guard as detailed in Division Order 32, (C.R.E. 62nd Division order 17) will move forward in the general direction of VILLERS LEZ CAGNICOURT via HENDENCOURT, gaining touch Northwards with the Cavalry Corps and covering the left of the Anzac Corps, who will be advancing towards CAGNICOURT.

   The 186th Infantry Brigade and the 213th M.G. Coy will be in position about MORY at 6.am. - Headquarters :- L'HOMME MORT and the 187th Infantry Brigade and the 208th M.G. Coy will be in position about BEHAGNIES - SAPIGNIES at 8 a.m. - Headquarters BEHAGNIES, ready to move on in support of the Advanced Guard.

   The 201st. M.G. Coy will be prepared to move from its billets at 6 a.m.

   Field Coys R.E. will be prepared to move from their present billets at 6 a.m.

   Orders for R.A. will be issued by G.O.C.R.A.

   Orders for Field Ambulances, Train, Mobile Veterinary Section will be issued by 'Q'

4. ACKNOWLEDGE.

A.Hore-Ruthven, Lieut.Col.
General Staff 62nd. Division

C.R.E. 62nd Division Order No 19.

10. 4. 17.

1. An attack will be made on the Hindenburg line on the morning of 11. 4. 17. in accordance with 62nd Division Order No 35 copies of which are issued herewith to Os.C. Field Coys R.E.

2. As previously ordered 1 Section 460th Field Coy complete with transport will be placed under the Orders of the G.O.C. Advanced Guard (Brigadier-General de Falbe, C.M.G., D.S.O.)

3. Two sections of the 461st Field Coy are placed at the disposal of G.O.C. 187th Infantry Brigade and will be in position about BEHAGNIES at 6 a.m. Senior Officer in Command of sections will report at 187th Inf.Bde H.Qrs at BEHAGNIES at 6 a.m.

4. Two sections of the 457th Field Coy are placed at the disposal of 186th Inf.Bde, and will be in position about MORY at 6 a.m. Senior in Command of these Sections will report to Headquarters 186th Inf. Brigade at L'HOMME MORT at 6 a.m.

5. The two sections of the 460th Field Coy detailed to assist the 4th Cavalry Division are now withdrawn and will be placed at the disposal of G.O.C. Advanced Guard for cutting gaps in wire and clearing road in U.21.a. to allow of passage of Corps Cavalry and Field Artillery attached to Advanced Guard.
The O.C. of these two sections will report forthwith to 185th Infantry Brigade Headquarters for instructions. He will receive his orders as to when to go forward to clear the wire from G.O.C. Advanced Guard.
When the Cavalry and Artillery have passed through the wire these two sections will return to their Unit headquarters and be in Divisional Reserve.

6. The names of the Senior Officers in command of Sections detailed under paras 3 & 4 and the officer in command of section with Advanced Guard will be reported to the Brigade concerned and to this office forthwith.

7. Troops will wear Jerkins and carry Haversacks. Packs will not be carried.
The unexpired portion of the days rations and the iron ration will be carried on the man.

8. Units, less sections detailed in paras 2,3,4,&5, will be in Divisional Reserve and will be prepared to move from their present Headquarters at 6va.m.

9. Each Unit will send a Mounted Orderly to report to these Headquarters at 5. a.m. Feeds for the day to be brought.

10. ACKNOWLEDGE.

Issued at   p.m.

Lieut.Colonel R.E.
C. R. E. 62nd Division.

Copies to
   O.C. 461st Field Co   187th Brigade
   O.C. 457th Field Co   62nd Divn G.
   O.C. 460th Field Co   2 War Diary
   185th Brigade   1 File.
   186th Brigade.

NOTE: - In the event of Field Coys in Divnl Reserve being ordered to move forward Pontoons will not be taken in the first instance unless definite orders are issued to this effect

Appendix 26

C.R.E. 62nd Division Order No 19.

10. 4. 17.

1. An attack will be made on the Hindenburg line on the morning of 11. 4. 17. in accordance with 62nd Division Order No 35 copies of which are issued herewith to Os.C. Field Coys R.E.

2. As previously ordered 1 Section 460th Field Coy complete with transport will be placed under the Orders of the G.O.C. Advanced Guard (Brigadier-General de Falbe, C.M.G., D.S.O.)

3. Two sections of the 461st Field Coy are placed at the disposal of G.O.C. 187th Infantry Brigade and will be in position about BEHAGNIES at 6 a.m. Senior Officer in Command of sections will report at 187th Inf. Bde H.Qrs at BEHAGNIES at 6 a.m.

4. Two sections of the 457th Field Coy are placed at the disposal of 186th Inf. Bde. and will be in position about MORY at 6 a.m. Senior Officer in Command of these Sections will report to Headquarters 186th Inf. Brigade at L'HOMME MORT at 6 a.m.

5. The two sections of the 460th Field Coy detailed to assist the 4th Cavalry Division are now withdrawn and will be placed at the disposal of G.O.C. Advanced Guard for cutting gaps in wire and clearing road in U.21.a. to allow of passage of Corps Cavalry and Field Artillery attached to Advanced Guard.
The O.C. of these two sections will report forthwith to 185th Infantry Brigade Headquarters for instructions. He will receive his orders as to when to go forward to clear the wire from G.O.C. Advanced Guard.
When the Cavalry and Artillery have passed through the wire these two sections will return to their Unit headquarters and be in Divisional Reserve.

6. The names of the Senior Officers in command of Sections detailed under paras 3 & 4 and the officer in command of section with Advanced Guard will be reported to the Brigade concerned and to this office forthwith.

7. Troops will wear Jerkins and carry Haversacks. Packs will not be carried.
The unexpired portion of the days rations and the iron ration will be carried on the man.

8. Units, less sections detailed in paras 2,3,4,&5, will be in Divisional Reserve and will be prepared to move from their present Headquarters at 6 a.m.

9. Each Unit will send a Mounted Orderly to report to these Headquarters at 6. a.m. Feeds for the day to be brought.

10. ACKNOWLEDGE.

Lieut.Colonel R.E.
C. R. E. 62nd Division.

Issued at   p.m.

Copies to
  O.C. 461st Field Co   187th Brigade
  O.C. 457th Field Co   62nd Divn G.
  O.C. 460th Field Co   2 War Diary
  185th Brigade   1 File.
  186th Brigade.

    NOTE: - In the event of Field Coys in Divnl Reserve being ordered to move forward Pontoons will not be taken in the first instance unless definite orders are issued to this effect

SECRET   Copy No ..8....

                        C. R. E. 62nd Divn Order No 20.

REF: Maps 51.b.S.W.)   14.4.17.
         57.c.N.W.)

1.   Provided the wire is sufficiently cut, the attack on the
HINDENBURGH LINE, ordered in 62nd Division Order No 31 (C.R.E.Order No 17)
will take place on a date (not before April 16th) and at an hour to be
notified later, unless the enemy withdraw previously on account of the
attack of the Third Army.

2.   In addition to the Objectives laid down in the above Order, the 62nd
Division will be responsible for the capture of BULLECOURT. This will be
carried out by the 185th Inf. Brigade less one Bn.

3.   The objectives, frontages and Boundaries of the 186th and 187th Inf.
Brigades will be as in C.R.E. Order No 17. 1 Bn of the 185th Inf. Bde
will be placed at the disposal of G.O.C. 186th Inf. Bde to hold the
second objective and release a battalion 186th Infantry Brigade to move
forward to the 3rd objective.

4.   The advance from the 1st objective to the 2nd objective will commence
at Zero plus 2 hours and 15 minutes. The hours mentioned in paras 3, of
CRE 62nd Division Order No 17 will be amended accordingly.

5.   Battalions of the 185 Infantry Bde attacking BULLECOURT will jump off
at 2 mins before Zero hour and will advance at the rate of 100 yards in
2 minutes to the 1st Objective.

6.   186th and 187th Infantry Brigades will form up under cover of their
own posts
        The 185th Infantry Brigade will form up under cover of the posts of
186th Inf. Bde which cover the frontage of their attack, and will form up
on the Railway Line in U.27.d. and the road running North in U.27.d.
U.27.c and U.27 a.
        The posts held by the 187th Inf. Bde West of U.20.a.4.0.will be taken
over by a battalion of the 7th Divn on the evening of the 14th April --
arrangements to be made direct between 187th Inf. Bde and 7th Divn.

7.   ~~The formations and method of attack will be as laid down in 62nd Divn
Order No 31, with the exception that the strong bombing party~~
        Os.C. Field Coys will detail two sections to be placed at the disposal
of their affiliated Infantry Brigades to assist in the consolidation of
the positions gained
        These sections will in no case be sent forward until the objectives
are securely in our hands.

8.   O.C. 460th Field Coy will detail two sections to be in readiness to
cut gaps in wire for the Corps Cavalry. Detailed instructions as to how
when and where these sections are to be employed will be issued to-morrow

9.   H.Q. and all sections not detailed under paras 7 & 8 will be in
Divisional Reserve and will hold themselves in readiness to move from
their present billets at very short notice. O.C. Units will get into
touch at once with the Infantry Brigade concerned with regard to the
location and employment of the two sections attached to their affiliated
Brigade during the attack.

10.   The numbers of the Sections detailed to Brigades and the names of
the officers in command to be reported to C.R.E.

11.   Watches will be synchronised at 12 noon and 5 p.m. on 'Y' day.

SECRET.

62nd DIVISION ORDER NO 35.

10. 4. 17.

Ref: Maps 51.b.S.W.)
          57.c.N.W.) 1/20,000

1. Unless it is discovered during the night that the enemy have evacuated the HINDENBURG LINE on our front, the 4th Australian Division will attack the line between U.30.a. and U.28.b. at an early hour on the morning of the 11th April, covered by Tanks.

    Zero hour will be notified later.

2. Liaison Officers will be detailed between :-
62nd Divnl Headquarters and 4th Australian Division.
185th Infantry Brigade and Left Brigade 4th Autralian Divn.
Right Battalion 185th Infantry Brigade and Left Battalion 4th Australian Division.

3. 62nd Division Order No 33 from line 13 - "The Objective of the 4th Australian Division" to the end - will now hold good.

4. ACKNOWLEDGE.

Issued 3 p.m.

                                                A.HORE RUTHVEN Lieut.Col,
                                                  General Staff, 62nd Division.

12. REPORT CENTRES:

        Divisional Report Centre :-   B.13.b.2.3.

    185 Inf. Bde.)
    186 Inf. Bde.)   B.17.a.8.7.
    187 Inf. Bde.)

13. ACKNOWLEDGE.

                                R.A. Gillam Lieut.Col R.E.
                          C. R. E. 62nd Division.

Copies to.
  1 457 Field Co   6 187 Brigade
  2 460 Field Co   7 62nd Divn G
  3 461 Field Co   8 Retained.
  4 185 Brigade   9 War Diary
  5 186 Brigade   10   do

R.E. Orders
and Instructions
for
Attack

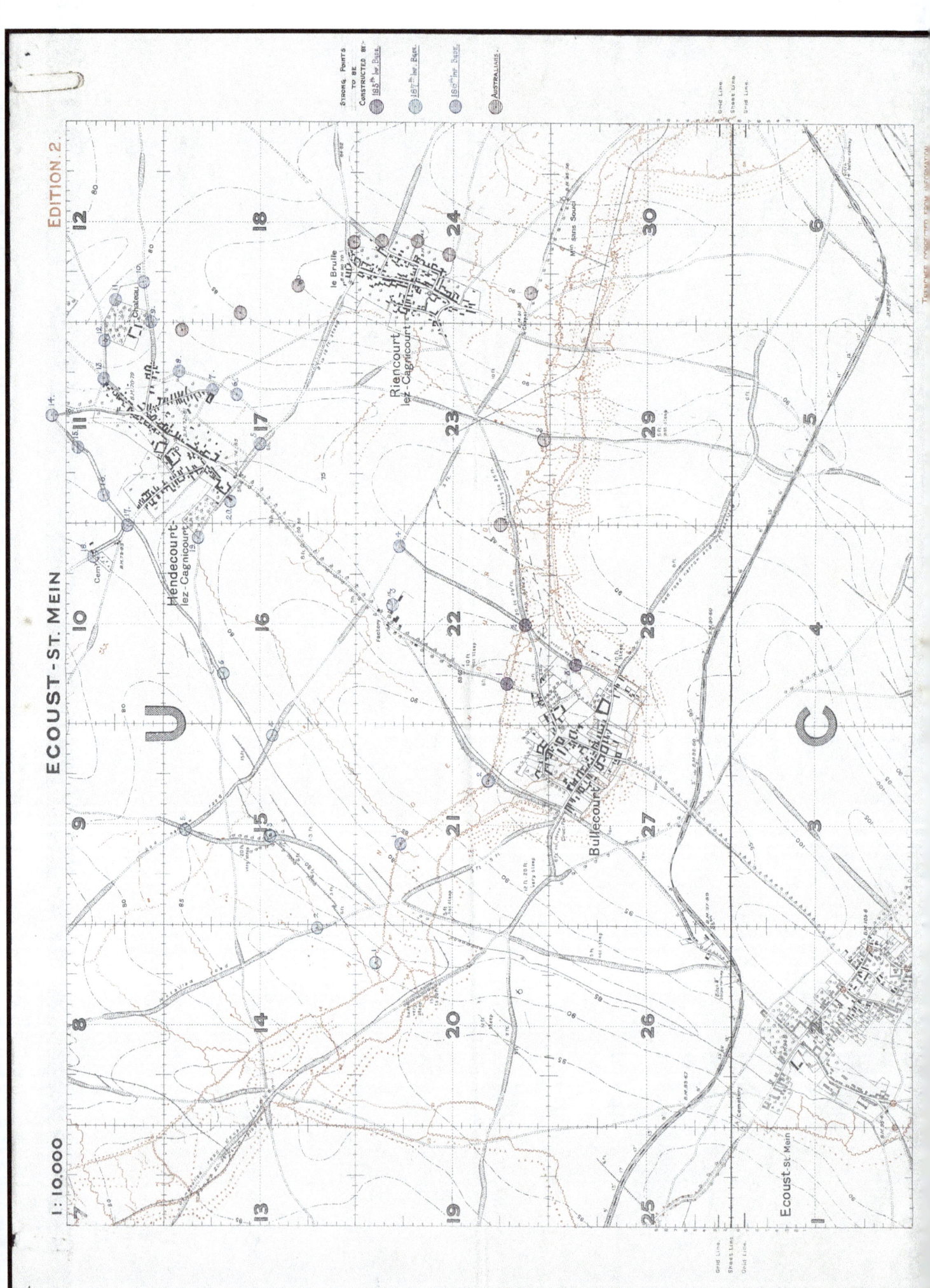

SECRET   Copy No. 7

AMENDMENTS TO C.R.E. 62nd Division Order No 20.

The amendments to C.R.E. 62nd Division Order No 20 dated 23.4.17 are cancelled and the following substituted.

7. Field Companies are placed at the disposal of G.Os.C. Infantry Brigades as under to assist in the work of consolidation and in constructing strong points.

    457th Field Coy - 4 Sections to 186th Brigade.
    460th Field Coy - 2 Sections to 185th Brigade.
    461st Field Coy - 2 Sections to 187th Brigade.

In the case of the 457th Field Coy and the 460th Field Coy this scheme provides for only 3 and 1 sections respectively being absorbed in the operations and for the remaining sections in each case to be held in readiness in the forward positions indicated hereunder in case they may be required.

2 sections 460th Field Coy and 2 Sections 461st Field Coy will be held in Divisional Reserve.

8. Working and carrying parties will be provided as already arranged by Os.C. Field Coys in direct communication with Brigades.

9. The R.E. Sections detailed to operate with Brigades will rendezvous on Y night, together with their working and carrying parties, at the places of assembly indicated hereunder. The hour of assembly to be arranged direct between Os.C. Field Coys and Brigades.

(a) 457th Field Coy - 4 sections - In the old system of German trenches existing at C.2.a.0.5.
(b) 460th Field Coy - 2 sections - In cellars in ECOUST near Battalion H.Q. at C.2.d.8.8.
(c) 461st Field Coy - 2 sections - In Railway Cutting between U.25.b.8.1. and U.25.b.2.4.

No R.E. will advance with the assaulting troops. In case of (a) above two sections R.E. will move forward after the first objective has been gained as directed in 186th. Brigade amended instructions for Attack No 4. para 5 (f) dated 20.4.17.

In the case of (b) 1 Section R.E. will similarly move forward after the 1st objective has been gained.

In the case of (c) 2 Sections R.E. will move forward after the 1st Objective has been gained, when one section will commence work on Strong Points 1, 2 and 3. The other section will remain with Battalion H.Q. until the 2nd objective has been gained when it will move forward for work on Strong Points 4 and 6.

The Officers Commanding sections engaged on Strong Points under (a), (b) and (c) will report at their respective Battalion H.Qs. at U.26.c.9.0., C.2.d.8.8. and U.25.b. at zero hour.

10. (a) Strong points will be constructed as under :-

Brigade & Field Coy responsible.	No and map ref of strong point.	Working Party	Garrison.
186th Brigade 457th Field Co	(1) U.21.a.8.5.	I Section R.E. with party of Brigade	1 M.G. & 1 Platoon.
	(2) U.21.d.5.6.	Mining Section attd under Lt. BROOK R.E.	1 M.G. & 1 Platoon.
	(3) U.22.b.1.7.	1 Section R.E. with party of Brigade	1 M.G. & 1 Platoon.
	(4) U22.b.7.5.	Mining Section attd under Lieut BEST R.E.	1 M.G. & 1 Platoon.

Copy No ....

AMENDMENTS TO C.R.E. 62nd Division Order No 20.
- - - - - - - - -

The amendments to C.R.E. 62nd Division Order No 20 dated 23.4.17. are cancelled and the following substituted.

7.

-2-

Brigade & Field Coy responsible.	No & Map ref of Strong Point	Working Party	Garrison.
185th Brigade 460th Field Co	(1) U.22.c.4.1.	) 1 Section R.E. with) 1 Officer and party) of Brigade Mining) Section attached.) The whole under Lt) FROGGATT R.E.	1 M.G. & 1 Officer and 10 O.R.
	(2) U.22.c.9.2.		1 M.G. 1 N.C.O. and 9 men
	(3) U.28.a.5.7.		1 M.G. 1 N.C.O. and 9 men.
187th Brigade 461st Field Co	(1) U.20.b.6.8.	) 1 Section R.E. with) 1 Off. and party of) Brigade Mining Section) attd. The whole) under 2/Lieut Collins) R.E.	1 M.G. & 12 O.R.
	(2) U.14.d.9.4.		1 M.G. & 12 O.R.
	(3) U.15.c.9.9.		1.M.G. & 12 O.R.
	(4) U.15.d.9.8.	) 1 Section R.E. with) party of Bde Mining) Section attd. The whole) under Lieut DYKE R.E.	1 M.G. & 12 O.R.
	(5) U.15.a.9.8.		1 M.G.& 12 O.R.
	(6) U.16.a.5.3.	Post with M.G. to be established By Infantry.	

WORKING PARTIES:

    1 Senior R.E. N.C.O. will be in immediate charge of the work on each Strong Point.

    The approximate strength of working party on each strong point will be

        R.E. - 10 Other Ranks.
    Infantry (including Mining Section) - 20 to 25 Other Ranks.

CARRYING PARTIES:

    457th and 461st Field Coys - 1 N.C.O. & 24 men for each strong point (1 journey).
    460th Field Coy. - 1 N.C.O. & 10 men for each strong point (2 journeys).

(b) As soon as the situation admits of it strong points for the defence of HENDECOURT will be established at the following points, each for a garrison of 1 platoon and 1 Lewis gun, with the addition of Machine Guns where stated.

    The garrisons of these posts will be furnished from the 2/4th and 2/7th Bns Duke of Wellington's Regt (2 Coys from each) which will be allotted for the defence of the village under the command of Lieut. Colonel H.E.P. NASH.

    5. U.17.a.8.0.   1 M.G.   ) -
    6. U.17.b.20.15.   ) 1 Company
    7. U.17.b.3.5.   1 M.G.   ) 2/7th Bn D. of W.
    8. U.17.b.5.9.   )

    9. U.11.d.9.1.   )
    10. U.12.c.4.2.   ) 1 Company
    11. U.12.c.2.5.   2 M.Gs.   ) 2/7th Bn D of W.
    12. U.11.d.8.6.   )

```
13.  U.11.d.4.6.       )
14.  U.11.b.1.2.   1 M.G.  ) 1 Company
15.  U.11.c.8.9.       ) 2/4th D. of W. Regt.
16.  U.11.c.4.6.       )

17.  U.11.c.0.4.       )
18.  U.10.d.7.7.   1 M.G.  )    1 Company
19.  U.18.b.9.7.       ) 2/4th D. of W. Regt.
20.  U.17.a.3.3.       )
```

Battn H.Q. of O.C. Garrisons: Vicinity of wood U.17.a.1.7.

The village will be sub-divided for purposes of responsibility into four parts as follows :-
i. A line running ~~east from~~ N.E. along BULLECOURT - BOIS DU MONT roadway.
ii. A line running west from Road junction U.11.c.0.4. - through Road junction U.11.d.1.2. - thence along the roadway which bounds the S. side of the Chateau VERAC.

Two senior Officers have been specially detailed by 186th Brigade to assist the O.C. Garrison in organising the defence of HENDECOURT and Brigade Orders on the subject are being issued to all concerned.

Lieut S.A. SMITH with 16 Other Ranks 457th Field Co R.E. is detailed to assist these Officers in the preparations for defence of HENDECOURT. This party will move forward at the earliest opportunity, closely following the battalions detailed for the capture of HENDECOURT Arrangements as to rendezvous and the exact hour of moving forward will be made direct between O.C. 457th Field Coy and 186th Brigade.

O.C. 457th Field Coy will arrange for Lieut SMITH to be put into communication with the 2 senior Officers above referred to forthwith.

On reaching HENDECOURT Lieut Smith will at once take steps to ascertain what suitable material (if any) is available locally for defence purposes.

(c) Provided the situation has become sufficiently clear to allow of work being carried out, 1 Field Coy (which is expected to be furnished from another Division) will be sent forward to HENDECOURT on the evening of Z day for the work of strengthening the strong points indicated under 10 (b) and (c) and for consolidating the defences of the village. Instructions for this Company will be issued later.

This Company will be relieved on the morning following Z day by four Sections of the 62nd Divisional R.E. which have been held in Divnl Reserve.

11. Strong Points will be prepared for all round defence and will be completely surrounded with wire entanglement.

The crucifix type (figs. 1 and 2) will be adopted where suitable to the configuration of the ground. This type will generally be found to be adoptable in conjunction with existing trenches, as in the case of those to be established in the support trench of the HINDENBURG LINE or the type shewn in Fig.3 may be employed in this latter connection.

In all cases M.G. Emplacements must be constructed and alternative M.G. positions provided.

12. Immediately on reaching the sites of strong points in the HINDENBURG support trench the R.E. Section Officers in charge will take steps to block the existing trench at a distance of 50 yards to each flank, and as soon as circumstances permit will dig a length of straight trench and construct loopholed traverses for enfilading same.

13. Strong Points will be established by the 2nd Australian Divn on our immediate right at

U.23.c.0.5.
U.18.c.3.6.
U.18.a.1.2.
and U.17.b.9.8.

14. The Sections of 460th and 461st Field Coys in Divisional Reserve will remain in their present billets at ERVILLERS and be ready to move in battle order at half an hour's notice from zero hour onwards.
NOTE - 1 Section 460th Field Coy R.E. of the two in Divisional Reserve will be held in readiness for wire cutting for Corps Cavalry in case of its being called upon to do so.

15. The positions of Os.C. Field Coys during the operations will be at their respective Brigade battle Headquarters.

16. Forward R.E. Dumps will be established as under :-

185th Inf. Brigade and 460th Field Coy — C.1.d.9.2.
186th Inf. Brigade and 457th Field Coy — C.2.a.9.9.
187th Inf. Brigade and 461st Field Coy — C.25.b.8.1. and
C.25.b.2.4.

Dumps to be supplied to the scale already communicated by drawing from the forward Divisional R.E. Dump at ERVILLERS.

17. The arrangements for the attack will be communicated by Field Coy Commanders to all Officers concerned, and the manner in which the R.E. will participate must be carefully explained in detail to all ranks engaged in the operations. Care must be taken that the orders issued to each Section officer are clearly understood by the two senior N.C.Os of his section.

18. The C.R.E. will be with Advanced Divisional Headquarters at ERVILLERS, B.13.b.2.3. from zero hour onwards.

Lieut.Colonel R.E.
C. R. E. 62nd Division.

27. 4. 17.

Copy No 1. 457th Field Co.
2. 460th Field Co.
3. 461st Field Co.
4. 185th Brigade
5. 186th Brigade.
6. 187th Brigade.
7. 62nd Division G.
8 & 9 War Diary
10. Retained.

TYPES OF STRONG POINTS.

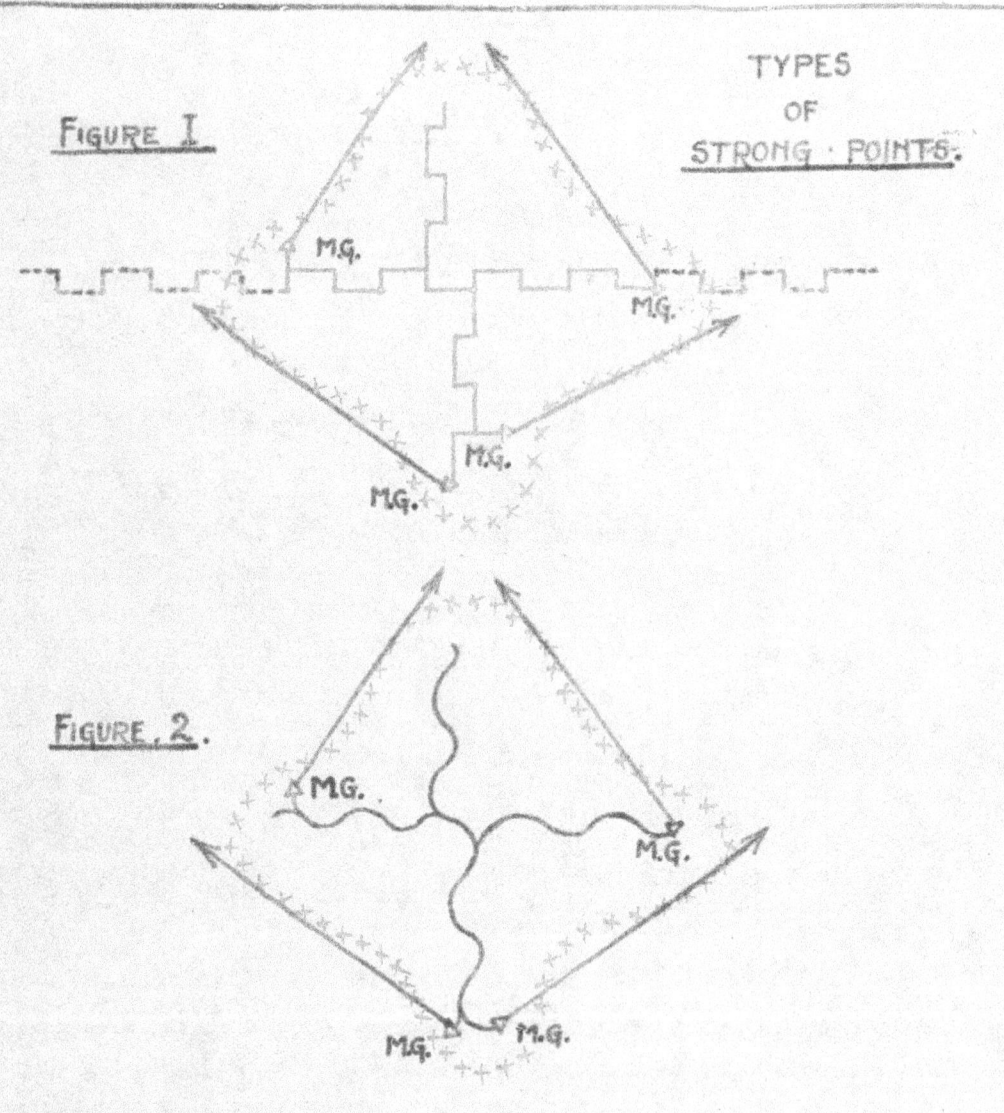

FIGURE 1.

FIGURE 2.

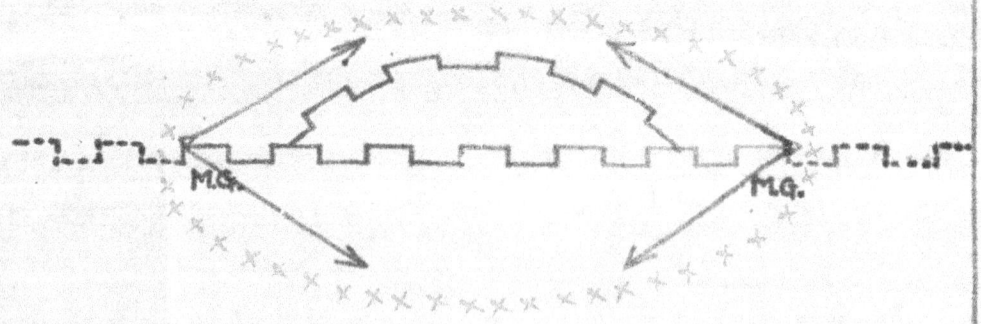

FIGURE 3

C.R.E. 62nd DIVISIONAL R.E.

Secret   Copy No ..4......

C.R.E. 62nd Division Order No 21.

30. 4. 17.

Reference Amendments to C.R.E. 62nd Division Order No 20 para 10 (b) and (c) of 27. 4. 17. and amendments of same dated 28. 4. 17, the following supplementary instructions are issued for the action to be taken to strengthen the defences of HENDECOURT, and all concerned will be prepared to proceed in accordance with these orders on 'Z' day as the situation develops.

1. O.C. 457th Field Coy R.E. will be responsible that there is a sufficient supply of barbed wire and pickets in the forward dump at ECOUST to allow of a total length of 2000 yards of single apron fence being erected as rapidly as possible during Z night, that is to say about 120 yards for each of the 16 strong points immediately surrounding HENDECOURT.

Any balance of material remaining over in the 460th Field Coy dump at ECOUST will be considered by O.C. 457th Field Coy as also available for this purpose.

2. 2/Lieut Smith R.E. (or the senior N.C.O. or Sapper of his party that circumstances may render it necessary to act for him) will keep O.C. 457th Field Coy informed as to the nature and quantities of material that have been found to be available in or about HENDECOURT so as to minimise or altogether obviate if possible the necessity for carrying material forward.

3. O.C. 457th Field Coy R.E. will arrange with 186th Brigade for carrying parties to be made available on Z evening to take forward the R.E. material that may be required for work during the night, in the event of none having been found to exist in or about HENDECOURT.

4. Captain L.H.C. DERMER who will be in command of the 4 sections (2 sections 460th Field Coy and 2 sections 461st Field Coy) which will be moving forward for work during the night will get into touch at once with O.C. 457th Field Coy and arrange details for the supply of material, reporting to C.R.E. by 10 p.m. 1st May the exact arrangements that have been made.

1.

5. The defences of HENDECOURT will be divided for the purposes of work into four sectors as under, and 1 Section R.E. will be allotted to each sector to provide the necessary R.E. supervision and technical assistance.

Sector	Strong Points		Garrison
A.	(5) U.17.a.8.0.	1 M.G.	
	(6) U.17.b.20.15.		1 Company
	(7) U.17.b.3.5.	1 M.G.	
	(8) U.17.b.5.9.		2/7th Bn D of W Regt.
B.	(9) U.11.d.9.1.		
	(10) U.12.c.4.2.		1 Company
	(11) U.12.c.2.5.	2 M.G's	
	(12) U.11.d.8.6.		2/7th Bn D of W Regt
C.	(13) U.11.d.4.8.		
	(14) U.11.b.1.2.	1 M.G.	1 Company
	(15) U.11.c.8.9.		
	(16) U.11.c.4.6.		2/4th Bn D of W Regt
D.	(17) U.11.c.0.4.		
	(18) U.10.d.7.7.	1 M.G.	1 Company
	(19) U.18.b.9.7.		
	(20) U.17.a.3.3.		2/4th Bn D of W Regt.

Captain DERMER to communicate early to C.R.E. the name of the R.E. Officer in Command of each Section allotted to the above Sectors A.B.C. & D.

6. Captain DERMER will report to-morrow (1st May) to Headquarters 186th Brigade who will kindly put him into communication with the Officers Commanding Companies providing the garrisons of the Strong points for the defence of HENDECOURT.

7. The garrisons of the strong points will supply the working parties for Z night.

All available R.E. will be employed on wiring, which must be proceeded with immediately the R.E. Sections arrive on the site on Z evening.

8. Orders for the 4 Sections R.E. from Divisional Reserve to move forward to HENDECOURT will be issued by C.R.E.

These sections will be held in readiness to leave Camp early on Z afternoon.

Copies to - 3 Field Coys
3 Brigades
62nd Division G.

Lieut. Colonel R.E.

SECRET.

Copy No .7...

AMENDMENTS TO C.R.E. 62nd Division Order No 20.

28. 4. 17.

Paras 10 (c) and 16 of Amendments to C.R.E. 62nd Division Order No 20 dated 27. 4. 17. are cancelled and the following substituted.

10.

(c) Provided the situation has become sufficiently clear to allow of work being carried out 2 sections 460th Field Coy and 2 sections 461st Field Coy which are being held in Divisional Reserve will be sent forward to HERMIESCOURT on the evening of Z day under the command of Captain L.H.C. Permer, 461st Field Coy, for the work of strengthening the strong points indicated under 10 (b) and for consolidating the defences of the village. Detailed instructions for these four sections will be issued later.

These four sections will be relieved on the morning following Z day by a Field Coy (which is expected to be furnished from another Division).

16. Forward R.E. Dumps will be established as under :-

185th Inf. Brigade and 460th Field Coy — C.1.d.9.2.
186th Inf. Brigade and 457th Field Coy — C.2.a.9.9.
187th Inf. Brigade and 461st Field Coy — U.25.b.8.1. and U.25.b.2.4.

Dumps to be supplied to the scale already communicated by drawing from the forward Divisional R.E. Dump at ERVILLERS.

Ack 29/4

Lieut.Colonel R.E.
C. R. E. 62nd Division. B.E.F.

Copy No 1 457th Field Co
        2 460th Field Co
        3 461st Field Co
        4 185th Brigade
        5 186th Brigade
        6 187th Brigade
        7 62nd Division G.
      8 & 9 War Diary
       10 Retained.

SECRET

The following Transport arrangements will be carried out on Z day to ensure getting forward a supply of R.E. material to HENDECOURT for work on Z night.

Each Field Company will detail 2 pontoon wagons to report at the Advanced Divisional dump at MORY at noon on Z day to be loaded up with 100 coils barbed wire, 2oo long and 200 short pickets.

(457th Coy will detail a Corporal to be in charge of these 6 wagons and 460th and 461st Field Coys will each detail a junior N.C.O. to accompany them)

When the wagons are loaded the N.C.O. in charge will report to O.C. 457th Field Co (Major COLLEY) at L'HOMME MORT and await instructions to move forward.

When giving him his orders to go forward O.C. 457th Field Coy will direct this N.C.O. to report to LIEUT HAMMOND R.E. on arrival at ECOUST and receive orders from that officer as to when he may take the wagons on to BULLECOURT. The Object to be aimed at will be to get the wagons up as far as point U.27.b.1.7. at the S.W. entrance to BULLECOURT, and it is thought that the conditions at some period of the afternoon will allow of this being effected by 5 p.m. on Z day.

In the event of Lieut SMITH R.E. having reported during the day that a supply of R.E. material has been found at HENDECOURT the above 6 wagons will only proceed as far as the ECOUST Road and there unload at the existing dump of the 186th Inf. Bde.

A carrying party of 300 will be required for taking forward the R.E. Material from the point above indicated in BULLECOURT to HENDECOURT and this will be detailed under orders to be issued by the Division.

The above draft for your approval

SECRET

REPORT ON R.E. SCHEME FOR ATTACK ON HINDENBURG LINE.

1. Field Coys are placed at the disposal of G.Os.C. Infantry Brigades as under to assist in the work of consolidation and in constructing strong points.

    457th. Field Coy. - 4 Sections to 186th Brigade.
    460th. Field Coy. - 2 Sections to 185th Brigade.
    461st. Field Coy. - 2 Sections to 187th Brigade.

NOTE:- In the case of the 457th. and 460th Field Coys this scheme provides for only 3 Sections and 1 Section respectively being absorbed in the operations and for the remaining Section in each case to be held in readiness in the forward positions indicated hereunder in case they may be required

2 Sections 460th Field Coy and 2 Sections 461st Field Coy will be held in Divisional Reserve.

2. Working and carrying parties will be provided as already arranged by Os.C. Field Companies in direct communication with Brigades. *(see + below)*

3. The R.E. Sections detailed to operate with Brigades will rendezvous on Y night, together with their working and carrying parties, at the places of assembly indicated hereunder. The hour of assembly to be arranged direct between Os.C. Field Companies and Brigades.

(a) 457th. Field Coy - 4 Sections with working and carrying parties - In the old system of German trenches existing at C.2.a.0.5.
(b) 460th. Field Coy - 2 Sections with working and carrying parties - In cellars in ECOUST near Battalion H.Q. at C.2.d.8.8.
(c) 461st. Field Coy - 2 Sections - In Railway Cutting between U.25.b.8.1. and U.25.b.2.4.

No R.E. will advance with the assaulting troops. In case of (a) above 2 Sections R.E. will move forward after the first objective has been reached as directed in 186th Brigade Amended Instructions for Attack No. 4. para 5 (f) dated 20.4.17.

In the case of (b) 1 Section R.E. will similarly move forward after the 1st objective has been gained.

In the case of (c) 2 Sections R.E. will move forward after the 1st objective has been gained, when 1 Section will commence work on Strong Points 1, 2 and 3. The other Section will remain with Battalion H.Q. until the 2nd objective has been gained when it will move forward for work on Strong Points 4 and 6.

The Officers commanding Sections engaged on Strong Points under (a), (b) and (c) will report at their respective Battalion Headquarters at U.26.c.9.0., C.2.d.8.8. and U.25.b. at zero hour.

4. (a) Strong Points will be constructed as under

Brigade and Field Coy responsible.	No. and map reference of strong point.	Working party.	Garrison.
186th Brigade. 457th. Field Coy.	(1) U.21.a.8.5.) (2) U.21.d.5.6.)	1 Section R.E. with party of Brigade Mining Section attd, under Lieut. BROOK R.E	1 M.G. & 1 platoon 1 M.G. & 1 platoon

(2)

Brigade and Field Coy responsible.	No. and map reference of strong point.	Working party.	Garrison.
186th. Brigade 457th. Field Co.	(3) U.22.b.1.7. (4) U.22.b.7.5.	1 Section R.E. with party of Brigade Mining Section attd, under Lieut. BEST R.E	1 M.G. & 1 platoon 1 M.G. & 1 platoon
185th. Brigade 460th. Field Co	(1) U.22.c.4.4. (2) U.22.c.9.2. (3) U.28.a.5.7.	1 Section R.E. with 1 Officer and party of Brigade Mining Section attached. The whole under Lt. FROGGATT, R.E.	1 M.G. & 1 officer and 10. O.R. 1 M.G. 1 N.C.O. and 9 men. 1 M.G. 1 N.C.O. and 9 men.
187th. Brigade 461st. Field Co	(1) U.20.b.6.8. (2) U.14.d.9.4. (3) U.15.c.9.9. (4) U.15.d.9.8. (5) U.15.a.9.8. (6) U.16.a.5.3.	1 Section R.E. with 1 Officer and party of Bde. Mining Sectn attd. The whole under Lt. COLLINS R.E. 1 Section R.E. with party of Brigade Mining Section attd. The whole under Lt. DYKE,R.E. Post with M.G. to be established by Infantry.	1 M.G. and 12 O.R. 1 M.G. and 12 O.R. 1 M.G. and 12 O.R. 1 M.G. and 12 O.R. 1 M.G. and 12 O.R.

WORKING PARTIES.

1 Senior R.E. N.C.O. will be in immediate charge of the work on each strong point.
The approximate strength of working party on each strong point will be
    R.E. - 10 other ranks.
    Infantry (including Mining Section) - 20 to 25 other ranks.

CARRYING PARTIES.

457th. and 461st. Field Coys. - 1 N.C.O. and 24 men for each strong point (1 journey)
460th Field Coy. - 1 N.C.O. and 10 men for each strong point (2 journeys).

    (b) As soon as the situation admits of it strong points for the defence of HENDECOURT will be established at the following points, each for a garrison of 1 platoon and 1 Lewis gun, with the addition of Machine Guns where stated.

    The garrisons of these posts will be furnished from the 2/4th. and 2/7th. Duke of Wellington's Regiments (2 Coys from each) which will be allotted for the defence of the village under the command of Lt. Colonel H.E.P. NASH.

    5. U.17.a.8.0.   1 M.G.)
    6. U.17.b.20.15.   ) 1 Company
    7. U.17.b.3.5.   1 M.G.) 2/7th. D. of W. Rgt.
    8. U.17.b.5.9.   )

    9. U.11.d.9.1.   )
    10. U.12.c.4.2.   ) 1 Company
    11. U.12.c.2.5.   2 M.G's) 2/7th. D. of W. Rgt.
    12. U.11.d.8.6.   )

    13. U.11.d.4.6.   )
    14. U.11.b.1.2.   1 M.G.) 1 Cmpany
    15. U.11.c.8.9.   ) 2/4th. D. of W. Rgt.
    16. U.11.c.4.6.   )

(3)

```
17. U.11.c.0.4.      )
18. U.10.d.7.7.  1 M.G. )        1 Company
19. U.18.b.9.7.      )        2/4th. D. of W. Regt.
20. U.17.a.3.3.      )
```

Battn. H.Q. of O.C. Garrisons: Vicinity of Wood U.17.a.1.7.

The village will be subdivided for purposes of responsibility into four parts as follows:-
i. A line running N.E. along BULLECOURT - BOIS DU MONT roadway.
ii. A line running west from road junction U.11.c.0.4. - through Road junction U.11.d.1.2. - thence along the roadway which bounds the S.side of the Chateau VERAC.

Two Senior Officers have been specially detailed by 186th Brigade to assist the O.C. Garrison in organising the defence of HENDECOURT and Brigade orders on the subject are being issued to all concerned.

Lieut. S.A. SMITH with 16 other ranks 457th. Field Coy. R.E is detailed to assist these Officers in the preparations for defence of HENDECOURT. This party will move forward at the earliest opportunity, closely following the battalions detailed for the capture of HENDECOURT. Arrangements as to rendezvous and the exact hour of moving forward will be made direct between O.C. 457th. Field Coy. and 186th Brigade.

O.C. 457th. Field Coy will arrange for Lieut. SMITH to be put into communication with the 2 Senior Officers above referred to forthwith.

On reaching HENDECOURT Lieut. SMITH will at once take steps to ascertain what suitable material (if any) is available locally for defence purposes.

(c) Provided the situation has become sufficiently clear to allow of work being carried out, 1 Field Company (which is expected to be furnished from another Division) will be sent forward to HENDECOURT on the evening of Z day for the work of strengthening the strong points indicated under 10 (b) and (c) and for consolidating the defences of the village. Instructions for this Company will be issued later.

This Company will be relieved on the morning following Z day by four Sections of the 62nd. Divisional R.E. which have been held in Divisional Reserve.

5. Strong Points will be prepared for all round defence and will be completely surrounded with wire entanglement.

The crucifix type (figs 1 and 2) will be adopted where suitable to the configuration of the ground. This type will generally be found to be adapted in conjunction with existing trenches, as in the case of those to be established in the support trench of the HINDENBURG LINE, or the type shewn in Fig. 3 may be employed in this latter connection.

In all cases M.G. Emplacements must be constructed and alternative M.G. positions provided.

6. Immediately on reaching the sites of strong points in the HINDENBURG support trench the R.E. Section Officers in charge will take steps to block the existing trench at a distance of 50 yards to each flank, and as soon as circumstances permit will dig a length of straight trench and construct loopholed traverses for enfilading same.

7. Strong Points will be established by the 2nd. Australian

Division on our immediate right at

              U.23.c.0.5.
              U.18.c.3.6.
              U.18.a.1.2.
    and U.17.b.9.8.

8. The Sections of 460th and 461st. Field Coys in Divisional Reserve will remain in their present billets at ERVILLERS and be ready to move in battle order at half an hour's notice from zero hour onwards.

NOTE: - 1 Section 460th Field Coy. R.E. of the two in Divisional Reserve will be held in readiness for wire cutting for Corps Cavalry in case of its being called upon to do so.

9. The positions of Os. C. Field Companies during the operations will be at their respective Brigade battle Headquarters.

10. Forward R.E. Dumps will be established as under:-

    185th. Inf. Brigade and 460th. Field Coy - C.1.d.9.2.
    186th. Inf. Brigade and 457th. Field Coy - C.2.a.9.9.
    197th. Inf. Brigade and 461st. Field Coy - C.25B.8.1. and
                                                                   C.25.b.2.4.

Dumps to be supplied to the scale already communicated by drawing from the forward Divisional R.E. Dump at ERVILLERS.

11. The arrangements for the attack will be communicated by Field Coy Commanders to all Officers concerned, and the manner in which the R.E. will participate must be carefully explained in detail to all ranks engaged in the operations. Care must be taken that the orders issued to each Section Officer are clearly understood by the two Senior Non-Commissioned Officers of his Section.

12. The C.R.E. will be with Advanced Divisional Headquarters at ERVILLERS, B.13.b.2.3. from zero hour onwards.

27.4.17.

                                                Lieut.Col.R.E.
                                        C.R.E. 62nd. Division.

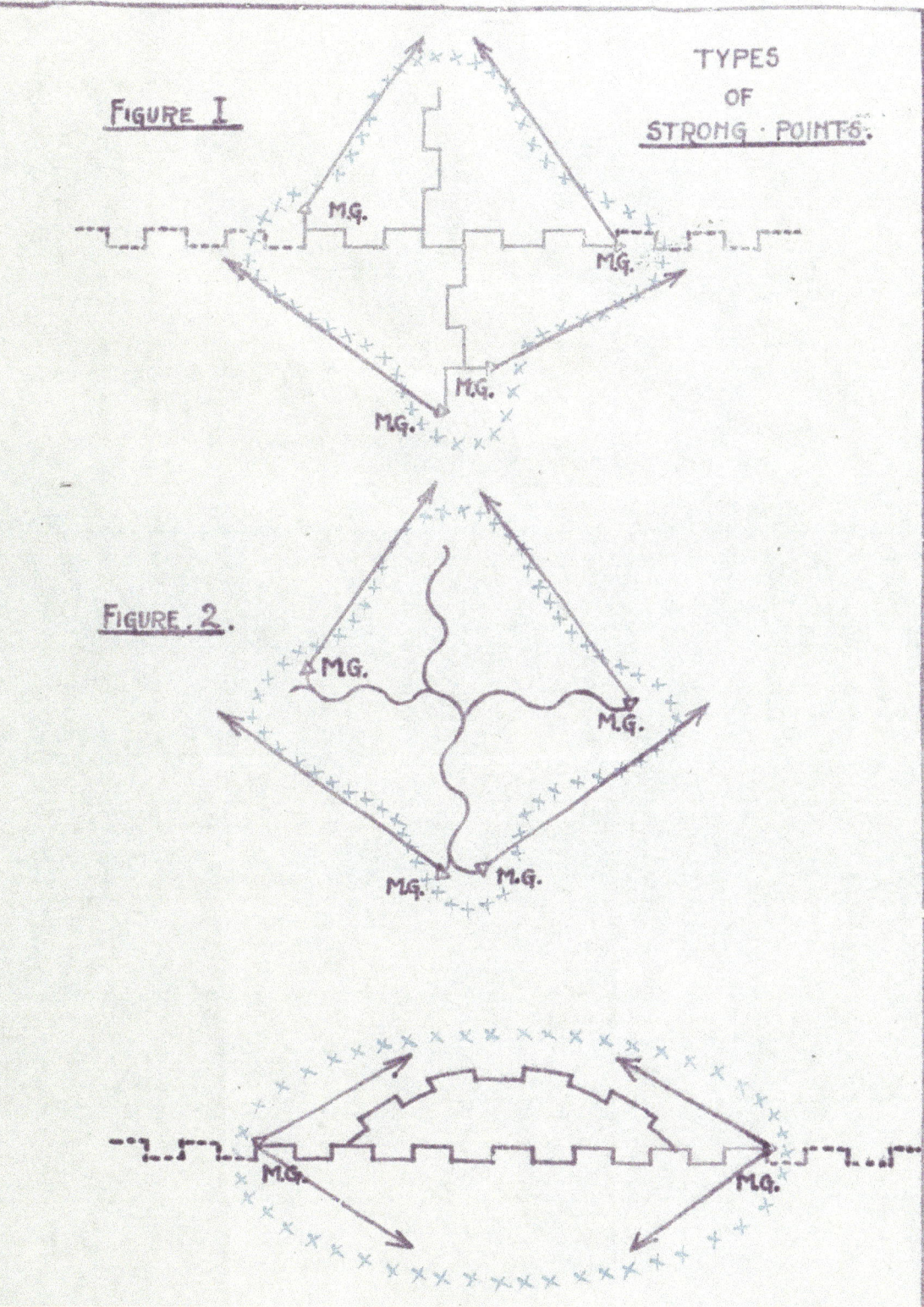

SECRET.

9149.

AMENDMENT TO G.R.A. ORDER NO 20.
----

23. 4. 17.

With reference to G.R.A. 62nd Division Order No.20 of 14.4.17 (Attack on the HINDENBURG LINE), paras 7,8,9, and 10 dealing with the disposition of R.E. Units are hereby cancelled and the following orders for their employment substituted.

7. Field Companies are placed at the disposal of O.Cs.C. Infantry Brigades as under to assist in the work of consolidation and in constructing strong points.

    457th Field Coy. - 4 Sections to 186th Brigade.
    460th Field Coy. - 2 Sections to 185th Brigade.
    461st Field Coy. - 2 Sections to 187th Brigade.

2 Sections 460th Field Coy and 2 Sections 461st Field Coy will be held in Divisional Reserve.

8. Os.C. Field Coys will get into communication at once with O.Cs.C. Brigades and arrange with them direct for the provision of working and carrying parties required.

9. Os.C. Field Coys will receive direct from O.Cs.C. Brigades orders as to places and hour of assembly for the Sections placed at the disposal of Brigades for the operations.

10. Strong points will be constructed as under.

Bde & Fd Coy responsible.	No & Map Ref: of Strong Point.	Working Party	Garrison.
186 Brigade. 457 Field Co.	(1) U.21.d.8.6. (2) U.21.a.8.5. (3) U.22.b.1.7. (4) U.22.b.7.5.	R.E. assisted by Mining Section. (attached)	1 N.C. with detachment & 12 Infantry.
	(5) U.17.a.7.6. (6) U.17.b.5.5. (7) U.12.c.2.5. (8) U.11.d.4.6. (9) U.12.c.7.7. 22.c.9.2.	Infantry under supervision of vision of R.E. (2 O.R.)	Infantry as ordered.
185 Brigade 460th Fd Co.	(1) U.22.b.4.6. (2) U.22.c.4.4. (3) 26.b.6.6.	R.E. assisted by Mining Section (attached.)	1 N.C. with detachment & 12 Infantry.
187 Brigade 461st Fd Co.	(1) U.20.b.2.8. (2) U.14.d.9.4. (3) U.15.c.9.9. (4) U.15.d.9.8. (5) U.15.a.9.9.	R.E. assisted by Mining Section (attached)	1 N.C. with detachment & 12 Infantry.

11. The sections of 460th and 461st Field Coys in Divisional Reserve will remain in their present billets at ENVILLERS and be ready to move in battle order at half an hour's notice from zero hour onwards.

12. The position of Os.C. Field Companies during the operations will be at their respective Brigade Battle Headquarters.

13. In accordance with the instructions already issued on the subject forward R.E. Dumps will be established as under

- 2 -

        185th Inf. Bde. & 466th Field Co. C.1.d.9.8.
        186th Inf. Bde. & 457th Field Co. C.2.a.9.9.
        187th Inf. Bde. & 401st Field Co. U.H2.b.8.1.
                                                    U.26.b.2.4.

Forward R.E. Dumps will be stocked in accordance with the instructions previously issued to Brigades by Divnl Headquarters.

Os.C. Field Coys will arrange for an additional supply of material to be supplied for their own use in those forward dumps, which material will include the following

    2,000 Sandbags
    125 - 205 Long Screw Pickets) Actual amount depending on
    200 - 400 Short do   ) rate at which dump can be
    30 - 60 Coils barbed wire.   ) stocked.

Above materials may be drawn from Forward Divisional R.E. Dump at ENVILLERS.

14. C.R.E. will be with Advanced Divisional R.A. ENVILLERS at B.13.b. 5.5. from zero hour onwards.

                                          Lieut.Colonel R.E.
                                C.R.E. 62nd Division.

NOTE:- Reference para 11 above, 1 Section 460th Field Coy of the two in Divisional Reserve will be held in readiness for wire cutting for Corps Cavalry in case of its being called upon to do so.

SECRET.

Appendix 28

AMENDMENT TO G.S.O. ORDER NO 20.

28. 4. 17.

With reference to G.S.O. 62nd Division Order No.20 of 14.4.17 (Attack on the HINDENBURG LINE), paras 7,8,9, and 10 dealing with the disposition of R.E. Units are hereby cancelled and the following orders for their employment substituted.

7. Field Companies are placed at the disposal of O.Cs.C. Infantry Brigades as under to assist in the work of consolidation and in constructing strong points.

    457th Field Coy. - 4 Sections to 186th Brigade.
    460th Field Coy. - 2 Sections to 185th Brigade.
    461st Field Coy. - 2 Sections to 187th Brigade.

2 Sections 460th Field Coy and 2 Sections 461st Field Coy will be held in Divisional Reserve.

8. Os.C. Field Coys will get into communication at once with O.Cs.C. Brigades and arrange with them direct for the provision of working and carrying parties required.

9. Os.C. Field Coys will receive direct from O.Cs.C. Brigades orders as to places and hour of assembly for the Sections placed at the disposal of Brigades for the operations.

10. Strong points will be constructed as under.

Bde & FE Coy responsible.	No & Map Ref: of Strong Point.	Working Party	Garrison.
186 Brigade. 457 Field Co.	(1) U.21.d.5.6. (2) U.21.a.8.b. (3) U.22.b.1.7. (4) U.22.b.7.5.	R.E. assisted by Mining Section. (attached)	1 N.C. with detachment & 12 Infantry.
	(5) U.17.a.7.5. (6) U.17.b.3.5. (7) U.16.a.6.5. (8) U.11.d.4.6. (9) U.10.d.7.7. U0.c.9.2.	Infantry under supervision of vision of R.E. (@ O.R.)	Infantry as ordered.
185 Brigade 460th FE Co.	(1) U.22.b.5.8. (2) U.22.c.4.6. (3) U0.b.6.5.	R.E. assisted by Mining Section (attached.)	1 N.C. with detachment & 12 Infantry.
187 Brigade 461st FE Co.	(1) U.20.a.9.9. (2) U.14.d.9.4. (3) U.15.c.9.9. (4) U.15.a.9.9. (5) U.15.a.9.9.	R.E. assisted by Mining Section (attached)	1 N.C. with detachment & 12 Infantry.

11. The sections of 460th and 461st Field Coys in Divisional Reserve will remain in their present billets at ERVILLERS and be ready to move in battle order at half an hour's notice from zero hour onwards.

12. The position of Os.C. Field Companies during the operations will be at their respective Brigade Battle Headquarters.

13. In accordance with the instructions already issued on the subject forward R.E. Dumps will be established as under

-2-

185th Inf. Bde. & 456th Field Co. G.1.d.9.2.
186th Inf. Bde. & 457th Field Co. G.8.a.9.9.
187th Inf. Bde. & 461st Field Co. G.21.b.8.1.
G.28.b.2.4.

Forward R.E. Dumps will be stocked in accordance with the instructions previously issued to Brigades by Divnl Headquarters.

13. Field Coys will arrange for an additional supply of material to be supplied for their own use in these forward dumps, which material will include the following

    2,000 Sandbags
    120 - 200 Long Screw Pickets   ) Actual amount depending on
    600 - 450 Short do   ) rate at which dump can be
    30 - 50 Coils barbed wire.   ) stocked.

Above materials may be drawn from Forward Divisional R.E. Dump at ENVILLERS.

14. C.R.E. will be with Advanced Divisional H.Q. ENVILLERS at B.13.b. 2.3. from zero hour onwards.

R.H.Gillman
Lieut.Colonel R.E.
G.S.O. 62nd Division.

NOTE:- Reference para 11 above, 1 Section 456th Field Coy of the two in Divisional Reserve will be held in readiness for wire cutting for Corps Cavalry in case of its being called upon to do so.

Appendix 29

Copy No........

AMENDMENTS TO C.R.E. 62nd Division Order No 20.

The amendments to C.R.E. 62nd Division Order No 20 dated 23.4.17 are cancelled and the following substituted.

7. Field Companies are placed at the disposal of O.Cs.C. Infantry Brigades as under to assist in the work of consolidation and in constructing strong points.

    457th Field Coy – 4 Sections to 186th Brigade.
    460th Field Coy – 2 Sections to 185th Brigade.
    461st Field Coy – 2 Sections to 187th Brigade.

In the case of the 457th Field Coy and the 460th Field Coy this scheme provides for only 3 and 1 sections respectively being absorbed in the operations and for the remaining sections in each case to be held in readiness in the forward positions indicated hereunder in case they may be required.

2 sections 460th Field Coy and 2 Sections 461st Field Coy will be held in Divisional Reserve.

8. Working and carrying parties will be provided as already arranged by Os.C. Field Coys in direct communication with Brigades.

9. The R.E. Sections detailed to operate with Brigades will rendezvous on Y night, together with their working and carrying parties, at the places of assembly indicated hereunder. The hour of assembly to be arranged direct between Os.C. Field Coys and Brigades.

  (a) 457th Field Coy – 4 sections – In the old system of German
       trenches existing at C.2.a.O.5.
  (b) 460th Field Coy – 2 sections – In cellars in ECOUST near Battalion
       H.Q. at C.2.d.8.8.
  (c) 461st Field Coy – 2 sections – In Railway Cutting between
       U.23.b.8.1. and U.22.b.2.4.

No R.E. will advance with the assaulting troops. In case of (a) above two sections R.E. will move forward after the first objective has been gained as directed in 186th. Brigade amended Instructions for Attack No 4. para 5 (f) dated 20.4.17.

In the case of (b) 1 Section R.E. will similarly move forward after the 1st objective has been gained.

In the case of (c) 2 Sections R.E. will move forward after the 1st Objective has been gained, when one section will commence work on Strong Points 1, 2 and 3. The other section will remain with Battalion H.Q. until the 2nd objective has been gained when it will move forward for work on Strong Points 4 and 5.

The Officers Commanding sections engaged on Strong Points under (a), (b) and (c) will report at their respective Battalion H.Qs. at U.26.c.9.0., C.2.d.8.8. and U.25.b. at zero hour.

10. (a) Strong points will be constructed as under :–

Brigade & Field Coy responsible.	No and map ref of strong point.	Working Party	Garrison.
186th Brigade 457th Field Co	(1) U.21.a.8.5.	1 Section R.E. with party of Brigade	1 M.G. & 1 Platoon.
	(2) U.21.d.5.6.	Mining Section attd under Lt. BROOK R.E.	1 M.G. & 1 Platoon.
	(3) U.22.b.1.7.	1 Section R.E. with party of Brigade	1 M.G. & 1 Platoon.
	(4) U.22.b.7.5.	Mining Section attd under Lt. BROOK R.E.	1 M.G. & 1 Platoon.

Copy No . . . .

AMENDMENTS TO C. R. E. 62nd Division Order No 20.
- - - - - - - -

The amendments to C.R.E. 62nd Division Order No 20 dated 23.4.17. are cancelled and the following substituted.

7.

-2-

Brigade & Field Coy responsible.	No & Map ref of Strong Point	Working Party	Garrison.
185th Brigade 480th Field Co	(1) U.22.c.4.4.	) 1 Section R.E. with) 1 Officer and party) of Brigade Mining) Section attached.) The whole under Lt) PROGGATT R.E.	1 M.G. & 1 Officer and 10 O.R.
	(2) U.22.c.9.3.		1 M.G. 1 N.C.O. and 9 men
	(3) U.23.a.5.7.		1 M.G. 1 N.C.O. and 9 men.
187th Brigade 461st Field Co	(1) U.20.b.6.8.	) 1 Section R.E. with) 1 Off. and party of) Brigade Mining Section) attd. The whole) under 2/Lieut Collins) R.E.	1 M.G. & 12 O.R.
	(2) U.14.d.9.4.		1 M.G. & 12 O.R.
	(3) U.15.c.9.9.		1 M.G. & 12 O.R.
	(4) U.15.c.9.9.	) 1 Section R.E. with) party of Bde Mining) Section attd. The whole) under Lieut DENE R.E.	1 M.G. & 12 O.R.
	(5) U.15.a.9.5.		1 M.G. & 12 O.R.
	(6) U.16.a.5.3.	Post with M.G. to be established by Infantry.	

WORKING PARTIES:
    1 Senior R.E. N.C.O. will be in immediate charge of the work on each Strong Point.

    The approximate strength of working party on each strong point will be
        R.E.   -   10 Other Ranks.
        Infantry (including Mining Section) - 20 to 25 Other Ranks.

CARRYING PARTIES:

    457th and 461st Field Coys - 1 N.C.O. & 24 men for each strong point
                                   (1 journey).
    480th Field Coy.   - 1 N.C.O. & 12 men for each strong point
                                   (2 journeys).

(b) As soon as the situation admits of it strong points for the defence of HEBUTERNE will be established at the following points, each for a garrison of 1 platoon and 1 Lewis gun, with the addition of Machine Guns where stated.

    The garrisons of these posts will be furnished from the 2/4th and 2/7th Bns Duke of Wellington's Regt (2 Coys from each) which will be allotted for the defence of the village under the command of Lieut. Colonel H.N.P. NASH.

    5. U.17.a.8.0.   1 M.G.   ) -
    6. U.17.b.80.15.   ) 1 Company
    7. U.17.b.3.5.   1 M.G.   ) 2/7th Bn D. of W.
    8. U.17.b.8.9.   )

    9. N.11.d.9.1.   )
    10. U.12.c.4.8.   ) 1 Company
    11. U.12.a.2.8.   2 M.Gs.   ) 2/7th Bn D of W.
    12. U.11.d.8.8.   )

13. U.11.d.4.8.   )
14. U.11.b.1.3.   1 M.G.) 1 Company
15. U.11.c.0.9.   ) 2/4th D. of W. Regt.
16. U.11.c.4.5.   )

17. U.11.c.0.4.   )
18. U.10.d.7.7.   1 M.G.)   1 Company
19. U.15.b.9.7.   ) 2/4th D. of W. Regt.
20. U.17.a.5.5.   )

Battn H.Q. of O.C. Garrisons: Vicinity of wood U.17.a.1.7.

The village will be sub-divided for purposes of responsibility into four parts as follows :-
i. A line running west from N.E. along BULLECOURT - BOIS DU MONT roadway.
ii. A line running west from Road junction U.11.c.0.4. - through Road junction U.11.d.1.5. - thence along the roadway which bounds the S. side of the Chateau VRAC.

Two senior Officers have been specially detailed by 185th Brigade to assist the O.C. Garrison in organising the defence of HENINCOURT and Brigade Orders on the subject are being issued to all concerned.

Lieut S.A. SMITH with 15 Other Ranks 457th Field Co R.E. is detailed to assist these Officers in the preparations for defence of HENINCOURT. This party will move forward at the earliest opportunity, closely following the battalions detailed for the capture of HENINCOURT. Arrangements as to rendezvous and the exact hour of moving forward will be made direct between O.C. 457th Field Coy and 185th Brigade.

O.C. 457th Field Coy will arrange for Lieut SMITH to be put into communication with the 2 senior Officers above referred to forthwith.

On reaching HENINCOURT Lieut Smith will at once take steps to ascertain what suitable material (if any) is available locally for defence purposes.

(c) Provided the situation has become sufficiently clear to allow of work being carried out, 1 Field Coy (which is expected to be furnished from another Division) will be sent forward to HENINCOURT on the evening of Z day for the work of strengthening the strong points indicated under 10 (b) and (c) and for consolidating the defences of the village. Instructions for this Company will be issued later.

This Company will be relieved on the morning following Z day by four Sections of the 62nd Divisional R.E. which have been held in Divnl Reserve.

11. Strong Points will be prepared for all road defence and will be completely surrounded with wire entanglement.

The crucifix type (figs. 1 and 2) will be adopted where suitable to the configuration of the ground. This type will generally be found to be adoptable in conjunction with existing trenches, as in the case of those to be established in the support trench of the HINDENBURG Line or the type shown in Fig.3 may be employed in this latter connection.

In all cases M.G. Emplacements must be constructed and alternative M.G. positions provided.

12. Immediately on reaching the sites of strong points in the HINDENBURG support trench the R.E. Section Officers in charge will take steps to block the existing trench at a distance of 50 yards to each flank, and as soon as circumstances permit will dig a length of straight trench and construct loopholed traverses for enfilading same.

13. Strong Points will be established by the 2nd Australian Divn on our immediate right at

-6-

     U.23.a.9.5.
     U.18.c.9.9.
     U.12.a.1.9.
  and U.17.b.9.9.

14. The Sections of 460th and 461st Field Coys in Divisional Reserve will remain in in their present billets at ENVILLERS and be ready to move in battle order at half an hour's notice from zero hour onwards.

NOTE – 1 Section 460th Field Coy R.E. of the two in Divisional Reserve will be held in readiness for wire cutting for Corps Cavalry in case of its being called upon to do so.

15. The positions of Os.C. Field Coys during the operations will be at their respective Brigade battle Headquarters.

16. Forward R.E. Dumps will be established as under :-

  185th Inf. Brigade and 460th Field Coy - C.1.d.9.5.
  186th Inf. Brigade and 457th Field Coy - C.2.a.9.9.
  187th Inf. Brigade and 461st Field Coy - C.25.b.6.1. and
                   C.25.b.2.4.

Dumps to be supplied to the scale already communicated by drawing from the forward Divisional R.E. Dump at ENVILLERS.

17. The arrangements for the attack will be communicated by Field Coy Commanders to all Officers concerned, and the manner in which the R.E. will participate must be carefully explained in detail to all ranks engaged in the operations. Care must be taken that the orders issued to each Section officer are clearly understood by the two senior N.C.Os of his section.

18. The C.R.E. will be with Advanced Divisional Headquarters at ENVILLERS, B.13.b.8.5. from zero hour onwards.

                R.H.Williams
                Lieut.Colonel R.E.
           C. R. E. 62nd Division.

27. 4. 17.

 Copy No 1. 457th Field Co.
    2. 460th Field Co.
    3. 461st Field Co.
    4. 185th Brigade
    5. 186th Brigade.
    6. 187th Brigade.
    7. 62nd Division G.
  8 & 9 War Diary
    10. Retained.

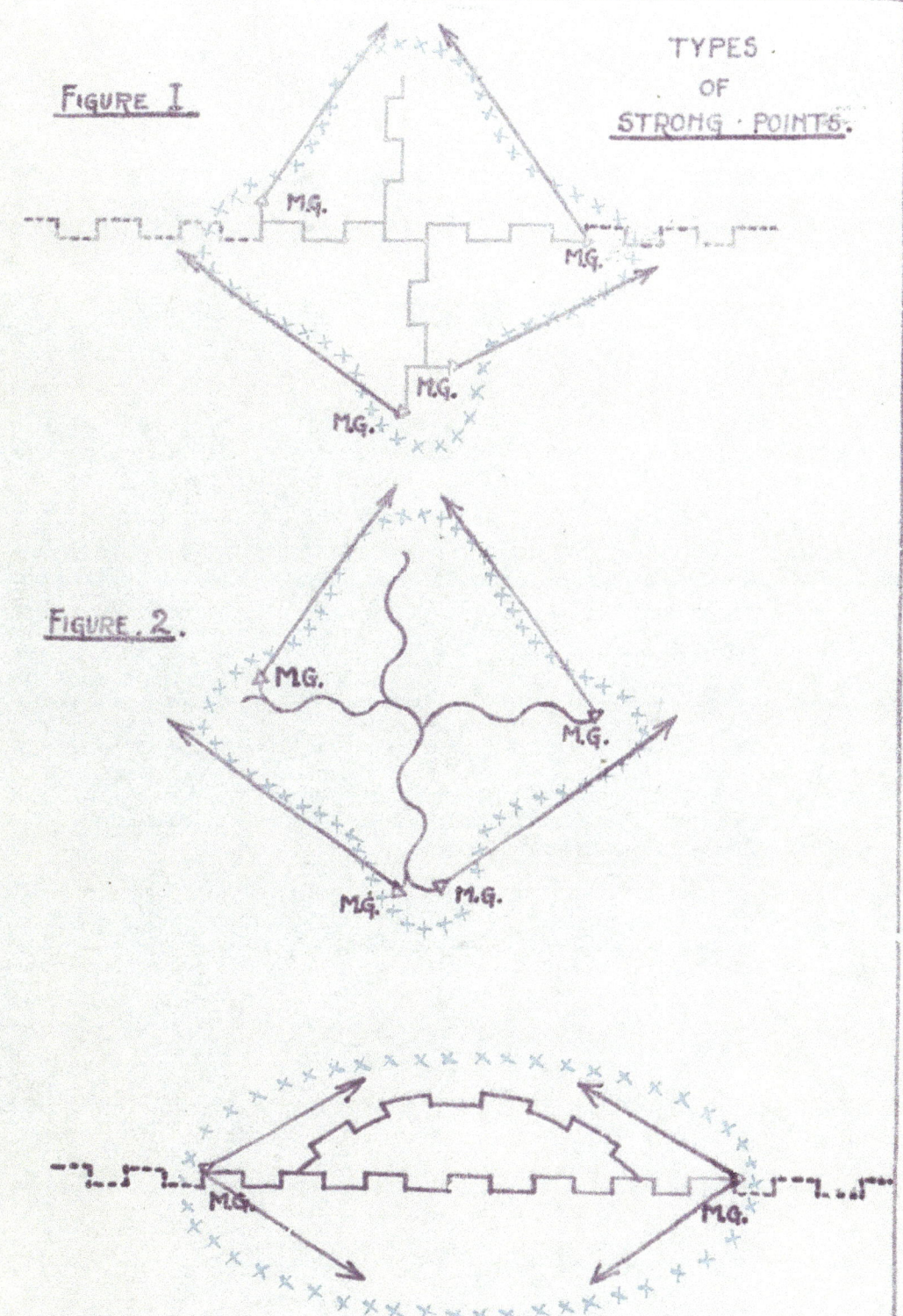

TYPES OF STRONG POINTS.

FIGURE 1

FIGURE 2

FIGURE 3

C.R.E. 62nd DIVISIONAL R.E.

Appendix 30

Copy No 8

AMENDMENTS TO C.R.E. 62nd Division Order No 26.

28. 4. 17.

Paras 10 (c) and 16 of Amendments to C.R.E. 62nd Division Order No 26 dated 27. 4. 17. are cancelled and the following substituted.

10.

(c) Provided the situation has become sufficiently clear to allow of work being carried out 2 sections 460th Field Coy and 2 sections 461st Field Coy which are being held in Divisional Reserve will be sent forward to NOREUIL on the evening of Z day under the command of Captain L.H.J. Perzor, 461st Field Coy, for the work of strengthening the strong points indicated under 10 (b) and for consolidating the defences of the village. Detailed instructions for these four sections will be issued later.

These four sections will be relieved on the morning following Z day by a Field Coy (which is expected to be furnished from another Division).

16. Forward R.E. Dumps will be established as under :-

185th Inf. Brigade and 460th Field Coy - C.1.d.9.2.
186th Inf. Brigade and 457th Field Coy - C.8.a.9.9.
187th Inf. Brigade and 461st Field Coy - U.25.b.8.1. and U.26.b.2.4.

Dumps to be supplied to the scale already communicated by drawing from the forward Divisional R.E. Dump at ERVILLERS.

[signature]

Lieut-Colonel R.E.
C. R. E. 62nd Division M.E.

Copy No 1   457th Field Co
         2   460th Field Co
         3   461st Field Co
         4   185th Brigade
         5   186th Brigade
         6   187th Brigade
         7   62nd Division G.
     8 & 9   War Diary
        10   Retained.

Secret

Appendix 31

Copy No 10

C. R. E. 62nd Division Order No 31.

30. 4. 17.

Reference Amendments to C.R.E. 62nd Division Order No 30 para 10 (b) and (c) of 27. 4. 17. and amendments of same dated 28. 4. 17, the following supplementary instructions are issued for the action to be taken to strengthen the defences of HEUDICOURT, and all concerned will be prepared to proceed in accordance with these orders on 'Z' day as the situation develops.

1. O.C. 457th Field Coy R.E. will be responsible that there is a sufficient supply of barbed wire and pickets in the forward dump at EQUANCOURT to allow of a total length of 2000 yards of single apron fence being erected as rapidly as possible during Z night, that is to say about 120 yards for each of the 16 strong points immediately surrounding HEUDICOURT.

Any balance of material remaining over in the 482th Field Coy dump at EQUANCOURT will be considered by O.C. 457th Field Coy as also available for this purpose.

2. 2/Lieut Smith R.E. (or the senior N.C.O. or Sapper of his party that circumstances may render it necessary to act for him) will keep O.C. 457th Field Coy informed as to the nature and quantities of material that have been found to be available in or about HEUDICOURT so as to minimise or altogether obviate if possible the necessity for carrying material forward.

3. O.C. 457th Field Coy R.E. will arrange with 186th Brigade for carrying parties to be made available on Z evening to take forward the R.E. material that may be required for work during the night, in the event of none having been found to exist in or about HEUDICOURT.

4. Captain L.R.E. BONNER who will be in command of the 4 sections (2 sections 482th Field Coy and 2 sections 481st Field Coy) which will be moving forward for work during the night will get into touch at once with O.C. 457th Field Coy and arrange details for the supply of material, reporting to C.R.E. by 10 p.m. 1st May the exact arrangements that have been made.

2.

5. The defences of HENINCOURT will be divided for the purposes of work management into four sectors as under, and 1 Section R.E. will be allotted to each sector to provide the necessary R.E. supervision and technical assistance.

Sector	Strong Points		Garrison
A.	(5) U.17.a.8.9.	1 M.G.	)
	(6) U.17.b.90.15.		) 1 Company
	(7) U.17.b.3.5.	1 M.G.	)
	(8) U.17.b.8.9.		) 2/7th Bn D of W Regt.
B.	(9) U.11.d.9.1.		)
	(10) U.12.c.4.8.		) 1 Company
	(11) U.12.c.8.5.	2 M.G's	)
	(12) U.11.d.8.5.		) 2/7th Bn D of W Regt
C.	(13) U.11.d.4.3.		)
	(14) U.11.b.1.2.	1 M.G.	) 1 Company
	(15) U.11.c.9.9.		)
	(16) U.11.c.4.5.		) 2/4th Bn D of W Regt
D.	(17) U.11.d.2.4.		)
	(18) U.10.d.7.7.	1 M.G.	) 1 Company
	(19) U.12.b.9.7.		)
	(20) U.17.a.3.3.		) 2/4th Bn D of W Regt.

Captain DERBER to communicate early to C.R.E. the names of the R.E. Officer in Command of each Section allotted to the above Sectors A. B. C. & D.

6. Captain DERBER will report to-morrow (1st May) to Headquarters 186th Brigade who will kindly put him into communication with the Officers Commanding Companies providing the garrisons of the Strong points for the defence of HENINCOURT.

7. The garrisons of the strong points will supply the working parties for E night.

All available R.E. will be employed on wiring, which must be proceeded with immediately the R.E. Sections arrive on the site on E evening.

8. Orders for the 4 Sections R.E. from Divisional Reserve to move forward to HENINCOURT will be issued by C.R.E.

These sections will be held in readiness to leave Camp early on E afternoon.

Copies to - 3 Field Coys
3 Brigades
62nd Division G.

R.H. Gillam
Lieut. Colonel R.E.
62nd Division.

ORIGINAL

WM 5

CONFIDENTIAL

WAR DIARY
of
H.Q. 62nd Div. R.E.

From May 1st 1917 to May 31st 1917

Vol V

WAR DIARY
or
INTELLIGENCE SUMMARY.

Army Form C. 2118.

Place	Date	Hour	Summary of Events and Information	Remarks and references to Appendices
ACHIET-LE-GRAND	1/5/17		HdQr 62nd Div. R.E. Information received from 62nd Div. that attack on HINDENBURG line will take place on 3rd April 1917. Entrenchments carried out before C.R.E. & left early. Bombs & ammunition charges contained 30lb. 20lb. 10lb of Ammonal. Bangalore torpedo made by filling a pilot tin with ammonal & inserting No. 8 Detonator & fuze not ammonal though. Both wooden plug fitting in to spout of tin was also used. All charges were fired by Bickmore lighters. The charges were thrown down the steps of some of the German Dugouts the exponents being warned not to wait a visit to the possibility of blocking the Dugout entrances with the charges. All charges detonated successfully but galleries not examined owing to gas.	
ERVILLERS	2/5/17		C.R.E. & ADJT moved to advanced Div HQ at ERVILLERS. Report received of effect caused by portable charges. Results	

WAR DIARY
or
INTELLIGENCE SUMMARY
(Erase heading not required.)

Army Form C. 2118.

Place	Date	Hour	Summary of Events and Information	Remarks and references to Appendices
			not satisfactory as though galleries were badly shaken they were not entirely blocked. In view of this, afternoon it was decided to use the 10 lb. charges (on account of their portability) during following afternoon a few 20 lb. charges (Bristol bar 25 lb.) were also made up with a view to their being exploded at the roof of the galleries before detonation of lb. charges at the end by infantry in charge by sappers.	September 22
ERVILLERS	2/6/15		Attack on HINDENBURG LINE by 2nd Div commenced at 3.30 am. All R.E. sections detailed, in addition to forward bombers by ZERO HOUR. Owing to failure of Infantry to clear objective R.E. sections did not advance & were ordered to return & was killed at 6 am. O/C the bombs charges sent forward now was wounded. 2nd Div relieved at dusk by 1st Div & attacked BULLECOURT at 10.30 pm. Attack not successful	Tyler

T.J. 134. Wt. W708-776. 500000. 4/15. Sir J. C. & S.

WAR DIARY or INTELLIGENCE SUMMARY

Army Form C. 2118.

(Erase heading not required.)

Place	Date	Hour	Summary of Events and Information	Remarks and references to Appendices
BERVILLERS	4.5.17		6th Div Order No 44 received detailing 183 of 6th Div from 1st line of defence sent by 7th Div. 6th Div to be responsible for 2nd line of defence from L'HOMME MORT to ST LEGER.	
ACHIET-LE-GRAND	5.5.17		H.Q. 6th Div C.R.E. returned to ACHIET LE GRAND. C.R.E. Order No 22 issued detailing work on new sector of 2nd line of defence. VRAUCOURT – L'HOMME MORT sector of 2nd line of defence handed over to C.R.E. 7th Div.	September 35
	6.5.17		Nil	
	7.5.17		Nil	
	8.5.17		Fifth Army Commander inspected 2nd line of defence. C.R.E. was present. Arrangement made with 174 (Tun) Coy R.E. to commence construction of dug outs in embankment near FROST W.& C.	
	9.5.17		Orders received that a rest line posn in rear of our Advanced Posn Rs. to be hand "dug". Tracing to be carried out night 10/11th and be the chg w/o K.O.Rs. & R. Officer hy B.B of bn. 1400 yds, working party all Bn.	

WAR DIARY
or
INTELLIGENCE SUMMARY.
(Erase heading not required.)

Army Form C. 2118.

Summary of Events and Information HQ 62nd Div RE

Place	Date	Hour	Summary of Events and Information	Remarks and references to Appendices
ACHIET LE GRAND	9.5.17 contd		300 men. Provided other work to unit	Appendix 34
	10.5.17		Conference of O.C. Field Coys & O.C. Working Parties at 10.0.a.m and engineers to choose sites of digging new head line. CRE & ADJT. went over 2nd line of defence with CRE Co. & Col. a M.G. officer to settle site of all M.Guns & additional works required. Orders issued with regard to digging of New Trench bet night 11/12. Trench & Communication trenches detailed in Appendix 35 successfully taken night of 10/11.	Appendix 35
	11.5.17			
	12.5.17		Trench from U20c45 – 8U27c 45 75 dug to a depth of 2ft (average)	
	13.5.17		Communication trench from U20c15 – to U26.6.7 45 dug to an average depth of 3ft 6 ins. Communication trench taken from U26.6.5 to U21 c4.	
	14.5.17		Communication trench from U26.6.65 to U21c4 dug to an average depth of 4ft on night 13/14. Deepening of communication trench from U20c45 – U25c 45 75 continued.	
	15.5.17		Work on forward areas continued.	
	16.5.17		ditto	

Army Form C. 2118.

WAR DIARY
or
INTELLIGENCE SUMMARY.
(Erase heading not required.)

Instructions regarding War Diaries and Intelligence Summaries are contained in F. S. Regs., Part II. and the Staff Manual respectively. Title pages will be prepared in manuscript.

Place	Date	Hour	Summary of Events and Information	Remarks and references to Appendices
Achiet-le-Grand	17.6.17		HQ. and D.H. R.E.	
	18.6.17		Nil	
	19.6.17		Nil	
			C.R.E, G.S.O.I. & ADJT R.E. visited Sunken Road in U21.c.5.0.t. reconnoitre work in progress in forward area.	
	20.6.17		Nil	
	21.6.17		ADJT R.E. proceeded on 10 days leave.	
			C.R.E. visited SECOND LINE DEFENCE works and met O.C. Companies and indicated alignment of COMMUNICATION TRENCH back to SUPPORT & RESERVE TRENCHES and pointed out positions of the latter.	
	22.6.17		Meeting of O.C. Companies at 461 FIELD C° discussed position of SUPPORT and RESERVE points in rear of FRONT LINE DEFENCE	
			SAPPER MIDDLETON N°460409 (Acting L/Cpl) awarded MILITARY MEDAL	
			Acting C.E. V. Corps called upon C.R.E. and discussed points of Scheme for MAIN and SECOND LINE	
	23.6.17		Nil	
	24.6.17		C.R.E. along with O.C. 457th FIELD C° visited Fire trench N.W. of ECOUST	

Army Form C. 2118.

WAR DIARY
or
INTELLIGENCE SUMMARY.
(Erase heading not required.)

Instructions regarding War Diaries and Intelligence Summaries are contained in F. S. Regs., Part II. and the Staff Manual respectively. Title pages will be prepared in manuscript.

Place	Date	Hour	Summary of Events and Information	Remarks and references to Appendices
ACHIET-LE-GRAND	25.5.17		NIL	H.Q. R.E. Div XL
	26.5.17		NIL	
	27.5.17		NIL	
	28.5.17		C.R.E. handed over work on LINE to C.R.E. 58th DIVISION	
	29.5.17		C.R.E. proceeded on 10 days leave. Major L.S.J. COLLEY acting C.R.E.	
	30.5.17		NIL	
	31.5.17		Major L.S.J. COLLEY acting C.R.E. along with C.E. I Corps visited, inspected + improved SECOND LINE DEFENCE. VRAUCOURT — ECOUST ROAD to L'HOMME MORT.	

W.A. Seaman
Major R.E.
Acting C.R.E. XLDiv

Appendix 32

RE/O/5.

C.R.E.
62nd Division.

Report on effect of Portable Bomb Charges :-

<u>No 1.</u> Petrol Tins, weight of charge 25 lbs Depth of Dug-out 30 feet.

The bomb fell to the bottom of the dug-out, completely breaking Two Stanchions and six Topsills, made a semi-circular hole in the top of roof 3 feet deep. All timbers in the whole of the Dug-out cracked or moved.

<u>No 2.</u> 10lb Portable Charge. Depth of Dug-out 25 ft. The Bomb fell to the bottom of the steps and made a hole in the ground sill, no other timbers were destroyed or even badly shaken.

<u>No 3.</u> 30lb Portable charge depth of Dug out 30 feet.

Bomb fell to the bottom of steps, every frame in Gallery was lifted and 5 frames completely ripped and destroyed.

The bottom of the Dug-out was blocked in with Soil and a hole in the roof 4 feet deep.

<u>No 4</u> 20 lb Portable Charge - depth of Dug-Out 25 ft.

Four Topsills moved, considerable amount of soil droped some of the Timbers were cnsiderably shaken.

The best results were obtained from 1 and 3 .

Naturally in the case of No 3 the length of the charge apparently prevented it from rolling to the very bottom of the Dug-out. This inference is drawn from the fact that the Timber in the centre of the steps, was more destroyed than at the bottom.

(Sd) E.I.Scott Capt, for
O.C.#57th Field Co.

2/5/17.

O.C. 460th Field Co
O.C. 461st Field Co.

For your information.

2/5/17

Lieut-Colonel R.E.

Appendix 33

Copy No. 8

C.R.E. 62nd Division Order No 22.

6.8.17.

Ref: Map FRANCE 1/20,000.
51 B.S.E. 57 C.N.W.

1. The Division will continue to hold the front line between the Corps Boundary on the left (JUDAS FARM exclusive - SENSEE RIVER to along road T.24.a.9.4. to U.14.c.5.9) and the MORY - ECOUST - BULLECOURT road on the right.

2. The Divisional Front will be held by the 186th Infantry Brigade on the right and the 187th Infantry Brigade on the left.
The dividing line between the right and left sub-sectors will be a line U.30.d.7.5. - U.25.b.0.8. - B.1C. central - B.13.a.0.9.

3. The second line of Defence will be from B.17.b.2.8. to ST LEGER and will be held by the Corps Motor Machine Gun Company.
The 7th Division will be holding the 2nd Line on our right.

4. The 62nd Divisional R.E. will be responsible for work on the defences of the 2nd Line held by the 62nd Division.

5. Field Companies will be responsible for carrying out work on this second line of defence on the sectors detailed hereunder.

 457th Field Co R.E. From ECOUST - MORY road (exclusive) to B.11.a.0/ (road inclusive)
 461st   do   From B.11.a.0.8*5 (road exclusive) to B.5.a.0.8. (road inclusive).
 460th   do   From B.5.a.0.8. (road exclusive) to T.29.a.2.4. (river inclusive).

A plan showing work executed by 7th Divnl R.E. will be issued to Units at an early date.

6. O.C. Field Coys will be responsible for any work that may be required in the front line by their affiliated Brigades and will keep in close touch with their respective Brigades accordingly. One section of each Field Coy will always be regarded as available for work on the sector of its affiliated Brigade in Front line. These sections will when not required by the Brigades work under orders of the C.R.E.

7. Progress reports will be rendered daily to C.R.E. for all work carried out both on front and second lines.

8. All forward R.E. Dumps established by Units for recent operations will be maintained with the exception of the Dump established in MORY by the 460th Field Coy R.E. which has already been handed over to 528th Field Coy R.E. (7th Division).

9. Arrangements will be made for carrying out all work on 2nd line by night commencing the night of the 6th inst. Steps will be taken to have new intermediate works and the trench connecting existing works laterally traced by day commencing the morning of the 6th inst. Infantry working parties will be detailed as and if available for the night of the 6/7th inst and onwards and instructions in regard to same will be communicated to Os.C. Units to-morrow. But in the event of its not being possible to find such working parties the work will be carried out by Field Coys and their attached Mining Sections.

10. ACKNOWLEDGE.

Lieut.Colonel R.E.
C.R.E. 62nd Division.

Copies to
1. 461 Field Co
2. 457 Field Co
3. 460 Field Co
4. 62nd Divn G.
5. 185 Bde.
6. 186 Bde.
7. 187 Bde.
8-9 War Diary
10 File.

RE/650/1039.

O.C. 461st Field Co.
O.C. 457th Field Co.
O.C. 460th Field Co.

Orders have been received for a new Line to be laid out and dug behind our advanced posts from approximately U.27.c.4.5,7.5 to U.26.b.7.4.5 and thence to U.20.c.5.4. with a small trench from U.20.c.2.5.5 to U.19.d.6.5.7, also a communication trench from approximately U.26.c.1.5.6.5 to U.26.b.7.4.5.

It has not yet been decided whether the main trench firstly noted will be traced and dug on the same night or traced on one night and dug on the following night, but the latter course will probably be adopted. In any case this main trench will have to be traced to-morrow night 10/11th May and also the communication trench.

Each Field Coy will detail an Officer and personnel for the work of tracing.

Orders as to the Companies from which Sections will be required to be provided for supervision of working parties will be issued later.

Working parties will probably consist of 200 Cavalry and 150 Corps Cyclists.

There will be a meeting of O.C. Units with the C.R.E. at the Mess of the 460th Field Coy, ERVILLERS, at 10 a.m. to-morrow 10th inst to arrange details.

Os.C. Units, if they wish it, may bring with them the officers they propose to detail for the work of tracing.

Sd R A Gillam
Lieut.Colonel R.E.
C.R.E. 62nd Division.

9.5.17.

Appendix 35

RE/650/1039/6.

O.C. 457th Field Co.   O.C. V Corps Cavalry.
O.C. 460th Field Co.   O.C. V Corps Cyclists.
O.C. 461st Field Co.   62nd Division 'G'

Reference this office letter RE/650/1039 - 9.5.17.

The work on the advanced trench from U.27.c.4.5. 7.5 to U.$\frac{1}{2}$20.c.5.4. and thence to U.19.d.6.5.7. will be carried out to-morrow night 11/12th.

2. The portion of the line from U.27.c.4.5.7.5 to U.26.b.7.4.5 will be under the direction of O.C. 457th Field Co and the extension of working parties will take place from the SUNKEN ROAD end (U.26.b.7.4.5).

The portion of the trench from U.26.b.7.4.5 to U.19.d.6.5. 7. will be under the direction of O.C. 461st Field Coy and the extension will be carried out from point U.20.c.5.4. on the Road.

3. The following working parties only can be counted upon for the execution of the above work:-

(a) For work under O.C. 457th Field Coy on right sector as above indicated.

Unit.	No of R.E. Offs. O.R.		No of Working Party. Offs. O.R.		
457th Field Co)					
2 sections.)	2	30			
Do)					
Mining Section)			1	40	
V Corps Cavalry			3	125	O. O.R.
	2	30	4	165	Totals 6. 195.

(b) Under O.C. 461st Field Co for work on Left Sector as above indicated.

Unit	No of R.E. Offs. O.R.		No of Working party Offs. O.R.		
461st Fd Co)					
2 sections.)	2	30			
Do))					
Mining Section)			1	40	
460th Fd Co)					
Mining Section)			1	30	
V Corps Cyclists			3	170	O. OR.
	2	30	5	240	7 270.

4. Work. All working parties should be extended on the line in time to commence work at 10 p.m. sharp. Work will be carried on until 2 a.m. and later if the moon will admit of it.

5. The type of trace to be adopted will be the German pattern of 30' Bays with Traverses 12' in the clear (total depth from front to rear 15'). It is essential that the trench should be dug to the full length to such a depth as the time available (4 hours minimum) will admit of attaining.

6. Each man will be allotted a task 15' in length and 3' wide which should enable him to dig to a depth of at least 1'6" in the 4 hours. It is hoped however that a depth of 2' at least will be reached.

7. Details as to hour and place of rendezvous will be arranged between Os.C. Field Coys and the Commanders of their respective working parties on the lines indicated at the meeting with the C.R.E. this morning.

8. There will be a meeting of the C.R.E. and Os.C. Units at 10 a.m. to-morrow at the 460th Field Coy Officers' Quarters ERVILLERS to discuss and decide on the final arrangements for work.

O.c. working parties are invited to attend this meeting.

9. The work of excavating the communication trench from U.25.c.1.5 4. to U.26.b.7.4.5. will be carried out under the direction of O.C. 460th Field Coy at a subsequent date which will be notified later.

10. Please acknowledge.

Sd. R A Gillam
Lieut.Colonel R.E.
C.R.E. 62nd Division.

10. 5. 17.

ORIGINAL
Vol 6

CONFIDENTIAL

WAR DIARY

H.Q. 62nd DIV. R.E.

From 1st June 1917 to 30th June 1917

Volume VI

Army Form C. 2118.

WAR DIARY
or
INTELLIGENCE SUMMARY.
(Erase heading not required.)

Summary of Events and Information Hdqrs R.E. 62nd Div

Place	Date	Hour		Remarks and references to Appendices
ACHIET-LE-GRAND	1/6/17		Major L.ST.J.COLLEY acting CRE and Major W.A.SEAMAN O.C. 461 Field Coy visited 2nd LINE DEFENCES with C.E. V CORPS.	
	2.6.17		Actg ADJT. returned from leave	
	3.6.17		N.I.	
	4.6.17		Acting C.R.E. visited 2nd LINE with C.E. V CORPS & Comdg M.G.O.	
	5.6.17		Acting C.R.E. visited 2nd line with Corps M.G. Officer	
	6.6.17		Major A.J. WALTHEW returned from leave & took over duty as acting CRE for Major W.A. SEAMAN.	
	7.6.17		N.I.	
	8.6.17		Major A.J. WALTHEW visited 2nd Line with B.G.G.S. & C.E. V Corps	
	9.6.17		N.I.	
	10.6.17		CRE returned from leave. Orders recd to attach one Coy for work on front system of 63rd Div	
	11.6.17		CRE visited 2nd LINE with C.E. V Corps (reference London Rd & 62 Rd [illegible])	
	12.6.17		N.I.	
	13.6.17		N.I.	
	14.6.17		N.I.	

Army Form C. 2118.

WAR DIARY
or
INTELLIGENCE SUMMARY.
(Erase heading not required.)

Place	Date	Hour	Summary of Events and Information	Remarks and references to Appendices
Achiet le Grand	15.6.17		R.E. H.Q. 61st Div	
	16.6.17	Nil	61st Div R.E. H.Q. moved to ACHIET-LE-PETIT. walk H.Q 61st Div owing to enemy shelling of ACHIET-LE-GRAND.	
			C.R.E visited 2nd line walls C.E I Corps.	
	17.6.17	Nil		
	18.6.17	Nil		
	19.6.17		Orders received from 61st Div that 61st Div will relieve 20th Div on immediate right of I Corps Sector on or about 23rd June.	
	20.6.17		C.R.E + A.d.R.E visited C.R.E 20th D.I.	
			C.R.E went up to front line of 20th Div sector with C.R.E 20th Div	
			C.R.E Order No. 23 issued	Appendix 36
	21.6.17	Nil		
	22.6.17		C.R.E visited right sector of line the taken over from 20th Div	
			C.R.E Order No 24 issued	
	23.6.17	Nil		
	24.6.17		C.R.E visited left sector of line to be taken over from 20th Div	Appendix 37

WAR DIARY
or
INTELLIGENCE SUMMARY.
(Erase heading not required.)

Army Form C. 2118.

Place	Date	Hour	Summary of Events and Information	Remarks and references to Appendices
Achiet le Petit	25.6.17	Nil	H.Q. Coy. D in rest.	
"	26.6.17	Nil		
"	27.6.17		2nd Phase of offence from VRAUCOURT & L'HOMME MORT transferred to 5th Div.	
FAVREUIL	28.6.17		R.E. H.Q. moved from ACHIET-LE-PETIT & recently of FAVREUIL	
"			C.R.E. 62nd Div took over from C.R.E. 5th Div.	
"	29.6.17		C.R.E. reconn'd Intermediate & new line north of S.O.S.	
"	30.6.17		C.R.E. reconn'd Intermediate line east of new "ridge top" offence line by night of this line	light

R.P.Williams
LIEUT.-COLONEL, R.E.
C.R.E. 62ND (W.R.) DIVISION.

Appendix 36

Copy No. 10.

G.R.E. 62nd. DIVISION ORDER No. 25.

1. With reference to RE/689/1188/4 of June 19th 1917, the relief of the 20th Division by the 62nd Division will now commence on the 26th June and will be completed by the 29th June.

2. Brigades will take over Sectors of the line as under, and the exact dates of relief by each Brigade will be communicated later.

    Right Sector   - 185th Inf. Brigade - H.Q., C.29.a.4.2.
    Left Sector   - 186th Inf. Brigade - H.Q., C.9.d.7.6.
    Brigade in
      Support   - 187th Inf. Brigade - H.Q., H.16.b.3.0.

3. Field Companies will move into their affiliates Brigade Sectors, and will be located as follows, taking over camps from Field Companies as stated below :-

    460th Field Coy - C.29.d.1.4. - (Transport at H.12.a.7.6)
                                      taking over from 93rd Field Coy.
    457th Field Coy - C.10.c.8.2. - (Transport at H.16.a.8.0)
                                      taking over from 84th Field Coy.
    461st Field Coy - I.8.a.2.2. - taking over from 96th Field Coy.

    It will be necessary for units to move into their positions in the line by night.

    Os.C. Field Coys will get into touch with Os.C. Field Coys of 20th Division as above at the earliest opportunity after the 21st instant to ascertain the work to be taken over, and will reconnoitre their respective Sectors before going into the line.

4. Os.C. Field Coys will make arrangements for their attached Brigade Mining Sections to be accommodated with their respective Units in the forward positions in the line indicated above.

    ACKNOWLEDGE.

20.6.17.

                                                    Lieut.Col.R.E.
                                            G.R.E. 62nd. Division.

Copy No.1. 457th Field Coy.
        2. 460th Field Coy.
        3. 461st Field Coy.
        4. 185th Inf. Brigade.
        5. 186th Inf. Brigade.
        6. 187th Inf. Brigade.
        7. 62nd. Division, 'G'
        8. Retained.
        9.)
       10.) War Diary.

Appendix 37
Copy No. 10

C.R.E. 62nd DIVISION.

No.........
Date.........

C. R. E. 62nd Division Order No 24.

22. 6. 17.

1. Field Coys of the 62nd Division will relieve the Field Coys of the 20th Division in the line as under

    460th Field Co   relieve   83rd Field Co night 25/26th
    457th Field Co   relieve   84th Field Co night 27/28th

Details of reliefs to be arranged by O.C. Units concerned.

2. Units will take over and occupy billets and transport lines as detailed hereunder and not as laid down in C.R.E. Order No 23 para 3.

Unit		Location	From
460th Field Coy	Forward billets	C.29.d.1.4.	83rd Field Coy.
	Transport Lines	I.8.a.2.2.	96th Field Coy.
457th Field Coy	Forward Billets	C.10.c.8.2.	84th Field Coy.
	Transport Lines	H.12.a.7.6.	83rd Field Coy.
461st Field Coy	Reserve Billets & Transport Lines.	H.16.a.8.1.	84th Field Coy.

3. Units will move into the new area in accordance with the following move table.

Date	Unit	From	To
25.6.17.	96th Field Coy	I.8.a.2.2.	GOMIECOURT
	460th Field Coy	GOMIECOURT	I.8.a.2.2.
Night 25/26	460th Field Coy (H.Q.&3 Sects).	I.8.a.2.2.	C.29.d.1.4.
Night 25/26	83rd Field Coy	C.29.d.1.4.	H.12.a.7.6.
26.6.17.	83rd Field Coy	H.12.a.7.6.	ACHIET LE PETIT
	457th Field Coy	ACHIET LE PETIT	H.12.a.7.6.
Night 27/28	457th Field Coy (H.Q & 3 Sects)	H.12.a.7.6.	C.10.c.8.2.
	84th Field Coy	C.10.c.8.2.	H.16.a.8.1.
28.6.17.	84th Field Coy	H.16.a.8.1.	BIHUCOURT
	461st Field Coy	MORY	H.16.a.8.1.

All camps must be vacated by 12 noon and arrangements made for their handing over to incoming unit.

Separate instructions will be issued to 461st Field Coy as regards the disposal of the canvas on charge of that Unit.

4. ACKNOWLEDGE.

R.C.Williams
Lieut.Colonel R.E.
C.R.E. 62nd Division.

```
Copy No 1 -  457th Field Co
        2    460th Field Co
        3    461st Field Co
        4    62nd Division 'G'
        5    C.R.E. 20th Division
        6    185th Inf. Bde.
        7    186th Inf. Bde.
        8.   187th Inf. Bde.
        9    Retained
     10 & 11 War Diary.
```

Original

Vol 7

Confidential

War Diary

of

H.Q. 62nd Division. R.E.

Vol VII

From 1st July 1917   To 31st July 1917.

Army Form C. 2118.

WAR DIARY
or
INTELLIGENCE SUMMARY.
(Erase heading not required.)

Instructions regarding War Diaries and Intelligence Summaries are contained in F. S. Regs., Part II. and the Staff Manual respectively. Title pages will be prepared in manuscript.

Place	Date	Hour	Summary of Events and Information	Remarks and references to Appendices
FAVREUIL	1/7/17		Nil	HQ 62nd Div R.E.
	2/7/17		Nil	
	3/7/17		CRE visited Right Brigade Sector	
	4/7/17		Nil	
	5/7/17		CRE visited Left Brigade Sector	
	6/7/17		461 Field Coy relieved 60th Field Coy in Left Brigade sector.	
	7/7/17		CRE visited Right Sector & Intermediate Line	
	8/7/17		Nil	
	9/7/17		Nil	
	10/7/17		CRE visited Left Sector & Intermediate Line	
	11/7/17		Nil	
	12/7/17		Nil	
	13/7/17		Nil	
	14/7/17		457 Field Coy relieved 460 Field Coy in Right Brigade Sector	
	15/7/17		CRE visited Left Brigade Sector	
	16/7/17		Nil	

Army Form C. 2118.

WAR DIARY
or
INTELLIGENCE SUMMARY.
(Erase heading not required.)

Instructions regarding War Diaries and Intelligence Summaries are contained in F. S. Regs., Part II. and the Staff Manual respectively. Title pages will be prepared in manuscript.

Summary of Events and Information   H.Q. 62nd Div. R.E

Place	Date	Hour	Summary of Events and Information	Remarks and references to Appendices
FAVREUIL	17/7/17		Nil	
	18/7/17		CRE visited Right Brigade Sector	
	19/7/17		Nil	
	20/7/17		Nil	
	21/7/17		CRE visited Left Brigade Sector	
	22/7/17		About 460 m Field by subaltern 460 m Field by an offr Left Brigade Sector	
	23/7/17		CRE visited Rt. Brigade Sector	
	24/7/17		CRE visited Back Areas to inspect camps being dismantled	
	25/7/17		CRE visited Left Brigade Sector with G.S.O.2.	
	26/7/17		Nil	
	27/7/17		Nil	
	28/7/17		CREs visited Right Brigade Outpost line with G.S.O.1.	
	29/7/17		Nil	
	30/7/17		CRE visited Right Brigade Sector	
	31/7/17		Nil	

R.H.Turner
LIEUT-COLONEL R.E.
C.R.E. 62nd (W.R.) DIVISION

ORIGINAL
Y8C 78

CONFIDENTIAL

WAR DIARY.

of

H.Q. 62nd Div. Eng.

From 1st Aug to 31st Aug 1917

Volume VIII

Army Form C. 2118.

WAR DIARY
or
INTELLIGENCE SUMMARY.
(Erase heading not required.)

Instructions regarding War Diaries and Intelligence Summaries are contained in F. S. Regs., Part II. and the Staff Manual respectively. Title pages will be prepared in manuscript.

Place	Date	Hour	Summary of Events and Information	Remarks and references to Appendices
FAVREUIL	1/8/17		HQ 62nd Div RE.	
			Provisional Orders received that the Right Brigade Sector was to be taken over by the 3rd Division & that the Division was to extend its left & take over the Right Brigade Sector of the 7th Div.	
	2/8/17		CRE 3rd Div. visited CRE 62nd Div. CRE 62nd Div. visited CRE 7th Div. 62nd Div Order No 57 received.	
	3/8/17		CRE visited sites Ath Pethem near with GSOI 62nd Div & GSOI 7th Div. CRE Order No 29 issued.	Appendix 38
	4/8/17		457th Field Coy relieved 410th Field Coy in in Eff (Morceul) Brigade Sector. 62nd Div Order No 58 received. CRE visited Ballencourt Sector.	
	5/8/17		Nil.	
	6/8/17			
	7/8/17		461st Field Coy relieved Morceul Sector by 3015 Field Coy. (3rd Div.)	
	8/8/17		CRE visited Morceul Sector with GSOI.	
	9/8/17		400 Field Coy relieved 95th Field Coy (7th Div.) in Bullecourt Sector.	
	10/8/17		CRE visited Bullecourt Sector. 62nd Div Order No 59 received. Addenby. CRE 62nd Div Order No 29 issued.	Appendix 39

Army Form C. 2118.

WAR DIARY
or
INTELLIGENCE SUMMARY
(Erase heading not required.)

Instructions regarding War Diaries and Intelligence Summaries are contained in F. S. Regs., Part II. and the Staff Manual respectively. Title pages will be prepared in manuscript.

Place	Date	Hour	Summary of Events and Information	Remarks and references to Appendices
			H.Q. 62nd Div. R.E.	
FAVREUIL	11/5/17		Nil	
	12/5/17		62nd Div Order No 60 recd allotting Army of Byde HQ in Noreuil sector	
	13/5/17		CRE visited Bullecourt sector	
	14/5/17		CRE visited Noreuil sector	
	15/5/17		Nil	
	16/5/17		CRE visited & on line with G.O.C. Division	
			62nd Div Order No 61 recd. CRE order No 31 issued allotting F.Coy subsp.	Appendix 40
	17/5/17		Nil	
	18/5/17		CRE visited front line	
	19/5/17		Nil	
	20/5/17		CRE visited Noreuil Sector. met Div Commander & G.S.O.I. 457 Field Coy about Fuler Coy in Bullecourt Sector	
	21/5/17		Nil	
	22/5/17		CRE visited Bullecourt sector with G.S.O.I.	
	23/5/17		Nil	
	24/5/17		Div Order No 62 recd allotting Brigade Relief. CRE Order No 32 issued	Appendix 41
	25/5/17		Nil	

Army Form C. 2118.

WAR DIARY
or
INTELLIGENCE SUMMARY.
(Erase heading not required.)

Instructions regarding War Diaries and Intelligence
Summaries are contained in F. S. Regs., Part II.
and the Staff Manual respectively. Title pages
will be prepared in manuscript.

Place	Date	Hour	Summary of Events and Information	Remarks and references to Appendices
FAVREUIL	26/8/17		Nil	
	27/8/17		Nil	
	28/8/17		466th Field Coy relieved 467th Field Coy in the MOEUVRES SECTOR	HQ 62nd Div. R.E.
	29/8/17		Nil	
	30/8/17		Nil	
	31/8/17		Nil	

R.F.Lumsden
LIEUT.-COLONEL, R.E.
C.R.E. 62nd (W.R.) DIVISION.

Copy No ....

C.R.E. 62nd Division Order No. 29. Appendix 35

3rd August 1917.

Reference :- Maps 1/20,000
    57c N.W.
    51b S.E.

1. On the night 7th/8th August, the 7th Division (less Artillery) is to be relieved by the 21st Division in the line U.21.c.5.1. to V.14.c.2.9.

    The 21st Division is to be transferred to VI Corps at noon on August 7th.

2. (a) The 186th Infantry Brigade will relieve the 185th Infantry Brigade in the NOREUIL Sector C.12.a.6.3. to U.23.c.9.1. on the night 3rd/4th August.
    186th T.M. Battery will remain in the Line and come under the tactical orders of 186th Infantry Brigade.
    457th Field Coy R.E. will relieve the 460th Field Coy R.E. on the night 4th/5th August.

    (b) The 187th Infantry Brigade will be relieved in the LAGNICOURT Sector by the 9th Infantry Brigade (3rd Division) on the night 7/8th August up to the River HIRONDELLE (inclusive) C.12.a.6.3.

    (c) The 185th Infantry Brigade will relieve the 20th Infantry Brigade (7th Division) in BULLECOURT Sector U.23.c.9.1. to U.21.c.5.1. on the night 8/9th August.

3. (a) The Command of the LAGNICOURT Sector will pass from G.O.C. 62nd Division (VI Corps) to G.O.C. 3rd Division (IV Corps) on completion of reliefs on night 7/8th August.

    (b) The Command of the BULLECOURT Sector will pass to G.O.C. 62nd Division from G.O.C. 7th Division on completion of reliefs on night 8th/9th August.

4. (a) The 460th Field Coy will be relieved in the Left (NOREUIL) sector by the 457th Field Coy R.E. on the night 4/5th August when 460th Field Coy will return to its billets at FAVREUIL.

    (b) The 461st Field Coy will be relieved in the Right (LAGNICOURT) Sector by the 56th Field Coy R.E. (3rd Division) on the night 7th/8th August when the 461st Field Coy will return to its rear billets at FAVREUIL.
    O.C. 56th Field Coy is being instructed to get into touch with O.C. 461st Field Coy in the line, and the latter will afford him all necessary information as to work in progress and new work proposed for execution.

    (c) The 460th Field Coy will take over the work in the BULLECOURT Sector from the 95th Field Coy (7th Division) on the night 9/10th August.
    The forward billets for the Field Coy working in the line in this sector will be notified later.
    O.C. 460th Field Co. will get into touch with O.C. 95th Field Coy at the earliest opportunity and ascertain work to be taken over.

5. Completion of all moves and reliefs will be reported by wire to these Headquarters.

6. Divisional Headquarters will remain in their present position.

7. ACKNOWLEDGE.

Lieut.Colonel R.E.
C.R.E. 62nd Divn.

Appendix 39

Copy No ....

C.R.E. 62nd DIVISION ORDER No 30.

REF: Maps 1/20,000
    57c.N.E.
    51b.S.W.

C.R.E.
62nd DIVISION.

1. Reference para 1 62nd Division Order No 58 issued to Units, the boundary between the 62nd and 21st Divisions will be U.21.c.35.15 along PELICAN AVENUE (inclusive to 21st Division) -- as far as N.26.c.3.5. - thence straight line to C.7.a.2.6. - thence straight line to B.17.b.2.6.

2. The 187th Infantry Brigade will relieve the 186th Infantry Bde in the Right (NOREUIL) Sector on the night 12/13 August.
    Command of the NOREUIL Sector will pass to G.O.C. 187th Infantry Brigade on night 12/13 August.

3. The 461st Field Coy will relieve the 457th Field Coy on the night 13/14 August, details of relief to be arranged between Os.C. Units concerned.

4. Duplicate copies of handing over Notes both of the 457th Field Coy for the NOREUIL Sector and of the 461st Field Coy for the back area will be forwarded to C.R.E.

5. Completion of relief will be reported to R.E. H.Q. by wire.

6. ACKNOWLEDGE.

                                Sd. R.A. Gillam
                                     Lieut.Colonel R.E.
                          C.R.E. 62nd Division.

10. 8. 17.

Copies to

No 1. 457th Field Co.
    2. 460th Field Co.
    3. 461st Field Co.
    4. 62nd Divn 'Q'
5 & 6. War Diary.
    7. File.

Copy No. 6   Appendix 40

C.R.E. 62nd Division Order No 31.

16. 8. 17.

1. (a) The 186th Infantry Brigade will relieve the 185th Infantry Brigade in the Left (BULLECOURT) Sector on the night 20/21st August

(b) The 457th Field Coy R.E. will relieve the 460th Field Coy on the night 21/22nd August.

(c) The Command of the BULLECOURT Sector will pass from G.O.C. 185th Infantry Brigade to G.O.C. 186th Infantry Brigade on completion of reliefs on night 20/21st August.

2. Os.C. 460th and 457th Field Coys will prepare and hand over Handing over notes on the Left (BULLECOURT) Sector, and on Back Area work, respectively. A copy of these notes will be sent by the Field Coy concerned to the C.R.E. for information.

3. Completion of relief to be report to R.E. Headquarters by wire.

4. ACKNOWLEDGE.

Sd R.A Gillam

Lieut.Colonel R.E.
C. R. E. 62nd Division.

Copies to

No 1. 457th Field Co.
   2. 460th Field Co.
   3. 461st Field Co.
   4. 62nd Divn G.
   5
   6 War Diary.
   7 File.

SECRET.

C.R.E.,
62nd DIVISION.

No..........
Date..........

Copy No ....

C.R.E. 62nd Division Order No 32.
----

24. 8. 17.

1. (a) The 185th Infantry Brigade will relieve the 187th Infantry Brigade in the Right (NOREUIL) Sector on the night 28/29th August.

   (b) The 460th Field Coy R.E. will relieve the 461st Field Co R.E. on the night 28/29th August.

   (c) The Command of the NOREUIL Sector will pass from G.O.C. 187th Infantry Brigade to G.O.C. 185th Infantry Brigade on completion of reliefs on night 28/29th August.

2. O.C. 461st Field Coy will hand over to O.C. 460th Field Coy Handing over Notes with regard to the NOREUIL Section and O.C. 460th Field Coy will hand over to O.C. 461st Field Coy Handing over Notes dealing with the whole of the Back Area work. forwarded
   Copies of these Handing Over Notes will be/forwarded by O.C. 461st Field Co and O.C. 460th Field Coy respectively to the C.R.E. for information.

3. Completion of move and relief to be reported to R.E. Headquarters by wire.

4. ACKNOWLEDGE.

Lieut.Colonel R.E.
C.R.E. 62nd Division.

Copies to
1. 460th Field Co
2. 461st Field Co.
3. 457th Field Co
4. 62nd Divn G.
5 & 6. War Diary.
7. File.

Vol 9 Original

CONFIDENTIAL

War Diary
of
H.Q. 6th Div. Engineers.

From Sept 1st 1917 to Sept 30th 1917

Volume VIII

Army Form C. 2118.

WAR DIARY
or
INTELLIGENCE SUMMARY.
(Erase heading not required.)

Instructions regarding War Diaries and Intelligence Summaries are contained in F. S. Regs., Part II. and the Staff Manual respectively. Title pages will be prepared in manuscript.

Place	Date	Hour	Summary of Events and Information	Remarks and references to Appendices
			H.Q. 62nd Div. Eng.	
FAVREUIL	1/9/17		Capt G.D.ASPLAND proceeded on 10 day leave. 62nd Div. Order No. 63 issued	
	2/9/17		C.R.E. Order No. 33 issued detailing Field Coy. schefs.	Appendix 1.2
	3/9/17		Nil	
	4/9/17		C.R.E. visited the Left SECTOR with O.C. 461 Field Co. and O.C. 457 Field Co. 461st Field Coy. relieved 457 Field Coy. in Bullecourt Sector	
	5/9/17		G.E. Corps visited R.E. WORKSHOPS, FAVREUIL and R.E. DUMP VAULX	
	6/9/17		Nil	
	7/9/17		C.R.E. visited ECOUST and portion of RIGHT SECTOR	
	8/9/17		62nd Div. Order No. 64 issued	
	9/9/17		C.R.E. Div. Order No. 34 issued detailing Field Coy. schefs.	Appendix 3
	10/9/17		Nil	
	11/9/17		C.R.E. proceeded on 10 days leave.	
	12/9/17		Capt G.D.ASPLAND ADJRE returned from leave. 467th Field Coy. relieved 460th Field Coy. in NOREUIL SECTION.	
	13/9/17		Nil	
	14/9/17		Nil	
	15/9/17		Nil	

WAR DIARY
or
INTELLIGENCE SUMMARY.
(Erase heading not required.)

Army Form C. 2118.

Summary of Events and Information HQ 11th Div. Eng

Place	Date	Hour		Remarks and references to Appendices
FAVREUIL 16/9/17	16/9/17		Nil	
	17/9/17		11th Div Order No 65 issued	
			CRE Order No 35 issued detailing task for whips.	Appendix 73 14
	18/9/17		Nil	
	19/9/17		Nil	
	20/9/17		Nil	
	21/9/17		Nil	
	22/9/17		CRE returned from leave.	
	23/9/17		CRE visited Left Section	
	24/9/17		CRE visited Right Section	
	25/9/17		82nd Div Order No 66 & 67 received	
			C.R.E. Order No 36 issued detailing task for salvage	Appendix 65
	26/9/17		Nil	
	27/9/17		CRE visited Left Section with Divisional Commander	
			11nd Div Order No 68 received detailing method of holding the Div	
			Sector. CRE Order No 37 issued.	Appendix 76

Army Form C. 2118.

WAR DIARY
or
INTELLIGENCE SUMMARY.
(Erase heading not required.)

Summary of Events and Information HQ 62nd Div Eng

Place	Date	Hour	Summary of Events and Information	Remarks and references to Appendices
FAVREUIL	28/9/18		461st Field Coy relieved 467th Field Coy in Right Section	
	29/9/18		CRE went to see the Right Section	
	30/9/18		Nil	

R.W. Munro
LIEUT.-COLONEL, R.E.
C.R.E. 62ND (W.R.) DIVISION

Instructions regarding War Diaries and Intelligence Summaries are contained in F. S. Regs., Part II. and the Staff Manual respectively. Title pages will be prepared in manuscript.

SECRET.

Copy No........ 5

C.R.E. 62nd Division Order No. 35.

2.9.17.

1. (a) The 187th Infantry Brigade will relieve the 186th Infantry Brigade in the Left (BULLECOURT) Section of the Divisional Sector on the night 5th/6th September.

   (b) The 461st Field Coy R.E. will relieve the 457th Field Coy on the night 4/5th September.

   (c) The command of the BULLECOURT Section will pass from G.O.C. 186th Infantry Brigade to G.O.C. 187th Infantry Brigade at ~~completion of relief on night~~ 9 a.m. 6th September.

2. O.C. 457th Field Coy will hand over to O.C. 461st Field Coy Handing Over Notes with regard to the BULLECOURT Section and O.C. 461st Field Coy will hand over to O.C. 457th Field Coy Handing Over Notes dealing with the whole of the Back Area work.
   Copies of these Handing Over Notes will be forwarded by O.C. 457th Field Coy and O.C. 461st Field Coy respectively to the C.R.E. for information.

3. Completion of move and relief to be reported to R.E. Headquarters by wire.

4. ACKNOWLEDGE.

[signature]
Lieut. Colonel R.E.
C.R.E. 62nd. Division.

Copies to
1. 461st Field Coy.
2. 457th Field Coy.
3. 460th Field Coy.
4. 62nd. Divn. G.
5 & 6. War Diary.
7. File.

SECRET.   Copy No... 5 ...

C.R.E. 62nd. Division Order No. 34.

9.9.17.

1. (a) The 186th Infantry Brigade will relieve the 185th Infantry Brigade in the RIGHT (NOREUIL) SECTION on the night 13th/14th September.

   (b) The 457th Field Coy R.E. will relieve the 460th Field Coy R.E. on the night 12th/13th September.

   (c) The Command of the NOREUIL Section will pass from G.O.C. 185th Infantry Brigade to G.O.C. 186th Infantry Brigade on completion of reliefs, on the night 13th/14th September.

2. O.C. 460th Field Coy will hand over to O.C. 457th Field Coy Handing Over Notes with regard to the BULLECOURT and NOREUIL Section and O.C. 457th Field Coy will hand over to O.C. 460th Field Coy Handing Over Notes dealing with the whole of the Back Area work.

   Copies of these Handing Over Notes will be forwarded by O.C. 460th Field Coy and 457th Field Coy respectively to the C.R.E. for information.

3. Completion of move and relief to be reported to R.E. Headquarters by wire.

4. ACKNOWLEDGE.

                                                  Lieut. Colonel R.E.
                                                  C.R.E. 62nd. Division.

Copies to
  1. 457th Field Coy.
  2. 460th Field Coy.
  3. 461st Field Coy.
  4. 62nd. Divn. 'Q'
5 & 6. War Diary.
  7. File.

Copy........5

C.R.E. 62nd. Division Order No. 35

17.9.17.

1. (a) The 185th Infantry Brigade will relieve the 187th Infantry Brigade in the Left (BULLECOURT) Section on the night 21/22 Sept.

   (b) The 460th Field Coy. R.E. will relieve the 461st Field Coy R.E. on the night 20/21 Sept.

   (c) The Command of the BULLECOURT SECTION will pass from G.O.C. 187th Infantry Brigade to G.O.C. 185th Infantry Brigade on completion of reliefs on the night 21/22 Sept.

2. O.C. 461st Field Coy will hand over to O.C. 460th Field Coy Handing Over Notes with regard to the BULLECOURT Section and O.C. 460th Field Coy will hand over to O.C. 461st Field Coy Handing Over Notes dealing with the whole of the Back Area work.

   Copies of these Handing Over Notes will be forwarded by O.C. 461st Field Coy and O.C. 460th Field Coy respectively to the C.R.E. for information.

3. Completion of move and relief to be reported to R.E. Headquarters by wire.

4. ACKNOWLEDGE.

Major R.E,
A/C.R.E. 62nd. Division.

Copies to :-
    1. 461st. Field Coy.
    2. 460th Field Coy.
    3. 457th Field Coy.
    4. 62nd. Divn. 'G'.
5 & 6. War Diary.
    7. File.

No. 5
28.9.19.

C.R.E. 62nd Division Order No 36.

1. (a) The 187th Infantry Brigade will relieve the 186th Infantry Brigade in the RIGHT (NOREUIL) SECTION on the night 29th/30th September.

   R.E.
   (b) The 461st Field Coy will relieve the 457th Field Coy R.E. on the night 28/29th September.

   (c) The Command of the NOREUIL SECTION will pass from G.O.C. 186th Infantry Brigade to G.O.C. 187th Infantry Brigade at 9 a.m. on 30th September.

2. O.C. 457th Field Coy will hand over to O.C. 461st Field Coy Handing Over Notes with regard to the NOREUIL SECTION and O.C. 461st Field Coy will hand over to O.C. 457th Field Coy. Handing Over Notes dealing with the whole of the Back Area work.

   Copies of these Handing Over Notes will be forwarded by O.C. 457th Field Coy and O.C. 461st Field Coy respectively to the C.R.E. for information.

3. Completion of move and relief to be reported to R.E. Headquarters by wire.

4. ACKNOWLEDGE.

                                    Lieut.Colonel R.E.
                                    C.R.E. 62nd Division.

Copies to :-
1. 461st Field Coy.
2. 457th Field Coy.
3. 460th Field Coy.
4. 62nd Divn. 'G'.
5 & 6. War Diary.
7. File.

C.R.E. 62nd Divn. Order No. 37.

Ref: Maps 1/20,000.
    57c. N.W.
    51b. S.W.

27.9.17.

1. On the relief of the 186th Infantry Brigade by the 187th Infantry Brigade on the 29th/30th September, the Divisional Front will be re-adjusted.

2. The 187th Infantry Brigade will, on the night 29th/30th September take over the Front of the right Battalion, 185th Infantry Brigade, from the present Inter-Brigade Boundary as far as FOX TROT Lane (exclusive)
All details of relief will be arranged between the Brigadiers concerned.

3. The Boundary between Brigades will, after relief, be :- FOX TROT Lane (to Left Brigade) - junction of TANK AVENUE with road in U.28.d. - TANK AVENUE (to Right Brigade) - thence to present Inter-Brigade Boundary.

4. The Right Section will be held by 3 Battalions in Front Line and 1 Battalion in Support.

    Right Battalion H.Q..........HOBART AVENUE.
    Centre   ----do----   )
    Left   ----do----   ) RAILWAY RESERVE.

The 186th and 187th Infantry Brigades will relieve each other every 8 eight days in the Right Section.

5. The Left Section will be held permanently by the 185th Infantry Brigade with 1½ Battalions in Front Line - one Battalion of this Brigade will be in Reserve at MORY.

6. The relief of Machine Gun Companies will not be affected, for the present, by the alteration of the Inter-Brigade Boundary.

7. The relief of the 457th Field Coy by the 461st Field Coy in the Right (HORNUIL) Section will take place on the 28th/29th September as previously ordered.

8. 460th Field Coy will remain permanently in the line in the Left (BULLECOURT) Section, keeping 3 Sections forward and 1 Section back at FAVREUIL.

9. Please ACKNOWLEDGE.

                                                              Lieut.Colonel R.E.
                                                              C.R.E. 62nd Division.

Copies to :-
    No.1. 457 Field Coy.
    No.2. 460th Field Coy.
    No.3. 461st Field Coy.
    No.4. 62nd Divn. 'G'.
  5 & 6. War Diary.
    No.7. File.

ORIGINAL

Vol 10

CONFIDENTIAL

WAR DIARY.

of

HdQrs 42nd Div. Engineers

From 1st Oct 1917 to 31st Oct 1917

VOLUME. IX.

Army Form C. 2118.

WAR DIARY
or
INTELLIGENCE SUMMARY.
(Erase heading not required.)

Instructions regarding War Diaries and Intelligence Summaries are contained in F. S. Regs., Part II. and the Staff Manual respectively. Title pages will be prepared in manuscript.

Summary of Events and Information HQ. 62nd Div Engineers

Place	Date	Hour	Summary of Events and Information	Remarks and references to Appendices
FAVREUIL	1/10/17		Nil	
	2/10/17		CRE visited Right & Left Sections and C.E. Third Army & C.E. II Corps.	
	3/10/17		CRE visited Right Section	
			Div. Operation Order No 69 issued. Detaching Bayonets Relief.	
			CRE 62nd Div Order No 38 issued. Detaching Field Coy Relief.	Appendices 41
			Div. Operation Order No 70 issued. Relief of 62nd Div by 3rd Div on 12/10/17.	
	4/10/17		Nil	
	5/10/17		CRE received notes of Relief to be taken over in hand over.	
	6/10/17		Nil	
	7/10/17		CRE 3rd Div visited CRE 62nd Div	
	8/10/17		CRE Order No 39 issued. Detaching Field by Relief.	Appendices 42
	9/10/17		CRE 62nd Div took CRE 3rd Div around handed of Div Sector.	
			457th Field Coy relieved by 53rd Field Coy. in MORCHIES SECTION.	
			461st Field Coy moved to YPRES.	
	10/10/17		460th Field Coy relieved by 529 Field Coy in BULLECOURT SECTION.	
			460th Field Coy moved to BARASTRE.	

Army Form C. 2118.

WAR DIARY
or
INTELLIGENCE SUMMARY.
(Erase heading not required.)

Instructions regarding War Diaries and Intelligence Summaries are contained in F. S. Regs., Part II. and the Staff Manual respectively. Title pages will be prepared in manuscript.

Place	Date	Hour	Summary of Events and Information	Remarks and references to Appendices
FAVEUIL	11/10/17		43rd Field Coy moved to BEAUCOURT. Camp's beds over hale taken over by 438th Field Coy	
"	12/10/17		3rd Div left are from 6th Div 10 am	
"	13/10/17		CRE 3rd Div taken over from 6th Div 10.30 am	
"	14/10/17		HQ 6th Div Eng moved to HAPLINCOURT	
HAPLINCOURT	15/10/17		Nil	
"	16/10/17		Nil	
"	17/10/17		Nil	
"	18/10/17		Nil	
"	19/10/17		Nil	
"	20/10/17		Nil	
"	21/10/17		Nil	
"	22/10/17		Nil	
"	23/10/17		Nil	
"	24/10/17		Nil	

Army Form C. 2118.

WAR DIARY
or
INTELLIGENCE SUMMARY.
(Erase heading not required.)

Instructions regarding War Diaries and Intelligence Summaries are contained in F. S. Regs., Part II. and the Staff Manual respectively. Title pages will be prepared in manuscript.

Place	Date	Hour	Summary of Events and Information	Remarks and references to Appendices
			H.Q. 6.ᵗʰ Div. Eng.	
HARINCOURT	24/9/17	Nil		
	25/9/17	Nil		
	26/9/17	Nil		
	27/9/17		Warning Order received from H.Q. 6ᵗʰ Div. that Division will move to III Corps area. Ordered that H.Q. & 2 & 3 Field Coys will remain in III Corps area for work under C.E. III Corps.	
			C.R.E. attended conference at C.E. III Corps.	Appendix 58
	28/9/17		Warning Order issued to units. Orders received that 460 Field Coy & 411ᵗʰ Field Coy will move to LESUCQUIERE & BEAUMETZ respectively on 29ᵗʰ Oct. & to work on entraining of BENGHY - BOURSIES Road. (Sheet 57 C)	
	29/9/17		460 Field Coy moved from BARASTRE to LESUCQUIERE. 411ᵗʰ Field Coy moved from YTRES to BEAUMETZ. 2 Section 450ᵗʰ Field Coy moved from BEAUMONT to METZ Blockade for work to C.R.E. 36ᵗʰ Div. Foot messages nightly & Horse Post for BERNAY - BOURSIES Road work commenced.	

T2134. Wt. W708-776. 50,000. 4/15. Sir J. C. & S.

Army Form C. 2118.

WAR DIARY
or
INTELLIGENCE SUMMARY.
(Erase heading not required.)

Instructions regarding War Diaries and Intelligence Summaries are contained in F. S. Regs., Part II. and the Staff Manual respectively. Title pages will be prepared in manuscript.

Place	Date	Hour	Summary of Events and Information	Remarks and references to Appendices
HAPLUI COURT	30/10/15		C.R.E. visited 2nd W. Coys.	
			5th Div. ableted 400 men + 20 carpenters for work on BEUGNY-BAPAUME Road.	Apps.
	31/10/15		Nil.	

HQ 62nd Div R.E.

R.H. Dunn
Lieut.-Colonel, R.E.
C.R.E. 62nd (W.R.) DIVISION.

Appendix 46
Copy... 5

C.R.E. 62nd DIVISION ORDER NO. 38.

3.10.17.

1. (a) The 186th Infantry Brigade will relieve the 187th Infantry Brigade in the Right (NOREUIL) Section on the night 7th/8th Octr.

   (b) The 457th Field Coy. R.E. will relieve the 461st Field Coy R.E. on the night 6th/7th Octr.

   (c) The Command of the NOREUIL Section will pass from G.O.C. 187th Infantry Brigade to G.O.C. 186th Infantry Brigade on completion of reliefs.

2. O.C. 461st Field Coy will hand over to O.C. 457th Field Coy all details of work in the NOREUIL Section and O.C. 457th Field Coy will hand over to O.C. 461st Field Coy all details of work in the back area.

   Copies of the Handing Over Notes embodying all the details above referred to will be forward by O.C. 461st and 457th Field Coys respectively to the C.R.E. for information.

3. Completion of relief will be wired to R.E. Headquarters.

4. ACKNOWLEDGE.

Lieut. Colonel R.E.
C.R.E. 62nd. Division.

Copies to
   No.1. - 457th Field Coy.
      2. - 461st Field Coy.
      3. - 460th Field Coy.
      4. - 62nd Divn. 'G'
   5 & 6. - War Diary.
      7. - Files

SECRET.   Copy No. 9.

C.R.E. 62nd Division Order No 39.
—————————

8. 10. 17.

1. The 62nd Division (less Divisional Artillery) will be relieved by the 3rd Division (less Divisional Artillery) on October 9th & 17th.

2. Reliefs of Field Coys will take place 24 hours in advance of Brigade Reliefs.

3. 461st Field Coy will hand over all work in back area to 457th Field Coy on morning of 9th inst.

4. 461st Field Coy will leave a rear party of 1 Officer and 1 N.C.O. to hand over billets (H.16.b.5.1.) to 56th Field Coy on arrival.

5. An advance party of 56th Field Coy (2 Officers & 4 N.C.Os) will report to O.C. 457th Field Coy MOREUIL at 10 a.m. on 9th inst to take over details of work in line. O.C. 457th Field Co will arrange accordingly.

6. 457th Field Coy will leave a small rear party under an Officer to hand over billets at MOREUIL to 56th Field Co on night 9/10th.

7. 460th Field Co will leave one section under an Officer at Forward billets until night 10/11 inst to carry on work in the line and to hand over billets to 9th Field Coy

8. 529th Field Coy will send an advance party (2 Officers & 4 N.C.Os) to 460th Field Coy Advance H.Q. (C.6.a.2.3.) at 10 a.m. on 9th inst to take over details of work in line. O.C. 460th Field Coy will arrange accordingly.

9. 460th Field Coy will leave a rear party of 1 Officer and 1 N.C.O. to hand over rear billets H.16.d.3.8. to 529th Field Co on arrival.

10. 438th Field Coy will send an Advance Party (1 Officer and 1 N.C.O.) to rear billets 457th Field Co H.12.b.4.4. at 10 a.m. 11th inst to take over details of work in back area.

11. 457th Field Coy will leave a Rear party of 1 Officer & 1 N.C.O. to hand over billets H.12.b.4.4. to 438th Field Coy on arrival.

12. Certificates signed by an Officer of the relieving Unit will be obtained in every case to the effect that Billets have been handed over in a clean condition. Certificates will be forwarded to this Office on completion of move.

13. ACKNOWLEDGE.

Copies to :-
1. 457th Field Co.
2. 460th Field Co.
3. 461st Field Co
4. 62nd Divn 'G'
5. C.R.E. 3rd Divn
6. 62nd Divn 'Q'
7½ 62nd Div Train
8. A.P.M.
9 & 10 War Diary
11 File.

Captain R.E. (T)
Adjutant to C.R.E. 62nd Division.

MOVE TABLE to go with C.R.E. Order No 39.

Item.	Date	Div.	Unit	From	To	Remarks.
1.	Oct.9	3rd	56th Field Co	VERTES Area O.26.b.5.3.	FAVREUIL - 461st Field Co Camp H.16.b.3.1.	To clear H.16.b.3.1. by 1 p.m.
2.	Oct.9	62nd	461st Field Co	H.16.b.3.1.	VERTES Area O.26.b.5.3.	To take over work from 457 Field Co.
3.	Oct.9/10	3rd	56 Field Co H.Q. & 3 sections	FAVREUIL H.16.b.3.1.	Fd Coy H.Q. NORMUIL C.10.c.7.1.	To be clear of C.10.c.7.1. by 9 p.m.
4.	Oct.9/10	62nd	457 Fd Coy H.Q. & 3 sections.	C.10.c.7.1.	Rear Billets H.12.b.4.4.	To be clear of C.8.a.2.3 by 9 p.m.
5.	Oct.9/10	62nd	460 Fd Coy less 1 section.	C.8.a.2.3.	Rear Billets H.16.d.3.8.	
6.	Oct.10th.	3rd	529 Fd Coy H.Q. & 3 sections.	BARASTRE Area O.16.d.2.8.	FAVREUIL 460 Fd Co Camp H.16.d.3.8.	
7.	Oct.10th.	62nd	460 Fd Coy (less 1 section).	H.16.d.3.8.	BARASTRE Area O.16.d.2.8.	To be clear of H.16.d.38 by 1 p.m.
8.	Oct.10/11.	3rd	529 Fd Co H.Q. & 3 sections.	H.16.d.3.8.	Fd Coy H.Q. C.8.a.2.3.	Take over from 460 Fd Coy.
9.	Oct.10/11.	62nd	1 Section 460 Fd Co	C.8.a.2.3.	BARASTRE Area O.16.d.2.8.	To hand over billets to 529 Fd Coy.
10.	11th Oct.	3rd	438 Field Coy	BEAULENCOURT Area N.18.c.5.2.	457th Fd Co Rear Billets.H.12.b.4.4.	
11.	11th	62nd	457 Field Coy	H.12.b.4.4.	BEAULENCOURT Area N.18.c.5.2.	To be clear of H.12.b.4.4. by 1 p.m.

C. R. E.   62nd Division.

PROVISIONAL ORDER.

27.10.17.

1. 62nd Division (less Artillery, R.E. H.Q. and 2½ Field Coys R.E. will move to area BARLY BASSEUX SIMENCOURT BERNEVILLE BEAUMETZ - LAHERLIERE as under :-

  Oct 29th 185th Inf. Bde. to GOMIECOURT
    30th do   to BARLY etc Area.

  Oct 30th 187th Inf. Bde. to GOMIECOURT
    31st do   to BERNEVILLE Area.

  Oct 31st 186th Inf. Bde. to BEAUMETZ Area.

It is possible that these dates may be ante-dated 24 hrs.

2. H.Q. R.E., 461, 460 and 2 Sections 457 Field Coy will remain in IV Corps Area and will be attached to IV Corps for work on forward roads.

H.Q. and 2 sections 457th Field Coy will move with 62nd Divn One of these sections will for the present remain at the 62nd Divnl Reinforcement Camp. The date on which H.Q. and 2 sections 457th Field Coy will move will be communicated as soon as ascertained.

461, 460 and 2 setions 457th Field Coys remaining in this area will move as under :-

  461st Field Co to BEAUMETZ J.13 & 14.
  460th Field Co to BEUGNY L.22
 2 sections 457th do to METZ   Q.20.

3. The 461st and 460th Field Coys will work under C.R.E, 62nd Divn on BEUGNY-CAMBRAI Road. 2 Sections 457th Field Coy will be attached to and carry out work for C.R.E. 36th Divn.

4. The provisional date of moves as above of Coys remaining in this Area will be Monday 29th October but definite orders for the date of move will be wired to Units as soon as arrangements for accommodation have been made.

5. R.E., H.Q. will remain at I.34.a.2.5. until further notice.

           R.A. Gillam Lieut.Colonel
            C.R.E. 62nd Divn

ORIGINAL
Vol II

CONFIDENTIAL

WAR DIARY
of
H.Q. 4th Divl. Engrs.

1st Nov. to 30th Nov. 1917.

VOL XI

Army Form C. 2118.

WAR DIARY
or
INTELLIGENCE SUMMARY
(Erase heading not required.)

Place	Date	Hour	Summary of Events and Information	Remarks and references to Appendices
HAPLINCOURT	1/11/17		H.Q. 3rd Div. Eng. CRE attended conference at CE's Office IV Corps re transport for work on Beugny - Boursies Road.	
	2/11/17		O.C. 3rd Pontoon Park started for duty with 25 London Regt. CRE visited Beugny - Boursies road with reference to A.D.L.R III Bde. & selection of loading point for stone & new railway.	
	3/11/17		CRE visited Beugny - Boursies Road with CE. Colonel Gray & CE III Corps.	
	4/11/17		CRE attended conference on Stores at Corps Headquarters.	
	5/11/17		CRE visited CRE 36 Div. with reference to Stores.	
	6/11/17		CRE visited CRE IV Corps to try & arrange to obtain wagons & infantry working parties for Beugny - Boursies Road. H.Q. 457 Field Co. & a section moved to RUYAULCOURT for work under CRE 36th Div.	
	7/11/17		CRE visited CRE 36th Div. & went over plans for his works.	
	8/11/17		Nil.	
	9/11/17		CRE visited Capt. NEVILLE with Camp Commandant Rev 3 Div. & settled accommodation for Cob. Div. H.Q.	

Army Form C. 2118.

WAR DIARY
or
INTELLIGENCE SUMMARY.
(Erase heading not required.)

Instructions regarding War Diaries and Intelligence Summaries are contained in F. S. Regs., Part II. and the Staff Manual respectively. Title pages will be prepared in manuscript.

Place	Date	Hour	Summary of Events and Information	Remarks and references to Appendices
HAPLINCOURT	10/1/17		CRE visited CRE 51st Div & CRE 36th Div.	H.Q. 62nd Div. R.E.
	11/1/17		CRE visited CRE 51st Div and inspected forward accommodation in forward area. CRE visited C.R.E. IV Corps & then proceeded with G.S.O.1 and Div. to 36th Div.	
	12/1/17		Information recd. that when BEUGNY - BOURSIES Road will be handed over to 51st Div on 15th CRE and new road with whereabouts of CRE 51st Div & O.C's 460 & 461st Field Coys.	
			CRE attended conference on forward Roads at office of C.E. IV Corps.	
	13/1/17		CRE visited rear area with reference to forward accommodation. Conference with O.C's 460 & 461st Field Coys at R.E. H.Q. with reference to work to be carried out during following operations.	
			62nd Div Instructions No 2 for following operations received	
			62nd Div Order No 74 & No 75 received detailing role of Div. Roch in IV Corps Area.	
	14/1/17		Orders received that Div R.E. will be engaged on main roads forward for 48 hours after Zero Hour.	

WAR DIARY
or
INTELLIGENCE SUMMARY.
(Erase heading not required.)

Army Form C. 2118.

Summary of Events and Information H.Q. 62nd Div. Eng.

Place	Date	Hour	Summary of Events and Information	Remarks and references to Appendices
HAPLINCOURT	14/11/17	contd	Orders issued to units to continue work till dark on forward roads. 100 men (Infantry) attached to each Field Coy the date for further covering operations.	Appendix 49.
	15/11/17		CRE Order No 40 issued detailing Mavis of 460 & 461st Field Coys to RUYAULCOURT & BERTINCOURT respectively on 16/11/17	Appendix 50.
			CRE inspected HAPLINCOURT WOOD and G.S.O.2 & remnants line & approved.	
			Last night of work by 2nd Div RE on BEUGNY-BOURSIES Road. Work handed over to 2/1st 5th Div.	
	16/11/17		Work on BEUGNY-BOURSIES road completed. A total of handing over to CRE 5th Div. 4260 yds of roadway & 3330 yds of tramway. 62nd Div Order No 77 issued detailing relief of 34th Div by 62nd Div. 460th Field Coy moved to RUYAULCOURT 461st Field Coy moved to BERTINCOURT CRE 62nd Div took ord CRE 34th Div to take over relief of works on hand.	

Army Form C. 2118.

WAR DIARY
or
INTELLIGENCE SUMMARY.
(Erase heading not required.)

Instructions regarding War Diaries and Intelligence Summaries are contained in F. S. Regs., Part II. and the Staff Manual respectively. Title pages will be prepared in manuscript.

(1)

Place	Date	Hour	Summary of Events and Information	Remarks and references to Appendices
HAVRINCOURT	17/11/17		C.R.E. visited new area to inspect progress on roads and tracks.	
	18/11/17		62nd Div Orders No. 78 & 79 received detailing attack to be carried out by 62nd Div.	
			R.E. Headquarters moved to NEUVILLE. (Adv. Div. H.Q.)	
			C.R.E. Order No 41 issued regarding forthcoming operations.	Appendix 51.
	19/11/17		Information received that Z day is to be Nov. 20th & Zero hour 6.20.A.M.	
			C.R.E. Order No 42 issued detailing Z day.	Appendix 52
			Units notified Zero hour will be 6.20.A.M.	
			Waggons for forward roads reported as ordered. Labour parties reported three hours late.	
	20/11/17	6.20.A.M.	Attack on HAVRINCOURT commenced.	
		9.15.A.M.	Orders wired for road waggons to move forward to roads.	
		9.45.A.M.	Report received that 464th Field Coy are moving on to work on roads. Reported to G.	
		10.15.A.M.	Report received 1st objectives gained excepting HAVRINCOURT.	
		10.55.A.M.	" " 461st Field Coy moved on to roads 9.40 a.m. Reported to G.	
		11.3.A.M.	Report sent to C.E. IV Corps. that work commenced on roads at 9.30 A.M.	
		12 Noon	C.R.E. Proceeded to visit work in progress on roads	
		12.55.P.M.	Report received from 461. Field Coy. that work is progressing satisfactorily. Reported to G.	

Army Form C. 2118.

(2)

WAR DIARY
or
INTELLIGENCE SUMMARY.
(Erase heading not required.)

Instructions regarding War Diaries and Intelligence Summaries are contained in F. S. Regs., Part II. and the Staff Manual respectively. Title pages will be prepared in manuscript.

Place	Date	Hour	Summary of Events and Information	Remarks and references to Appendices
NEUVILLE	20/11/17	1.15 PM.	Report recd that HAVRINCOURT has been cleared of enemy.	
		2.5 PM.	Report recd from 460th Fld.Coy. that roads in right sector are passable for traffic.	
		"	Large Crater reported in HAVRINCOURT. Reported to G.	
		3.30 PM.	Report received from 461st Field Coy. that Clayton Cres. HAVRINCOURT. ROAD. is passable for Traffic. Reported to G.	
		"	Report received that 62 Div have gained all objectives.	
		3.45 PM.	Road reports wired to C.E. IV. Corps.	
		6.10 PM.	Graincourt reported captured.	
		6.35 PM.	62nd Division reported to have gained 3rd (final) objectives	
		6.45 PM.	Orders received that 62nd Div. will advance on 21st and capture BOURLON WOOD. Repeated to Units.	
		7 PM.	Two sections 457. Fld.Coy. with 50 attached infantry ordered forward for work on HAVRINCOURT. — GRAINCOURT. ROAD.	
		10 PM.	Reports from 460 & 461 Fld Coys. report roads badly cut up, & being maintained with difficulty.	
		10.10 PM.	Orders wired to 460 Fld.Coy. allowing roads to be maintained. SHROPSHIRE SPUR being no longer required. Units instructed that the opening up of roads to GRAINCOURT. is absolutely vital.	Appendix 3

Army Form C. 2118.
(3)

WAR DIARY
or
INTELLIGENCE SUMMARY.
(Erase heading not required.)

Place	Date	Hour	Summary of Events and Information	Remarks and references to Appendices
NEUVILLE	20.11.17	10.25 PM	Report sent to C.E. IV Corps that roads are being maintained but with great difficulty.	
	21.11.17	3.10 AM	Attack on 21st to commence 10 a.m. Units informed. Wire received from C.E. IV Corps in response to telephonic request that no more Labour can be placed at C.R.E.s 62nd Div. disposal.	
		3.43 AM	62nd Div. G. asked to send forward Traffic Control men to regulate traffic on roads which are blocked.	
		9.30 AM	Road reports received from 466th & 461st Field Coy. Roads being maintained but with great difficulty. Reports forwarded to 62nd Div. G. and C.E. IV Corps.	
		10. a.m.	C.R.E. proceeded to visit work on roads.	
		11.10 am	51st Division report Capture of FLESQUIERES.	
		3.35 PM	Notification received from 62nd Div. Q. that 34 waggons allotted for work on roads can remain on work until further orders.	
		4.40 PM	C.R.E.s 62nd Div. Order No. 43 issued detailing distribution of work after advancement of D.G.T. line.	Appendix 52
		9.30 PM	461st Field Coy. notified that 2 Sections can proceed to HAVRINCOURT.	
		10. PM	Road reports upon HAVRINCOURT — FLESQUIERES Road. HAVRINCOURT — GRAINCOURT Road + To be continued next page.	

Army Form C. 2118.

WAR DIARY
or
INTELLIGENCE SUMMARY.
(Erase heading not required.)

Instructions regarding War Diaries and Intelligence Summaries are contained in F. S. Regs., Part II. and the Staff Manual respectively. Title pages will be prepared in manuscript.

(4)

Place	Date	Hour	Summary of Events and Information	Remarks and references to Appendices
NEUVILLE	21.11.17	10. p.m.	Continued (Direct Road) forwarded to C.E. IV Corps and 62. Div. "G".	Appendix 55
	22.11.17	3. a.m.	C.R.E. IV. Corps wires. D.G.T. Line will be advanced at 6 A.M. 22nd November.	
		8. a.m.	C.R.E. left H.Q. to visit work on roads and reconnoitre roads forward from HAVRINCOURT & GRAIN COURT.	
		9. a.m.	Road report received from all Field Coys. Roads still open to traffic. Reports repeated to 62nd Div "G" and C.E. IV Corps.	
		10. a.m.	Report forwarded to "G" strongly recommending that all traffic should go forward by METZ - TRESCAULT - BUTLERS CROSS Road to HAVRINCOURT.	
		10.30 a.m.	Enemy reported counter attacking 62nd Div.	
		11 a.m.	O.C. 258 Tunnelling Coy reported as his unit has instructions to work under 62nd Div on roads.	
		2.45 p.m	Information received that 62nd Div is to be relieved by 40th Div.	Appendix 56
		4 p.m.	CRE Order No 44 issued detailing work on roads	Appendix 57
		5 p.m.	CRE Order No 45 issued detailing work on relief by 40th Div	Appendix 58
	23.11.17		Contained to CRE Order No 45 issued.	
			CRE visited C. IV Corps to ascertain object of new work & to arrangement	

WAR DIARY
or
INTELLIGENCE SUMMARY.
(Erase heading not required.)

Army Form C. 2118.

Instructions regarding War Diaries and Intelligence Summaries are contained in F. S. Regs., Part II. and the Staff Manual respectively. Title pages will be prepared in manuscript.

HQ 2nd Div. Eng.

Place	Date	Hour	Summary of Events and Information	Remarks and references to Appendices
NEVILLE	23.11.17		A.D.S. Ref. visited CRE 40th Div and handed over sketch of road in hand.	
			CRE 2nd Div Order No 48 issued regarding taking over work of CRE 40th Div	Appendix 57
	24.11.17		60th Field Coy. commenced work on TRESCAULT – RIBECOURT ROAD.	
			No working parties available for the road in afternoon.	
		1.0 am	Information recd that 2nd Div will relieve 40th Div at night 25/26.11	
			A/CRE Div HQ & Companies move to HAVRINCOURT	
		2.10 am	Information recd that Div relief will be per Field Coys.	
	25.11.17	11.0 am	Information recd that CRE 40th Div will continue to carry out street work in Flesquières	
			4 CRE 2nd Div will take over No 81 recceived. Detailing relief of 40th Div by 2nd Div.	Appendix 60
			2nd Div Order No 51 issued	
			CRE 2nd Div Order No 49 issued	
	25.11.17	11.35/a	2nd Div Order No 52 received stating attack by 2nd Div on BOURLON	
	27.11.17		CRE moved into billets with 2nd F.A. by night at HAVRINCOURT.	
	28.11.17		2nd Div Order No 53 received detailing relief of 2nd Div by 47th Div	
			CRE Order No 48 issued	
	29.11.17		HQ 2nd Div Engineers moved to HAVRINCOURT	Appendix 59

WAR DIARY
or
INTELLIGENCE SUMMARY.

Army Form C. 2118.

Place	Date	Hour	Summary of Events and Information H.Q. 12th Div. R.E.	Remarks and references to Appendices
HAVRIN COURT	29.11.17		62nd Div. relieved by 25th Div. H.Q & 3 Field Coys 12th Div RE remained in area to continue work on hand. 460 & 459 Field Coys on Railways Reserve Line. 461 Field Coy on repairing TRESCAULT–RIBECOURT Rd. Heavy rain to attended very heavily.	1919
	30.11.17			

R. L. Wann
LIEUT. COLONEL, R.E.
C.R.E. 62nd (2nd) DIVISION.

CRE 62nd Div Instructions for work on Forward Roads

SECRET.

Appendix 49.

457th Field Co.
460th Field Co.
461st Field Co.

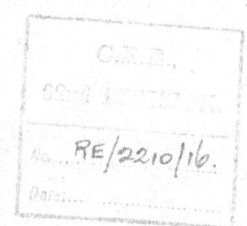
RE/2210/16.

The work on forward roads for which the 62nd Division will be responsible during the forthcoming operations will be carried out by Field Coys under the direction of C.R.E. 62nd Division in accordance with the following instructions.

1. The following roads on the 62nd Division line of advance will be made good and rendered practicable for the passage of Field Artillery and all horsed transport, and the necessary arrangements will be completed beforehand to ensure work commencing at the earliest possible opportunity after zero hour, which it is thought will be at about zero plus 2 hours.

   (i).(a) BUTLERS CROSS (Q.3.b.2.1.) - HAVRINCOURT
        via Q.3.a.7.9.

      (b) Q.8.b.9.6. - Q.3.a.7.9.

      (c) Q.8.d.2.7. - SHROPSHIRE SPUR (through K.34.c.)

   (ii) Q.8.a.1.7. - HAVRINCOURT.

2. O.C. 460th Field Coy will be in immediate charge of and responsible for the work on roads defined under 1 (i) a,b,& c.

O.C. 461st Field Coy will be similarly responsible for the work on road under 1 (ii).

3. During the period intervening between their arrival in the new area (on the 16th inst) and the commencement of operations O's.C. 460th and 461st Field Coys will take steps to ensure that the following lengths of road are rendered in a fit state for use by Field Artillery and all horsed transport.

    460th Field Coy - Q.8.d.2.7. - Q.8.b.9.6.
    461st Field Coy - Q.8.a.1.7.(HUBERTS CROSS) - Q.2.a.5.8.

During the same period O.C. 457th Field Coy R.E. will be responsible for keeping the road from Q.14.d.1.5. to Q.8.d.2.7.

(PLACE MORTEMART) open for the passage of Field Artillery, by maintaining a party of sappers and attached Infantry always in readiness to make good bad places.

Os.C. Field Coys must be prepared to use their own transport for the work mentioned in this paragraph.

Stone metal for this work will be drawn from METZ Dump and Q.14.a.8.1., and pit props from KANTARA dump.

4. WORKING PARTIES AND TRANSPORT.

The attached Table shews the distribution of the Working parties and Transport detailed for the work on the roads specified under 1.

On Y/Z night the R.E. Field Companies and attached Infantry will be located as under :-

```
460th Field Co -  H.Qs. & 2 sections      )
                  50 attached Infantry    ) RUYAULCOURT.

    Do         -  2 Sections              ) Forward billets in
                  50 attached Infantry    ) Q.7.d.

461st Field Co -  H.Q. & 2 sections       )
                  50 attached Infantry    ) RUYAULCOURT

    Do         -  2 Sections              ) Forward Billets in
                  50 attached Infantry    ) Q.17.d.
```

Instructions as to location of labour parties will be issued later.

Transport will be loaded up by the night of Y day and parked at RUYAULCOURT ready for hooking in and moving off at zero hour on Z day.

5. DUMPS:

```
    B.W. 62.       Q.7.b.9.3.     Sleepers.
    B.W. 60.       Q.7.d.9.3.     Pitprops & sleepers.
    B.W. 080.      Q.8.d.1.6.     Sleepers.
KANTARA DUMP       Q.14.b.1.8.    Pitprops & sleepers.
    B.W. 50        Q.14.b.1.3.    Stone & Pitprops.
```

Loading and unloading parties will be detailed from the labour attached to Field Coys.

6. WORKING HOURS.

Work will be carried out continuously by day and night for 48 hours after zero hour, and will be carried out by two reliefs of 8 hours each.

When once commenced the work will be maintained continuously no matter what the conditions may be.

7. The roads above specified must be made good and maintained in such a state of repair as will allow of the continuous flow of Artillery and horsed transport without interruption.

Special attention will be paid in the first instance to the following points -

    (1) Clearing of obstacles.
    (2) Filling in shell holes.
    (3) Deviations round craters.

8. About 48 hours after Zero the D.G.T. Line will be advanced as far as the situation allows, and Divisions will be informed as to the new location of the line and the time of change.

9. Os.C. 460th and 461st Field Coys will each mark the wagons allotted to him for roadwork with a special distinguishing sign, in order to obviate their being diverted to the wrong roads.

10. Notice Boards should be prepared beforehand, and some special blank ones made ready, together with preparations for rapid painting.

11. Each man should carry two sandbags.

12. Special wire cutting parties will be formed.

13. SANDBAGS FILLED WITH BRICK OR STONE WILL BE FILLED AND LOADED UP BEFOREHAND FOR QUICK FILLING OF SHELL HOLES.

14. Crosscut saws and road scrapers will be provided.

15. Os.C. 460th and 461st Field Coys will each arrange for an

-4-

Officer to be attached to the Headquarters of their respective Brigades to maintain liaison and inform their Units immediately the situation admits of the work on roads being commenced.

16. ACKNOWLEDGE.

Sd. R.A. Gillam.

Lieut.-Colonel R.E.
C. R. E. 62nd Division.

14. 11. 17.

TABLE OF LABOUR AND TRANSPORT TO ACCOMPANY IV Corps No 15/5 G. -13.11.17.

RIGHT SECTOR.

	R O A D.	R.E.	Attached Infantry.	Pioneers.	Labour.	Wagons. Each with 2 teams.	Divn.
1. (a)	BUTLERS CROSS - HAVRINCOURT	460 Field Co 2 Sections ½ Pan.Coy.	50	-	150	15	62nd
(b)	Q.8.b.9.6. - Q.3.a.7.9.	do 1 Section.	-	-	50	2	62nd
(c)	Q.8.d.2.7. - SHROPSHIRE SPUR through K.34.c.	do 1 Section.	50	-	50	2	62nd
11.	Q.8.a.1.7. - HAVRINCOURT.	461 Field Co 4 Sections.	100	-	100	15	62nd

NOTE:— 100 Labour at METZ DUMP will do all loading required (under 36th Division).

Appendix 50

Copy No .....7......

C.R.E. 62nd Division Order No 40.

14/11/17

1. 460th and 461st Field Coys will move from their present stations on the evening of the 16th inst as under.

   (a) <u>460th Field Coy R.E. with 100 Infantry attached.</u>

      H.Q. & 2 sections & 100 Infantry attached to RUYAULCOURT.

      Billets for H.Q. and 2 Sections will be taken over from 122nd Field Coy R.E. Billets for attached Infantry will be obtained from the Town Major RUYAULCOURT.

      2 Sections to billet in HAVRINCOURT WOOD at Q.7.d.8.3. These billets to be taken over from 122 Field Coy R.E.

   (b) <u>461st Field Coy R.E. with 100 attached Infantry.</u>

      H.Q. & 2 sections and 100 Infantry attached to BERTINCOURT.

      Billets for H.Q. & 2 Sections will be taken over from 150th Field Coy R.E. Billets for attached Infantry will be obtained from the Town Major BERTINCOURT.

      2 Sections to billet in HAVRINCOURT WOOD at Q.7.d.8.3.

2. Attention is called to 'Regulations for Traffic, Fires & Lights IV Corps Area issued to Units this date, which must be strictly complied with.

   460th and 461st Field Coys will not move from their present billets before 5 p.m.

3. 460th Field Coy will march via VELU, ~~VELU CHATEAU~~ direct to RUYAULCOURT by road in J.32 and Q.3.a.

   461st Field Coy will march via VELU, VELU CHATEAU and road through P.1. to BERTINCOURT.

4. 460th and 461st Field Coys will send forward small advance parties under an Officer to their new stations on the morning of the 16th inst to take over billets.

5. 2 Sections 457th Field Coy now stationed at METZ will rejoin H.Q. 457th Field Coy at RUYAULCOURT on the evening of the 17th inst O.C. 457th Field Coy will arrange to construct the necessary accommodation.

6. ACKNOWLEDGE.

                                        Lieut.Colonel R.E.
C. R. E. 62nd Division.

Copies to -
      1.- 457th Field Co
      2.- 460th Field Co
      3.- 461st Field Co.
      4.- 62nd Div G.
      5.- 62nd Div Q
      6.- C.R.E. 36th Div
7 & 8   - War Diary.
      9.- File.

Appendix 51

Copy No. 5

C. R. E. 62nd Division Order No 41.

1. INTENTIONS.

To break through the enemy's line between GONNELIEU and HAVRINCOURT and open a way through his defensive system by which the Cavalry can pass to exploit the success gained by the Infantry.

2. DIVISIONAL OBJECTIVES:

1st Objective.

Enemy's front line system & HAVRINCOURT (The Blue Line).

2nd Objective.

Hindenburg support line and FLESQUIERES Ridge (The Brown Line).

3rd Objective.

Line GRAINCOURT - FACTORY - HINDENBURGH SUPPORT LINE where it cross the spur in E.22. Trench running 250 yards North of CAMBRAI - BAPAUME Road and Bridge where this road crosses the Canal du NORD.

The 62nd Division will carry out the attack on the 1st and 2nd objectives with two Brigades abreast. 185th Infantry Brigade on Right and 187th Infantry Brigade on left.

186th Inf. Bde will pass through the leading Brigades after the Capture of the 2nd Objective to capture the 3rd Objective.

3. The 51st Division will attack on our right and the 36th on our left.

4. The Divisional Boundaries are as under -

Right Boundary.
K.35.a.0.0. - K.17.c.6.0. - K.11.d.4.0. - F.25.c.5.0.

Left Boundary.

The Line of the Canal du Nord up to BAPAUME - CAMBRAI Road.

The inter Brigade boundary is approximately K.33.Central - K.22.c.2.0. - K.16. c.5.0. - K.16.central.

5. TANKS.

30 Tanks will be at the disposal each of 185 and 187 Inf. Brigades, 6 tanks in each Brigade being kept back for the attack on the 2nd objective.

-1-

-2-

Tanks will be at their starting positions (approximately our outpost line) at Zero their advance to these positions will be covered by desultory firm Machine Gun fire ad Artillery fire.

6. CAVALRY.

2 squadrons of King Edwards Horse are at the disposal of the Division and will be at the disposal of 186th Inf. Bde. after the capture of the 2nd objective.

7. ARTILLERY.

(a) The Artillery will open fire at Zero hour.

(b) As soon as the Brown Line is captured the Field Artillery will be moved forward to the HAVRINCOURT-FLESQUIERES Ridge to cover the advance of the 186th Inf. Bde.

A zero hour for this advance will be fixed after the capture of the Brown Line.

8. HEADQUARTERS:

The following will be the position of Headquarters at Zero -

62nd Division	NEUVILLE.
185th Inf. Bde.	COSY COPSE Q.3.d.5.3.
186th Inf. Bde.	NEUVILLE.
187th Inf. Bde.	K.31.c.2.3.

9. ZERO HOUR.

Zero hour will be notified later.

10. SYNCHRONISATION OF WATCHES.

Field Coys will send an Officer at 11 a.m. and 5 p.m. to R. E. H.Q. to synchronise watches on Y day.

11. OPENING UP ROAD COMMUNICATIONS:

The undermentioned roads will be opened up for traffic. The will be cleared to enable guns and limbered G.S. Wagons to pass an will be improved for general traffic later.

It is of the utmost importance that these roads should be passable for the passage of Artillery as far as HAVRINCOURT shortl after the capture of the Brown line.

(1) (a) BUTLERS CROSS - HAVRINCOURT.

 (b) Q.8.B.9.6. - Q.3.a.7.9.

 (c) Q.8.d.2.7. - SHROPSHIRE SPUR - through K.34.c.

(11) Q.8.a.1.7. - HAVRINCOURT.

O.C. 460th Field Coy will be in immediate charge of and responsible for the work on the roads defined under para (1) (a) (b) and (c).

O.C. 461st Field Coy will be responsible for the work on roads under (ii).

457th Field Coy will be in reserve.

12. LABOUR AND TRANSPORT will be allotted to roads as under :-
460th Field Co
(1) (a) 2 Sections R.E. and half 258 Tunnelling Coy, 50 attached Infantry and 150 men of labour units with 15 G.S. Wagons.

(b) 1 Section R.E. and 50 men of labour Units with 2 G.S. wagons.

(c) 1 Section R.E. and 50 attached Infantry, 50 men of labour Units with 2 G.S. Wagons.

The above distribution of the 19 wagons may be re-adjusted to meet the exact requirements when ascertained.

(ii) 4 Sections R.E., 100 attached Infantry and 100 men of labour Units with 15 G.S. Wagons.

The Labour party of 350 men will report to O.C. 460th Field Coy at RUYAULCOURT at 10 p.m. on Y night. O.C. 460th Fd Coy will arrange to take over billets for this party from the billets vacated by the Infantry. He will also detail off the various parties for the respective roads.   O.C. 461st Field Coy will arrange guides for the labour allotted to his Unit. Half Company 258 Tunnelling Coy allotted to 460th Field Coy will be under the command of Capt Henwood and will be located in HAVRINCOURT WOOD/P.18.b. on Y/Z night   O.C. 460th Field Co will get into touch with Capt Henwood and issue the necessary orders direct to that officer.

TRANSPORT (34 G.S. Wagons) will report to 457th Field Coy on Y night as follows - 17 wagons at 8 p.m. 17 wagons at 9p.m. O.C. 457th Field Coy will load these wagons with broken brick in sandbags, pitprops, tools, etc. in accordance with instructions issued to him direct by O.C. 460th & 461st Field Coys.

O.C. 457th Field Co will arrange to park the loaded wagons

-4-

until required, and to send them forward as required by Os.C. 460th and 461st Field Coys.

13. Dumps of road materials are established at

      (a) KANTARA DUMP Q.14.b.
      (b) ROMANI DUMP Q.7.d.
      (c) PLACE MORTEMARE (fascines)
      (d) B.W. 50 - Q.14.b. (Stone) and pit props small.
                                                                                                                             quantity.

Owing to lack of Light Railway Transport the stocks at the dumps are small but materials will be sent forward at every available opportunity. O.C. 460th and 461st Field Coys will take into consideration the stocks at forward Dumps in deciding what materials to send forward by transport from RUYAULCOURT on Y/Z night.

The two considerations to be arrived at are (1) to open up the roads for artillery as rapidly as possible (2) to maintain the roads to permit of the passage of horse transport.

14. Work will be continued in 2 reliefs of 8 hours for 48 hours, after which time the roads detailed will be taken over by the Transportation Dept. When the roads are so taken over by the Transportation Dept the half Company 258 Tunnelling Coy allotted to this Division will again come under the direct orders of the Chief Engineer IV Corps and will return to their present billets.

Location of Units.

Units will be located at Zero hour as follows.

460th Field Coy. -

    2 Sections and 100 attached Infantry at Q.7.d.

H.Q. 2 Sections at RUYAULCOURT.

after work has commenced the latter party will be moved forward to Q.7.d.

461st Field Coy -

    2 Sections and 50 attached Infantry (100 if accommodation is available) at Q.7.d.
    H.Q. & 2 sections and remaining attached Infantry (if any) at RUYAULCOURT

after work has been commenced the latter 2 sections and attached infantry will move forward to Q.7.d.

(The above parties are a minimum only and there is no objection to larger parties being forward at Q.7.d. at Zero hour if the accommodation permits.

457th Field Coy with all such attached Infantry as are not detailed for forward dumps will remain at RUYAULCOURT in reserve, and await orders from the C.R.E.

15. The first sections will be sent forward for work on the roads as soon as the rear Battalions of the Assaulting Brigades have advanced to the attack.

16. O.C. 460th/Field Coy will be located at Zero hour as under - and 461st

    O.C. 460th Field Coy at Right Brigade H.Q. at Q.3.d.5.3.

    O.C. 461st Field Coy at Right Battn H.Q. HUBERT TRENCH Q.2.c.8.5.

17. COMMUNICATIONS:

Up to zero hour no telephones will be used in front of Divnl H.Q.

Up to zero hour Divnl code names will be used in the body of messages, but after zero hour all messages will be sent in clear.

The main forward report centre will be at Forward billets Q.7.d. and O.C. 460th and 461st Field Coys will arrange to keep in touch with this point throughout.

A regular D.R. Service will be maintained as under commencing Z day.

    To reach Kantara Dump   7. 30 a.m.
                                             1. 0 p.m.
                                             8. 0 p.m.

460th and 461st Field Coys will each maintain an orderly at Kantara Dump from Zero hour onwards. This orderly will know the route from Kantara to forward R.E. billets and will deliver all messages received by the D.R.

O.C. 460th and 461st Field Coys will forward all reports (except those of an urgent nature) by this D.R. Service.

Each Unit will detail a Mounted Orderly to report at

SECRET.

Appendix 52

C.R.E. 62nd Division Order No 42.

19.11.17.

1. Z Day will be November 20th.

2. Zero hour will be notified later by special D.R.

   Zero hour is on no account to be mentioned on the telephone.

                                    Captain, for
                                    Lieut.Colonel R.E.
                         C. R. E. 62nd Division.

RE/2241/2.

457th Field Co.
460th Field Co.
461st Field Co.

Owing to the change in the situation and the necessity for advancing to-morrow, work on the SHROPSHIRE SPUR Road is to be abandoned at once

All available labour for 460th Field Coy is to be put at once on the PLACE MORTMARE - BUTLERS CROSS - Q.3.c.7.9. Q HAVRINCOURT Rd and forward through HAVRINCOURT towards GRAINCOURT.

O.C. 460th Field Coy will be responsible for having this road passable for Field Artillery and limbers by 6.30 a.m. to-morrow 21st inst.

The deviation round the large crater at K.27.b.5.0. at the entrance to HAVRINCOURT must be completed by that hour sufficiently to allow of vehicles to pass somehow as Artillery must move through HAVRINCOURT to GRAINCOURT.

2. 461st Field Coy will continue to press on with the work on the HUBERTS CROSS - HAVRINCOURT ROAD and improve the surface of the deviations round Etna and Vesuvius Craters and after allotting sufficient men to this road to ensure that it is passable he will give such help as he can to the 460th Field Co with the crater at K.27.b.5.0.

3. It is of the utmost urgency that the above two roads should be passable for Field Artillery to-morrow morning especially that through BUTLERS CROSS and HAVRINCOURT.

4. 457th Field Coy will continue with work on the HAVRINCOURT - GRAINCOURT road and must try and get a communication through from about K.28.d.0.7. to K.27.d. 4. 7.

5.   The above work is absolxutely imperative owing to the further advance which is to take place to-morrow.

(Sd) R.A. GILLAM

Lieut.Colonel R.E.
C. R. E.   62nd Divn.

20.11.17.

C.R.E.
62nd DIVISION.

No................
Date..............

Secret   Appendix 54

Copy No ....7......

C. R. E. 62nd Division Order No 43.

21.11.17.

1. The D.G.T. Line will be advanced to the line of the road from K.27.d.4.9. to VESUVIUS CRATER (inclusive) from 7 a.m. to-morrow 22nd inst.

2. 2 Sections 457th Field Coy and remainder of attached Infantry not employed on dumps will move forward to-night and join the other 2 sections under Lieut Smith for work on the HAVRINCOURT – GRAINCOURT Road which runs through K.16.d.8.5. in accordance with instructions already issued to Lieut Smith.
It is imperative that this road should be kept open for Field Artillery and Horse transport.

460th Field Coy and attached Infantry will also commence work on the HAVRINCOURT – GRAINCOURT road to-morrow morning.

The division of responsibility on this road will be –

        457th Field Coy from Crater K.27.b.5.0. to K.16.d.8.5.
                trench inclusive

        460th Field Coy from K.16.d.8.5. to GRAINCOURT.

461st Field Coy and attached Infantry will commence work to-morrow morning 22nd inst. on the Western road from HAVRINCOURT to GRAINCOURT which runs through K.9.b.6.1. to K.4.d.6.5. (or through K.3.d.7.1. and K.4.d.6.5. whichever is the better road.) 460th Field Coy is now making a reconnaissance of this road and will furnish a copy direct to 461st Field Coy as well as to this office.

461st Field Coy will detail at least 1 Section RE and 25 Infantry forthwith for the essential work necessary to make this Western HAVRINCOURT – GRAINCOURT Road passable by 8 a.m. to-morrow morning.

3. Transport on Roads will be redistributed for work as under from 6 p.m. this evening

        To 457th Field Co - 10 Wagons.
           460th Field Co - 12 Wagons.
           461st Field Co - 12 Wagons.

4. MOVES:
With reference to para 2 above, H.Q. of 457th Field Coy will move to HAVRINCOURT by 5 p.m. to-morrow evening 22nd inst. Transport Lines of 457th Field Coy will remain at RUYAULCOURT.

Locations of 460th and 461st Field Coys will remain as at present until further orders. It is hoped to change locations of these Units on the lines suggested by Os.C. at a very early date.

5. It is hoped to relieve Companies of some of the pressure of work on roads at an early date but in the meantime every effort must be made to concentrate on this absolutely essential requirement in connection with the advance.

6. ACKNOWLEDGE.

Lieut. Colonel R.E.
C. R. E. 62nd Division.

(C.E. IV Corps.) D.G.T line advanced

"A" Form
MESSAGES AND SIGNALS.

Army Form C. 2121
(in pads of 100).

This message is on a/c of: Appendix 55

TO | C R E

Sender's Number.	Day of Month.	In reply to Number.	AAA
ER/1714	21/11/17		

D.G.T. Line to advanced from 6 am 22nd aaa New line runs aaa cross roads L.25.d.4.2 to to K.28.a.9.9 including RIBECOURT — HAVRINCOURT Road to J set central to cross roads J.9.b.4.3 to rejoin existing D.G.T. J.10.c

From: C.E. IV Corps.
Time: 11.40 pm

Copy No ...7...

C. R. E.   62nd Division Order No 44.

22.11.17.

1.   The D.G.T. Line has advanced to the line I.10.c. to J.9.b.6.3. - J.24. central - L.25.d.4.2. - H.2.d.8.6. from this morning the 22nd inst inclusive.

2.   The work on forward roads will proceed as under from to-morrow 23rd inst inclusive -

   460th and 461st Field Coys with their attached Infantry will (subject to the requirements of para 3) continue tonbe employed on the HAVRINCOURT - K.9.b.6.1. - K.3.d.6.0. - GRAINCOURT Road in accordance with verbal instructions issued by the C.R.E. to Os. C. 460th and 461st Field Coys this morning.

   457th Field Coy with their attached infantry will continue to be employed on the direct HAVRINCOURT - GRAINCOURT Road through K.16.d.7.0. with a view to keeping this road open for the passage of artillery and limbers.

3.   Until the work on that portion of the road is actually taken over by the D.G.T. the 461st Field Coy will continue to detail one section with a proportion of attached Infantry to carry on with the completion of the deviations round Etna and Vesuvius Craters with a view to ensuring that the road from HUBERTS CROSS to HAVRINCOURT which passes through these craters is kept open.

4.   258th Tunnelling Coy will commence to-morrow morning (23rd) filling in craters SNOWDEN amd K.27.b.5.0.   When the D.G.T. are ready to take in hand the road up to and including those craters the 258 Tunnelling Coy will move forward for work on the HAVRINCOURT - K.23.b.6.5. - GRAINCOURT Road, commencing from K.22.c.6.0. on the work of filling in craters.

5.   ACKNOWLEDGE.

Lieut.Colonel R.E.
C.R.E. 62nd Division.

Eopies to

1. 457th Field Co.
2. 460th Field Co.
3. 461st Field Co.
4. 62nd Divn G.
5. C.R.E. 40th Divn.
6. File
7 & 8. War Diary.
9. 258 Tun: Co.

Copy No ....7......

C. R. E.   62nd Division Order No 45.

22.11.17.

1. The 62nd Division is being relieved by the 40th Division on the night 22/23rd and the 23rd inst.

2. Field Coys of the 40th Division will relieve the Field Coys of the 62nd Division on work on forward roads at a date to be notified later.   Further details will be communicated later.

3. On completion of the relief by the 40th Divisional Engineers 2 Field Companies of the 62d Division will commence work on a new Reserve Line of Defence on the approximate line FLESQUIERES- - HAVRINCOURT - CANAL.

4.
457th and 460th Field Coys will be employed on this work and will commence work on this line after a day or two has been allowed for rest.

Headquarters and 4 Sections and 100 attached Infantry of both of these Field Coys will be located at HAVRINCOURT.

461st Field Coy with attached Infantry after handing over work on roads will return to RUYAULCOURT and take over the billets vacated by both 460th and 457th Field Coys.

Transport Lines under Seconds-in Command will remain in their present locations i.e. 457th and 460th Field Coys in RUYAULCOURT, 461st Field Coy in BERTINCOURT.

5.   ACKNOWLEDGE.

Lieut.Colonel R.E.
C. R. E. 62nd Division.

Copies to
1. 457th Field Co
2. 460th Field Co
3. 461st Field Co
4. 62nd Divn 'G'
5. File
 & 7 War Diary.

Copy No ....

AMENDMENT TO C.R.E. 62nd Division Order 45.

23.11.17.

1.   Para 4 of C.R.E. Order No 45 is cancelled.

457th Field Coy and 460th Field Coy with the 208 M.G. Coy will on the completion of relief by the 40th Division remain as a nucleus garrison of the FLESQUIERE RIDGE - K.17. - GEORGE STREET line and will put it into a state of defence under the orders of the C.R.E. 62nd Division.

The work will be carried out under the immediate supervision of the senior Field Coy Commander (Major E.J. Walthew).

One Field Coy and ½ M.G. Coy will be accommodated in trenches near FLESQUIERS and one Field Coy and ½ M.G. Coy in trenches in K.16. and K.17.

461st Field Coy will stand fast for the present until receipt of further orders.   Transport lines of all Units will remain in their present locations.

2.   Headquarters R.E. will remain at xxxxxxxx NEUVILLE.

3.   ACKNOWLEDGE.

                                        R.J. Cullen
                                        Lieut.Colonel R.E.
                    C. R. E. 62nd Division.

Copies to all recipients of C.R.E. 62nd Divn Order No 45.

SECRET.

Copy No...7....

C.R.E. 62nd Division Order No. 46.

1. C.R.E. 40th Division will take over all work on roads in advance of the D.G.T. Line from after work to-day 23rd instant.
    Field Coys will withdraw labour on these roads accordingly.

2. 258th Tunnelling Coy R.E. will from this date work under orders of C.R.E. 40th Division.

3. 15 wagons of the 14th Reserve Park which it was arranged to hand over to C.R.E. 40th Division on the 24th instant will remain attached to the 62nd Division and are placed at the disposal of 461st Field Coy for work on the FLESQUIERES - RIBECOURT Road. 461st Field Coy will arrange to collect these wagons on the 24th instant from 229th Field Coy located at HAVRINCOURT, and will detail these wagons for work in accordance with instructions to be issued later.
    Indents have been rendered for personnel and horses of these wagons by 460th Field Coy up to and including the 27th inst.
    O.C. 461st Field Coy will arrange to submit ration indents from the 28th inclusive.
    One of these wagons will be detailed by 461st Field Coy to report each day at 7.30 a.m. at the Divisional Troops Refilling Point NEUVILLE to draw rations for these 15 wagons.

4. All wagons of the 62nd Divisional Train will be returned to the 62nd. Divisional Train after work to-day.

5. C.R.E. 40th Division will relieve all Storekeepers and working parties at the BROKENHOUSE, ROMANI and KANTARA Dumps tomorrow morning the 24th instant.
    O.C. 457th Field Coy will warn all parties that they are being so relieved and will arrange for these parties to rejoing his Unit.
    The party of 1 N.C.O. (R.E) and 10 Infantry will remain at RUYAULCOURT Dump for the present.

6. ACKNOWLEDGE.

23/11.17.

Lieut. Colonel R.E.
C.R.E. 62nd Division.

Copy No.1. - 457th Field Coy.
        2   460th Field Coy.
        3   461st Field Coy.
        4   258th Tunnelling Coy.
        5   C.R.E. 40th Division.
      6 & 7 War Diary
        8   Filed.

SECRET.

C.R.E.
62nd DIVISION.
No.
Date.

Copy No ......6......

C. R. E. 62nd Division Order No 47.

Ref:-
Sheet 57c 1/40000
and MOEUVRES Sheet 1/20,000.

23.11.17.

1. The 62nd Division (less Artillery and R.E.) will relieve the 40th Division (less Artillery and R.E. & Pioneers Battn) in the BOURLON Sector of the line to-night.
The 186th Inf. Bde will be on the Right and the 187th Inf. Bde on the Left.
The Headquarters of both these Brigades will be in GRAINCOURT.
The 185th Inf. Bde will be in Divisional Reserve.

2. The boundaries of the Divisional Sector are, approximately, as follows, but are liable to alteration :-

(a) Between the Guards Division and 40th Division F.14.d.7.0.

(b) Between the 119th and 121st Infantry Brigades of 40th Divn about F.1.c.4.4. (BOURLON Village believed inclusive to Left Brigade).

(c) Between 40th and 36th Divisions E.21.b.8.0. and along the North and South Grid Line between E.28. and 29.
These boundaries are only approximate.

3. The R.A.M.C. of 40th Division will be relieved by the R.A.M.C. of 62nd Division under orders to be issued by the A.D.M.S.

4. There is a dump of explosives in GRAINCOURT which is available for use of both Brigades in the line.

5. Advanced Divisional H.Q. will open at HAVRINCOURT CHATEAU at 5 p.m. Divnl H.Q. H.Q. will remain at NEUVILLE for the present

6. Field Companies will continue work under C.R.E. 62nd Division in accordance with instructions issued in C.R.E. 62nd Division Orders No 45 and 46.

7. ACKNOWLEDGE.

Lieut.Colonel R.E.
C. R. E. 62nd Division.

Copies to
1. 457th Field Co
2. 460th Field Co
3. 461st Field Co
4. 62nd Divn G.
5. File
6 & 7. War Diary.

SECRET. Copy....4....

G.R.E.,
62nd DIVISION.

28.11.17.

G.R.E. 62nd Division Order No. 48.

1. The 62nd Division (less Artillery and M.G. Companies) will be relieved by 47th Division (less Artillery) tonight 28/29th inst.

2. On completion of relief the 62nd Division will be distributed as follows :-

  Divisional H.Q. - HAPLINCOURT.

  185th Inf. Brigade. - Vicinity of HAVRINCOURT.
  186th Inf. Brigade. - Old German front line trenches in K.3. and K.9.
  187th Inf. Brigade. - LEBUCQUIERE.

3. Separate instructions will be issued as to the reliefs and work of the R.E.

4. The Command of the Sector will pass to the G.O.C. 47th Division at 10 a.m. on 29th inst.

5. ACKNOWLEDGE.

           Lieut. Colonel R.E.
         G.R.E. 62nd Division.

Copies to:

  1. 457th Field Coy.
  2. 460th Field Coy.
  3. 461st Field Coy.
 4 & 5. War Diary.
  6. File.

ORIGINAL.

WAR DIARY.

DECEMBER 1917.

HEADQUARTERS

62nd (W.R) DIVISIONAL R.E.

Army Form C. 2118.

Original

WAR DIARY
or
INTELLIGENCE SUMMARY.
(Erase heading not required.)

Instructions regarding War Diaries and Intelligence Summaries are contained in F. S. Regs., Part II. and the Staff Manual respectively. Title pages will be prepared in manuscript.

Summary of Events and Information H.Q. 62nd Div Engineers

Place	Date	Hour	Summary of Events and Information	Remarks and references to Appendices
HAVRINCOURT	1.12.17		A/A IV Corps hand over to V Corps.	
	2.12.17		CRE V Corps called upon CRE R of Div.	
	3.12.17		CRE V Corps held conference at H.Q. 62nd Div RE. 62nd Div Order No 85 received to make CRE 62nd Div Order No 49 urgent. R.E.H.Q. and 3 Field Coys march & entrain at HAVRINCOURT for following	Appendix 62
	4.12.17		R.E H.Q. and 3 Field Coys entrained at HAVRINCOURT for following Destinations. R.E. H.Q. BASSEUX. 457th Field Coy BAILLEULMENT, 460th Field Coy ARRAS, 461st Field Coy BLAIREVILLE. 62nd Div Order No 86 received detailing move of 186th + 187th Inf Bdes. tonight. CRE 62nd Div Order No 50 issued.	Appendix 63
	6.12.17		62nd Div Order No 87 received detailing move of 62nd Div to XIII Corps Res. area. on 6.12.17. Field Coys to move under orders of Brigades to which they are affiliated.	
	6.12.17		R.E.H.Q. moved to MINGOVAL. CAPT H.W. WEBSTER 460th Field Coy left to command 497 Field Coy detaching move of Div H.Q. Cancelled later. 62nd Div Order No 88 issued.	
	7.12.17		Information received that 62nd Div in Field staff in readiness to proceed at	

T2134. Wt. W708-776. 500000. 4/15. Sir J. C. & S.

Original

Army Form C. 2118.

WAR DIARY
or
INTELLIGENCE SUMMARY.
(Erase heading not required.)

Instructions regarding War Diaries and Intelligence Summaries are contained in F. S. Regs., Part II. and the Staff Manual respectively. Title pages will be prepared in manuscript.

Place	Date	Hour	Summary of Events and Information	Remarks and references to Appendices
Mingoval	2/12/17		2nd Div Order No. 89 received detailing move of Div to 1st Corps area.	H.Q. 2nd Div Eng.
	8/12/17		2nd Div Order No. 90 received detailing move of Div to 1st Corps area	
	9/12/17		Nil.	
	10/12/17		Capt E.I. Scott 453rd Field Coy proceeded to command 155 Field Coy. Lt A.B. Paul 410th issued for transferred to 457th Field Coy of assume duties of 2nd in Command of that unit from 11/12/17 with seking rank of Capt.	
	11/12/17		Nil	
Lezouvrierres	12/12/17		Rt H.Q. moved with Div H.Q. to Lezouvrierres.	
	13/12/17		CRE visited CE 1st Corps.	
	14/12/17		CE 1st Corps visited CRE 2nd Div.	
	15/12/17		Nil	
	16/12/17		Nil	
	17/12/17		Warning order recd that 2nd Div was back into XIII Corps commencing 65 inf. D.O. 91 recd detailing move of XIII Corps area on 18th & 19th Dec.	
	18/12/17		Nil.	
Mingoval	19/12/17		RE H.Q. moved to Mingoval.	

Original

Army Form C. 2118.

WAR DIARY
or
INTELLIGENCE SUMMARY.

(Erase heading not required.)

Instructions regarding War Diaries and Intelligence Summaries are contained in F.S. Regs., Part II. and the Staff Manual respectively. Title pages will be prepared in manuscript.

Place	Date	Hour	Summary of Events and Information	Remarks and references to Appendices
MINGOVAL	20/12/17		Nil	
	21/12/17		Nil	
	22/12/17		CRE proceeded on leave. MAJ. F.J. WALTHEW acting C.R.E.	
	23/12/17		Information received that 2 Field Coys are to move out forward areas for work on different lines about 26th Dec. A/CRE visited C.E. XIII Corps.	
	24/12/17		A/CRE visited C.E. XIII Corps to obtain details of work & went over ground really to make & for any useful reconnaissance to be done	
	25/12/17		Xmas Day. Not information and that Field Coys will not be required in forward areas before 28th Dec.	
	26/12/17		Nil	
	27/12/17		Capt G.D. ASPLAND proceeded on leave	
	28/12/17		Information received that LIEUT. COLONEL R.A. GILLAM has been appointed C.E. VIII Corps.	
	29/12/17		2/LIEUT T.W. NOTT reported for duty with 461 Field Coy.	
	30/12/17		LIEUT. COL. R.A. GILLAM returned from leave. LIEUT. N. ADAMSON reported for duty with 457 Field Coy. A/CRE visited Defence Line work. C.E.XIII Corps.	
	31/12/17		LIEUT. COL. R.A. GILLAM left to take over duties C.E. VIII Corps. A/CRE visited Defence Line work	Comm. by C.R.E.
			O.C. 460 Field Coy and O.C. 461 Field Coy and pointed out their sectors of work. LIEUT. B.F.O'DOWDA & LIEUT. C.L. CLARKSON awarded M.C.	RE 62 - 12-25

Appendix 52
Copy No. 5

C.R.E. 62nd Division Order No. 49.

1. R.E. Headquarters and 3 Field Coys will move tomorrow 4th December to the area ARRAS - BAILLEULMONT - BLAIRVILLE.

2. (a) The move will be carried out in accordance with the attached Tables 'A' and 'B'.

   (b) Personnel will be moved by rail, entraining at FREMICOURT, in accordance with attached Table 'A'.

   (c) Transport will march through to the new area in one day, in accordance with the attached Table 'B'.

3. Troops will reach the entraining station 60 minutes before the time of departure of their train, and will halt outside the station until the R.T.O. gives permission to enter.
   Each Unit will send an Officer to report to the R.T.O. without delay on arrival at the Station.

4. Each Unit will furnish the R.T.O. with a complete marching out state shewing total to be entrained :-

   (a) Officers.   (b) Other Ranks.

5. The Senior Officer with each train will be O.C. Train. He will be responsible that picquets are told off before the train starts, who will prevent men from leaving the train without permission during the journey.
   He will be responsible for the discipline of the troops during the journey.

6. Each train will consist of 50 covered trucks to hold 40 men each, and the train will be loaded accordingly.
   Blankets and dogchies will be the only baggage carried on the train and lorries will be provided for this purpose as soon as possible.

   R.E. H.Q.   1 lorry at NEUVILLE.
   457th Fld Coy.   1 lorry at RUYAULCOURT.
   460th Fld Coy.   1 lorry at RUYAULCOURT.
   461st Fld Coy.   1 lorry at BERTINCOURT.

   As there is only half an hour allowed for entraining, parties will be told off (2 men per Field Coy) to load blankets beforehand, and should go with the blankets in the lorry to Station.

7. Rations for consumption on December 5th will be issued after arrival in new area.

8. Arrival of Units in billets in new area will be reported to R.E. Headquarters.

9. A table of accommodation in new area will be issued later.

10. R.E. Headquarters will close at HAVRINCOURT at 9.30 p.m. 3.12.17.

11. On arrival in new area the Division will come under the orders of the XVII Corps.

12. ACKNOWLEDGE.

Lieut.Col.R.E.
C.R.E. 62nd.Division.

Copy No.1.   457th Field Coy.
      2.   460th Field Coy.
      3.   461st Field Coy.
      4 and 5. War Diary.   6. File.

ENTRAINING.   TABLE 'A' to accompany C.R.E. 62nd Division Order No.49.

ENTRAINING STATION - FREMICOURT.

No.of train.	Entraining COMMENCES.	Train leaves.	Units.	Destination.	Remarks.
1.	7.30 a.m.	8.a.m.	2 Battns. 185th. Brigade.	ARRAS.	Billets in ARRAS.
2.	8.30 a.m.	9 a.m.	Bde. H.Qrs. 185th Brigade. 2 Bns. 185th Brigade. 460th Field Coy. R.E.	ARRAS.	Billets in ARRAS.
4.	10.30 a.m.	11.a.m.	2 Battns. 187th Brigade. 451st Field Coy. R.E. R.E. Headquarters.	BEAUMETZ	March to BLAIREVILLE. March to BASSEUX.
6.	12.30 p.m.	1 p.m.	2 Battns. 186th Brigade. 457th Field Coy. R.E.	BEAUMETZ.	March to BAILLEULMONT.

Troops in BEAUMETZ will march via VELU - 1.30.d.2.2. - 1.29.b.4.2.

MARCH TABLE 'B' OF TRANSPORT TO ACCOMPANY C.R.E. Order No. 49.

Serial No.	Unit.	From	To	Route.	Remarks.
1.	450th Field Coy.R.E.)	)	ARRAS.	BAPAUME thence direct to ARRAS.	) Three Coys to march
2.	461st Field Coy.R.E.)	BANCOURT.)	BAIREVILLE.	BAPAUME - BOIRY BECQUERELLE- BOISLEUX ST MARQ FICHEUX.	) as one Unit as far) as BAPAUME, to enter
3.	457th Field Coy.R.E.		BAILLEULMONT.	BAPAUME-ACHIET LE GRAND-ACHIET LE PETIT- BUCQUOY - BIENVILLERS AU BOIS	BAPAUME at 7 a.m.

SECRET.   Copy No 7

                C.R.E.   62nd Division Order No 30.

Reference: Sheet LENS 11.
           1/100,000.

                                                4. 12. 17.

1.   The 62nd Division (less Divisional Headquarters, Artillery and 185th Brigade Group) will move to-morrow, 5th December in accordance with attached march table.

     Brigade Groups will march complete as such.

2.   457th and 461st Field Coys will move with and form part of the 186th and 187th Inf. Brigade Groups respectively.

3.   Details of accommodation in the new area will be arranged direct with the H.Q. Infantry Brigade concerned.

4.   Details as to lorries for the move of extra kit will be issued later.

5.   Completion of moves together with map location of new Coy H.Q. will be reported to C.R.E. 62nd Division by wire by Os.C. Units immediately on completion of move.

6.   ACKNOWLEDGE.

                                            Lieut.Colonel R.E.
                                    C.R.E. 62nd Division.

Copies to -
    1. 457th Field Co.
    2. 460th Field Co.
    3. 461st Field Co.
    4. 62nd Divn G.
    5. 186th Brigade.
    6. 187th Brigade.
    7. File.
 8 & 9. War Diary.

MARCH TABLE TO ACCOMPANY C.R.E. 62nd Division Order 50.

Serial No.	Unit.	From	To	Distance	Route	Remarks.
1.	185th Brigade Group including 201 M.G. Coy	BAILLEULMONT	HARBARCQ-GOUVES -MONTENESCOURT.	About 8 miles.	BEAUMETZ- BERNEVILLE- WARLUS.	Head of column to be at BEAUMETZ Cross Roads on Main DOULLENS-ARRAS Road at 2.30 p.m. To be clear of these Cross Roads by 3.45 p.m. To be clear of WARLUS by 5.15 p.m.
2.	187th Brigade Group.	BLAIREVILLE	ETRUN-AXGNEZ LEZ DUISANS -"Y" Huts. do.		BRETENCOURT Beaumetz. Berneville Warlus.	Head of column not to cross Main DOULLENS - ARRAS Rd at BEAUMETZ before 3.50 p.m.

Note - A distance of 100 yards to be maintained between Units on the March.

VA/3

Original

Confidential

Headquarters
62nd Divnl Engineers.

War Diary — Jan 1. to Jan 31.
1918.

VOLUME XIII

WAR DIARY or INTELLIGENCE SUMMARY

Army Form C. 2118.

(Erase heading not required.)

Summary of Events and Information: **H.Q. 63rd Divisional Engineers**

Place	Date	Hour	Summary of Events and Information	Remarks and references to Appendices
MINGOVAL	1/1/18		Received orders to move to ECURIE WOOD CAMP. Lieut Colonel L. CHENEVIX TRENCH	P.M.
"	2/1/18		reported to take over duties of C.R.E.	P.M.
"	3/1/18		C.R.E. visited defence line. R.E. Headquarters moved to ECURIE WOOD CAMP.	C.B.N.
"			C.R.E. visited defence line with C.E. XIII Corps.	P.M.
"	4/1/18		C.R.E. visits regt. Deln of Rird with O.C. 460th Coy & O.C. 513th Coy. 56th Div.	P.M.
"	5/1/18		C.R.E. visited C.R.E. 56th Div. re handing over. Orders received for recalling	P.M.
			Capt G.R. Copland from leave as no appointment as SO.R.E. VIII Corps.	
			Major Walker 460th Field Coy, and Major Seaman 461st Field Company awarded M.C.	
	6/1/18		461st Field Coy moved forward and relieved 513th Field Coy by R.E.	P.M.
	7/1/18		Nix. Lieut J.A. Smith transferred to TANK CORPS.	P.M.
	8/1/18		Capt. G.R. Copland R.E. 15 takes over duties as SO.R.E. XIII Corps. 460th Field Coy R.E. relieves 513th Field Coy.	P.M.
			Lt. E.B. Hammond appointed Adj. 62nd Div. R.E. from 457th Field Coy R.E.	P.M.
	9/1/18		R.E. Headquarters moved to PORTSMOUTH CAMP. Closed at ECURIE WOOD CAMP. 11 A.M.	P.M.
			re-opened at PORTSMOUTH CAMP at the same hour.	
			457th Field Coy R.E. relieved 416th Field Coy.	
	10/1/18		C.R.E. visited Coy Sectors.	P.M.

Army Form C. 2118.

WAR DIARY
or
Original INTELLIGENCE SUMMARY.
(Erase heading not required.)

HQ 62nd Divl Engineers

Instructions regarding War Diaries and Intelligence Summaries are contained in F. S. Regs., Part II. and the Staff Manual respectively. Title pages will be prepared in manuscript.

Place	Date	Hour	Summary of Events and Information	Remarks and references to Appendices
	11/1/18		G.S.O.I. and C.R.E. visited the high vector front line works and support also Bys. sectors	MA
			457th Field Coy commenced work on Corps Wiring Scheme	
	12/1/18		LT ADAMSON 457th Coy took over duties of Corps Roads Officer at XIII CORPS	PA
			Relieving 2/Lt PALMER.	
	13/1/18		LT GRAHAM took over duties of Corps Defence Scheme Officer XIII Corps	PA
	14/1/18		C.R.E. visited dug-outs and front-line	PA
	15/1/18		C.R.E. and O.C. 460th Field Coy visited second line	PA
	16/1/18		C.R.E. inspected wiring done by 457th Field Coy R.E.	PA
	17/1/18		C.R.E. visited left sector	PA
	18/1/18		O.C. 460th Field Coy Left for BOULOGNE for trans. to England.	PA
			LT MACAULEY reported to 461st Field Coy from Hospital	
	19/1/18		C.R.E. took an American Colonel round the Suvauros front and defences	PA
	20/1/18		C.R.E. visited Ctr Sector	SN
	21/1/18		G.O.C. 62" Division visited rear Billets of 62" Divisional R.E. Companies	PA
			with C.R.E.	
			C.R.E. gave a lecture to 187th BRIGADE INFANTRY OFFICERS at LOUEZ.	
			on "CO-OPERATION OF INFANTRY with ROYAL ENGINEERS"	

WAR DIARY
or
INTELLIGENCE SUMMARY.

Army Form C. 2118.

(Erase heading not required.)

Original HQ 62nd Divl Engineers

Place	Date	Hour	Summary of Events and Information	Remarks and references to Appendices
PORTNOUTH CAMP	22/1/18		461st FIELD COY LT A.EGGLEDHILL left for 556th ARMY TROOPS COY own posten and LT.R.B. MURRAY	WM
	23/1/18		O.C. 461st FIELD COY returned from leave in England. C.R.E. visited from Ebro	WM
			LT. FOX 460th FIELD COY left to take over duties at ROUEN TRAINING SCHOOL	TBR
"	24/1/18		C.R.E. visited wiring parties on CORPS WIRING SCHEME at night.	WM
			C.R.E. with O.C. 461st FIELD COY visited right Sector	WM
"	25/1/18		C.R.E. visited 460th and 461st FIELD COYs.	SW
	26/1/18		Atte. C.R.E. inspected no-man's land in Battery Positions with CRE Officer.	SW
	27/1/18		C.R.E. visited Camps in rear trenches.	SW
	28/1/18		C.R.E. visited Infantry H.Q. in the line	SW
	29/1/18		C.R.E. visited Left Sector	TBR
	30/1/18		Nil	TBR
"	31/1/18		C.R.E. visited front line Left Sector with O/C 460th Field Coy.	TBR

R Kennard McOR
Lt Col
CRE 62nd Div

2.2.18

"Confidential"
Original

H.Q. 62nd Divnl R.E.

War Diary.

February 1918.

Original. Vol XIV

Army Form C. 2118.

WAR DIARY
or
INTELLIGENCE SUMMARY.
(Erase heading not required.)

Instructions regarding War Diaries and Intelligence Summaries are contained in F. S. Regs., Part II. and the Staff Manual respectively. Title pages will be prepared in manuscript.

Place	Date	Hour	Summary of Events and Information	Remarks and references to Appendices
	FEB			
PORTSMOUTH	1st		C.R.E. went round DUG-OUTS with O.C. 461 Field Coy and O.C. 176 Tunnelling Coy.	
CAMP	2nd		NIL	
	3rd		C.R.E. visited new billets	
	4th		NIL	
	5th		C.R.E. went on leave to U.K. Major Matthew saw C.R.E. 56th	
	6th		Estimate of monthly allotment. Corps order no 52 sent out.	
	7th		A/C.R.E. went round 56th Div work with C.E. Corps.	
	8th		A/C.R.E. visited wiring scheme with C.R.E 56th prior to handing over.	
	9th		A/C.R.E. visited left section	
	10th		Meeting at Div H.Q. at 2.30. A/C.R.E. went round wiring scheme.	
	11th		Handed over to 56th Div. A/C.R.E. went round Defence scheme with Corps Commander and C.E.	
	12th		A/C.R.E. visited right Sector with Corps wiring officer and B.G.G.S.	
	13th		A/C.R.E. visited wiring with Capt Paul in No Shircourt sector.	
	14th		A/C.R.E. visited wiring scheme.	
	15th		A/C.R.E. on Corps wiring scheme with wiring officers.	Appendix C.1B = 6 2nd Lts = OR.E. 6 2nd Lts M.G. 3

Army Form C. 2118.

WAR DIARY
or
INTELLIGENCE SUMMARY.
(Erase heading not required.)

Instructions regarding War Diaries and Intelligence Summaries are contained in F. S. Regs., Part II. and the Staff Manual respectively. Title pages will be prepared in manuscript.

Place	Date	Hour	Summary of Events and Information	Remarks and references to Appendices
	FEB			
	16th		A/C.R.E. on Corps wiring scheme.	
	17th		A/C.R.E. on Corps wiring scheme.	
	18th		A/C.R.E. on Corps wiring scheme.	
	19th		A/C.R.E. on Corps wiring scheme.	
	20th		C.R.E. returned from leave. A.C.R.E. visited wiring scheme.	
	21st		C.R.E. and Major Walthew on wiring scheme.	
	22nd		C.R.E. visited ST. CATHERINE Switch.	
	23rd		C.R.E. with B.G.G.S. and C.E. sited new ARMY BROWN LINE.	
	24th		C.R.E. visited ECURIE Defences.	
	25th		C.R.E. visited ECURIE Defences. Ordered to take over from 31st DIV coppice R.E.	
	26th		NIL	
	27th		NIL	
	28th		NIL	

French
LIEUT.-COLONEL, R.E.
C.R.E. 2ZND WRD DIVISION
3.3.18

WAR DIARY

C. R. E.

62nd DIVISION

MARCH 1918

Vol 15
A

Headquarters - 62nd Divisional R.E.

from March 1st 1918.
to March 31st 1918.

ORIGINAL.
VOL XV

INTELLIGENCE SUMMARY.
(Erase heading not required.)

War Diary 62nd Div R.E.

Place	Date	Hour	Summary of Events and Information	Remarks and references to Appendices
ROELINCOURT	MARCH 1st	10 AM	62nd Div. relieved 31st Div.	9A/1
	2nd		C.R.E. went round line with Field Coy. Commanders	9A/2
	3rd		NIL	9A/3
	4th		NIL	9A/4
	5th		C.R.E. went round line with G.S.O.I 62nd DIV.	9A/5
	6th		C.R.E. visited front line	9A/6
	7th		NIL	9A/7
	8th		NIL	9A/8
	9th		C.R.E. went round line & support lines	9A/9
	10th		C.R.E. game within selous. Adjutant and Lieut Pearson returned from leave	9A/10
	11th		CRE up the line with G.S.O.I. Lieut Collin returned from leave	9A/11
	12th		CRE inspected rear Roller	9A/12
	13th		CRE visited 457 Field Company advanced H.Q.	9A/13
	14th		CRE visited line with Bdr Gen 185 Brigade	9A/14
	15th		CRE inspected Torpedo Trials in breaking wire	9A/15
	16th		CRE visited Right Brigade H.Q. and line later by the Baggage	9A/16

Place	Date	Hour	Summary of Events and Information	Remarks and references to Appendices
ROCLINCOURT	MARCH 17th		CRE up the Line	SAA
	18th		CRE up the Line	SAA
	19th		WARNING ORDER received to relieve 56th DIV at PORTSMOUTH CAMP.	SAA
	20th		O.O. received for RELIEF on 25th MARCH. and 3rd DIV to relieve 62nd Div @ ROCLINCOURT	SAA
	21st		WIRE cancelling order to relieve 56th DIV. Received	SAA
	22nd		WARNING ORDER received 62nd DIV. to be relieved by 3rd CANADIAN DIV: on 22nd	SAA
	23rd		O.O. 62nd DIV received. 62nd DIV: to be relieved by 3rd CANADIAN DIV 2 Days later to Brigades for night 23/24th MARCH	SAA
	24th		O.O. received 62nd DIV: to move into 17th CORPS AREA.	SAA
	25th		H.Q. and FIELD COMPANIES moved to RONVILLE NR ARRAS	SAA
	26th		Moved to FONQUEVILLERS via AYETTE and BUCQUOY.	SAA
	26th to 27		CRE up the Line	SAA
	28th		RE.H.Q. moved to SOUASTRE CRE up the Line	SAA
	29th		CRE up the Line	SAA
	30th		WARNING ORDER received 62nd DIV. to be relieved by 37th DIV. night 2/3rd April	SAA
	31st		O.O. 62nd DIV received 62nd DIV to be relieved by 57th DIV. relief complete by night 1/2nd April	SAA

Dawnach ???
CRE 62 ???
3.4.18

62nd Divisional Engineers

WAR DIARY

C. R. E.

62nd DIVISION

APRIL 1918

WD 16

Confidential

War Diary.

of

Headquarters - 62nd (W.R.) Divnl. R.E.

from April 1st 1918.
to April 30th 1918.

Original

VOLUME. 16.

Army Form C. 2118.

Instructions regarding War Diaries and Intelligence Summaries are contained in F. S. Regs., Part II. and the Staff Manual respectively. Title pages will be prepared in manuscript.

WAR DIARY
or
INTELLIGENCE SUMMARY.
(Erase heading not required.)

Place	Date	Hour	Summary of Events and Information	Remarks and references to Appendices
SOUASTRE	APRIL 1st	10 AM	Relieved by 37th Div.	PBM
PAS	2nd		C.R.E. inspected proposed SWITCH LINE. SOUASTRE - FONQUEVILLERS	SBM
"	3rd		CRE with Fwd Eng Commander on SOUASTRE - SAILLY SWITCH.	SBM
"	4th		CRE round defence lines with G.S.O. 62nd Div.	SBM
"	5th		WARNING Order received ref relief by 42nd Div.	SBM
"	6th		OO. CRE sent to Company ref relief by Field Coy of 42nd Div, night 7/8th April	SBM
PAS - HENU	7th		Relieved by 42nd Div. relief complete 6 p.m. 62nd Div H.Q. moved to HENU.	SBM
HENU.	8th		Companies silenced.	SBM
"	9th		NIL.	SBM
"	10th		C.R.E. inspected WATER POINTS	SBM
"	14th		CRE visited forward BILLETS of Field Companies.	SBM
"	16th		CRE. a FONQUEVILLERS defences	SBM
"	17th		" with G.S.O. 69th Div.	SBM
"	18		"	SBM
"	20th		CRE. FONQUEVILLERS and ESSARTS.	SBM
"	21st		CRE visited water points.	SBM

WAR DIARY or INTELLIGENCE SUMMARY

Army Form C. 2118.

Place	Date	Hour	Summary of Events and Information	Remarks and references to Appendices
HENU.	APRIL 21st		62nd Div. D.O. received ref: relief by 37th Div:	SR11
	22nd		C.R.E. D.O. issued ref: Companies relief	SR11
	22nd		C.R.E. took C.R.E. 37th Div. around the Sector.	SR11
	23rd		C.R.E. took over work from C.R.E. 37th Div	SR11
HENU-PAS	24th		Hd. R.E. moved to PAS. Relieves 37th Division C.R.E. visited RED LINE	SR11
PAS.	25th		C.R's on RED LINE defences LOUVENCOURT – COUIN.	SR11
"	26th		ditto ditto	SR11
"	27th		C.R.E. on RED LINE. Gave Letters to Officers and N.C.O's 185th Regoes	SR10
			on DISTRIBUTION of WORK and INFANTRY WORKING PARTIES	
"	28th		C.R.E. on RED LINE defences	SR11
"	29-30th		ditto	SR10

Armstrong A.C.
CRE 62nd Div
2.5.18

Copy No ...11.

62nd Divnl R.E. Order No 60.

6. 4. 18.

1. The 62nd Division will relieve the 42nd Division (less Artillery) in the left Sector of the Corps front on the night 7/8, 8/9th inst:

2. The 185th Brigade will relieve 125th Brigade in the Right Section on night 7/8th.
  The 186th Brigade will relieve 127th Brigade in left section on night 8/9th.
  The 187th Brigade will relieve 126th Brigade in Divisional reserve on night 8/9th.

  The relief of Left Section Brigade will precede that of Reserve Brigade on 8/9th.

3. The reliefs of Field Companies R.E. will take place on the night of 7/8th as follows-

62nd Div Fd Co RE	Location.	Relieves 42nd Div; Fd. Co RE	Location. Forward	Rear.
460th	VAUCHELLES.	427th	F.26.a.8.3. (3 Sects)	D.20.b.2.8.
457th	PAS	428th	F.21.b.9.6. (3 Sects)	D.21.c.7.7.
461st.	AUTHIE	429th	E.23.c.3.4. (3 Sects)	D.21.b.4.1.

Reliefs to be completed by 6 a.m. 8th inst. Company Commanders will arrange details of relief direct with the Commanders of the companies to be relieved.

4. The 9th Bn D.L.I. (Pioneers) will take over work and billets from Pioneer Bn 42nd Division, on night of 7/8th inst under arrangements made direct.
  The location of 9th Bn D.L.I. is VAUCHELLES. and that of the Pioneer Bn of 42nd Divn is SOUASTRE.

1.

8. All maps, sketches and defence Schemes will be handed over on r

9. Completion of reliefs will be notified to R.E. H.Q. 62nd Div by wire.

10. ACKNOWLEDGE.

Lieut.Colonel R.E.
C. R. E. 62nd Division.

Copy No 1. 457th Fd Co
2. 460th Fd Co
3. 461st Fd Co
4. 9th D.L.I.
5. C.R.E.37 Div.
6. 62nd Div. G.
7. 62nd Div. Q.
8. 62nd Div. Train.
9. A.P.M.
10 & 11. War Diary.
12. File.

62nd Divnl R.E. O.O. No 80.

5. H.Q. 62nd Div R.E. will take over from H.Q. 42nd Div R.E. on 7th inst: completing relief by 6 p.m. 7th.
Locations
62nd Div. R.E. H.Q.   Billet No 183 PAS
42nd Div. R.E. H.Q.   HENU

6. Os.C. Field Coys and Pioneer Battn will report completion of relief to R.E. H.Q. by wire.

7. ACKNOWLEDGE.

Lieut.Colonel R.E.
C. R. E. 62nd Division.

ies to
1. 457 Field Co
2. 460 Field Co
3. 481s Field Co
4. 9th D.L.I.
5. C.R.E. 42nd Div.
6. 62nd Div. G.
7. 62nd Div. A.
8. A.P.M.
9. 62nd Div. Train.
10,11. War Diary
12. File.

Copy No. 10

62nd Divisional R.E. Operation Order No 61.

21. 4. 18.

1. The 62nd Division will be relieved by the 37th Division on nights 23rd/24th and 24th/25th inst.

2. The reliefs of Field Companies R.E. will take place on eve of 23rd as follows:—

Fd Coys. 62nd Div.	Location Forward.	Rear.	Relieved by Fd Coy 37th Div	Loc
457th	FONQUEVILLERS. Caves under Church.	D.22.c.8.7. No 73 SOUASTRE.	153rd.	BOIS WARNI I.23.b
460th	FONQUEVILLERS.	D.22.a.8.2. No 3 SOUASTRE.	152nd.	AUTHIE I.16.c
461st	Do. E.21.d.8.7.	D.22.a.4.4. No 141 SOUASTRE.	154th.	LOUVEN I.35.c

Reliefs to be completed by 8 p.m. 23/24th. Company Commande will arrange details of relief direct with Commanders of relieving Companies.

3. Each Field Company of 62nd Division will attach an Officer to relieving Company of the 37th Divn till 6 p.m. 25th in order to po out on the ground all work in hand.
Each Field Company of 62nd Division will send an Officer to th corresponding Field Coy of 37th Division to arrive by 10 a.m. and over work of 37th Division on the ground.

4. O.C. 9th (Pioneer) Battn D.L.I. will arrange direct with O.C. North Staffs: details of relief of Pioneer Battns.

5. R.E. H.Q. 62nd & 37th Divns will relieve each other on 24th in completing by noon.

6. Work will be carried on by Field Coys and attached Infantry up 1 p.m. on 23rd and by those of the 9th Bn D.L.I. engaged on day wo to the same hour.

7. Busses, if available, will be provided at SOUASTRE to transpor personnel of Field Coys and attached Inf. to their new locations.

8. All maps, sketches and defence Schemes will be handed over on

9. Completion of reliefs will be notified to R.E. H.Q. 62nd Div by wire.

10. ACKNOWLEDGE.

Lieut.Colonel R.E.
C. R. E. 62nd Division.

Copy No 1. 457th Fd Co
2. 460th Fd Co
3. 461st Fd Co
4. 9th D.L.I.
5. C.R.E.37 Div.
6. 62nd Div. G.
7. 62nd Div. Q.
8. 62nd Div. Train.
9. A.P.M.
10 & 11. War Diary.
12. File.

WO 17

Original.
Confidential.
War Diary.
of
H.Q. 62nd. Divisional R.E.

from May 1st 1918
to May 31st 1918

VOLUME XVII.

Original   H.Q. 62nd Divnl. R.E.

Army Form C. 2118.

WAR DIARY
or
INTELLIGENCE SUMMARY.

VOLUME XVII

(Erase heading not required.)

Place	Date	Hour	Summary of Events and Information	Remarks and references to Appendices
PAS.	May 1st	—	C.R.E. attended conference at Corps H.Q. visited RED LINE defences	ISM
"	2"		Visited Companies	SM
"	3.		C.R.E. with G.S.O.I in Purple Line	SM
"	4.		" "	SM
"	5th		C.R.E. in Purple Line	SBM
"	6th		C.R.E. visited C.R.E. New Zealand Div. Keuer to Purple Line.	SBM
"	7"		C.R.E. in Purple Line	SBM
"	8"		Companies and Divnl. Bath.	SBM
"	9–11		C.R.E. visited Purple Line	SBM
"	12		Warning order received ref. Div. relief.	SM
"	13		Div. Ordr received stating date of relieving 37th Div. in the Left Sector.	SM
"	14		C.R.E. O.O. 62 issued.	SM
"	15.16		Ord. Nil. Relief of field companies	SM
PAS–HENU	17.	10am.	Relief of Divison H.Q. 62nd Div. moved to HENU. Relieved by 37th Divl. H.Q.	SM
HENU	18.		Corps Conference.	SM
"	19		C.R.E. up to Line	SM

Original
H.Q. 62nd Divn. R.E.

Army Form C. 2118.

WAR DIARY
or
INTELLIGENCE SUMMARY.

VOLUME XVII

(Erase heading not required.)

Place	Date	Hour	Summary of Events and Information	Remarks and references to Appendices
HENU	MAY 20	—	CRE. at Corps Conference (Q)	9RH
"	21		CRE. up the line — and at ORVILLE (62nd Div. hdqrs)	SM
"	23		CRE. with G.S.O, I Edjarts Defences	SMA
"	24-25		CRE. up the Line	DSA
"	26		CRE. at ORVILLE CAMP and Div: Rifle Ranges	SM
"	27		CRE. attended the "Trial of Verlies Staple" at St. Leger.	SLR
"	28-29		CRE. up the line	SRH
"	31		CRE. up the line	DSH

Frederick Col
R.E. 62nd Divn
2.6.18.

AMENDMENT TO 62nd Divnl R.E. ORDER No 62.

For '32nd Divn' line 1 para 1   read '37th Divn'.

                                    Capt R.E. for
                                    Lieut.Col R.E.
                            C.R.E. 62nd Divn.

14. 5. 18.

Copies to all recxipients of Order No 62.

Copy No. 11

62nd Divisional R.E. Order No 62.

1. 62nd Division will relieve 32nd Division in Left Sector of Corps Front on the nights of 16th/17th and 17th/18th inst.

2. Relief of Field Coys will take place as follows :-

   457th Field Coy relieves 152nd Field Coy.
   460th   do   153rd   do
   461st   do   154th   do

   All reliefs will take place on afternoon and evening of 16th inst and will be completed by 6 a.m. 17th.
   Company Commanders will arrange with the Commanders of corresponding Companies of 37th Division all details of relief, which is to be arranged in such a way that any Day work in hand can be carried on on 17th inst without delay.

3. In order that the tactical responsibilities of the Field Companies R.E. may be fulfilled without any interval during the relief, Field Company Commanders 62nd Div: will arrange with Commanders of corresponding Companies of 37th Div: to move up to the forward billets of the latter before these are vacated by 37th Div:

4. The Pioneer Battalion relief will be carried out under arrangements made between Pioneer Battalion Commanders.

5. R.E., H.Q., will close at PAS and open at HENU at 10. a.m. 17th May.

6. List of Locations is attached.

7. Completion of relief by Field Coys and Pioneer Battalion will be notified to this office by wire.

8. Acknowledge.

14. 5. 18.

Lieut.Colonel R.E.
C. R. E. 62nd Division.

Copy No 1 - 457 Field Co.
      2   460   do
      3   461   do
      4   C.R.E. 37 Divn.
      5   62nd Divn G.
      6   62nd Divn A & Q.
      7   62nd Divnl Train.
      8   A.P.M. 62nd Divn.
      9   File.
   10. 11. War Diary.

LOCATION LIST.
-;-;-;-

62nd Divnl R.E.

H.Q. R. E.	Billet 119 PAS.
457th Field Co.	BOIS DU WARNIMONT (I.23.b.5.8).
460th Field Co.	AUTHIE WOOD (I.16.c.9.9.).
461st Field Co.	LOUVENCOURT (I.35.c.3.0.).
9th (P) Bn D.L.I.	BOIS DU WARNIMONT (I.24.b.).

- - - - - - - - - - -

37th Divnl R.E.

H. Q. R. E.	HENU (Chateau Grounds).
152nd Field Co.	PIGEON WOOD (E.30.a.4.4.).
153rd Field Co.	(Normal - FONQUEVILLERS CHURCH (Caves). (present - CHATEAU de la HAIE SWITCH ((D.30.b.8.7.).
154th Field Co.	(PIGEON WOOD (E.30.a.70.55.).
9th N.Staffs. Bn H.Q. (Pioneers).	Normal - FONQUEVILLERS Billet 52. Present - SOUASTRE Billet 74.
A. Coy.	E.23.c.9.5.
B. Coy.	Normal - FONQUEVILLERS CHURCH Present D.23.b.5.5.
D. Coy.	E.23.c.75.50.

-      -   -   -

ORIGINAL

CONFIDENTIAL

WAR DIARY.
of
HEADQUARTERS - 62nd. DIVNL. R.E.

From: JUNE 1st 1918.
To: JUNE 30th 1918.

Vol. XVIII

ORIGINAL

Army Form C. 2118.

Instructions regarding War Diaries and Intelligence
Summaries are contained in F. S. Regs., Part II.
and the Staff Manual respectively. Title pages
will be prepared in manuscript.

WAR DIARY
or
INTELLIGENCE SUMMARY.
(Erase heading not required.)

HEADQUARTERS,
62ND
DIVL ENGINEERS.

VOL. XVIII

Place	Date	Hour	Summary of Events and Information	Remarks and references to Appendices
HENU	JUNE 1st		C.R.E. up the Line	S.B.M
"	2-6		C.R.E. up the Line	S.B.M
"	6		C.R.E. with G.S.O.I. Scouts Officers	P.B.M
"	7-8		C.R.E. up the Line	S.B.M
"	9		C.R.E. working 10th Tank Batt. with G.S.O.I. to make arrangements for Tank raid.	S.B.M
"	10-11		NIL	S.B.M
"	12		C.R.E. up the Line	S.B.M
"	13.14	X	O.O's at Tank Operations	S.B.M
"	15		NIL	S.B.M
"	16.17		C.R.E. up the Line	P.B.M
"	19		C.R.E. with G.S.O.2. up the Line	S.B.M
"	20.21		C.R.E. up the Line	P.B.M
"	22 "		C.R.E. up the Line. Warning order received stating the relief between 23rd and 26th	P.B.M
"	23 "		C.R.E. O.O issued No. 64.	S.B.M
"	24 "		460th & 461st Field Companies relieved by Field Companies of 37th Div.	P.B.M
H- PAS	25th		DIV. HQ. relieved by DIV. HQ. 37th Div. 457 Field Coy relieved by Field Coy 37th Div. Relief Complete 4 p.m	S.B.M

ORIGINAL

Army Form C. 2118.

WAR DIARY
or
INTELLIGENCE SUMMARY.
(Erase heading not required.)

VOL. XVIII

HEADQUARTERS,
62ND
DIVL. ENGINEERS.

Instructions regarding War Diaries and Intelligence
Summaries are contained in F. S. Regs., Part II.
and the Staff Manual respectively. Title pages
will be prepared in manuscript.

Place.	Date	Hour	Summary of Events and Information	Remarks and references to Appendices
PAS	JUNE 26.27		CRE visited Rifle Ranges allotted for div. use.	SBW
"	28		CRE visited CHATEAU de la HAIE switch defences with G.S.O.I.	SBW
"	29		CRE visited Field Companies Camps.	PBW
"	30		CRE visited CHATEAU de la HAIE defences.	MN

Arnold McIne
Lt=Col=RE
2.7.18

T2134. Wt. W708-776. 5@000. 4/15. Sir J. C. & S.

SECRET.

Copy No. 13

62nd Divisional Engineers Order No 64.

23. 6. 18.

1. The 62nd Division will be relieved by the 37th Division between the 23rd and 26th inst.

2. The 62nd Divisional Artillery will be relieved at the same time by the 37th Divisional Artillery.

3. 186th Infantry Brigade will be relieved on the night of the 24/25th by the 111th Inf. Brigade.

   185th Infantry Brigade will be relieved on the afternoon of the 25th by the 112th Infantry Brigade.

   187th Infantry Brigade will be relieved on the 25/26th by the 63rd Infantry Brigade.

4. The 153rd Field Coy R.E. will relieve the 457th Field Coy R.E. on the morning of the 25th at 9 a.m. After being relieved the 457th Field Coy will march to SOUASTRE and get into busses which have brought 153rd Field Coy and go back in them to AUTHIEULE near DOULLENS.
   457th Field Coy to have representatives at SOUASTRE de-bussing point -
   1. To hold on to Busses. when they arrive and see that they do not depart until the rest of 457th Field Coy can get into them.
   2. To provide guides to take 153rd Field Coy forward to 457th Field Coy billets.

   153rd Field Coy should arrive at SOUASTRE de-bussing point at about 8.30 a.m. 25th.

   154th Field Coy R.E. relieves 460th Field Coy R.E. by march route on the afternoon of the 24th. 154th Field Coy will move into 460th Field Coy Billets at FONQUEVILLERS at 2 p.m. 24th at which hour 460th Field Coy will go to FAMECHON.

   152nd Field Coy R.E. will move into billets of 461st Field Coy R.E. at 2 p.m. 24th at which hour 461st Field Coy will march to the R.E. Dump SOUASTRE, where it will find lorries which have brought up R.E. Stores, ready to pick them up and take them back to MARIEUX.

5. Each Field Coy will leave one Officer and 2 O.R. to remain with the Companies relieving them for 24 hours after relief to complete details of handing over.

6. 9th Battn D.L.I. (Pioneers) will be relieved by Pioneer Battalion 37th Division on the afternoon of the 24th and will move back to DOULLENS on relief.
   O.C. 9th.D.L.I. will arrange to hand over to O.C. Pioneer Battn 37th Division all details of work in hand and projected.

-2-

7.   H.Q. R.E. 62nd Division will be relieved by H.Q.R.E. 37th Division at 4 p.m. 25th June.

8.   Location Table attached.

9.   All movement East of SOUASTRE during daylight will be by sections at 200 yards intervals.
A similar interval will be maintained between every 3 vehicles.

10. The usual Advance and Clearing up parties to be detailed and certificates as to cleanliness of billets obtained.

11. Completion of relief to be wired to this office.

12. Acknowledge.

S.B. Hammond Capt
Lieut.Colonel R.E.
C.R.E. 62nd Division.

DISTRIBUTION.

No	
1.	457th Field Co
2.	460th Field Co
3.	461st Field Co.
4.	9th Bn D.L.I.
5.	C.R.E. 37th Div.
6.	Lieut Clarson, R.A.R.E.
7.	62nd Division 'G'
8.	62nd Division 'A'
9.	C.E. IV Corps.
10.	A.P.M. 62nd Divn
11.	62nd Div. Train.
12.)	
13.)	War Diary.
14.	File.

LOCATIONS OF 62nd DIVISIONAL R. E.
AND PIONEERS ON COMPLETION OF
-- RELIEF. --

H.Q. R.E.	Billet 183 - PAS.
457th Field Coy	AUTHIEULE - Billet 41.
460th Field Coy	HURTEBISE FARM (near FAMECHON)
461st Field Coy	MARIEUX - Billet 15.
9th Bn D.L.I. (Pioneers)	DOULLENS - Billet 53, Rue St LA

457th Field Co.
460th Field Co.
461st Field Co.

The following is an outline

Divl. Engineers,

62nd Division.

C. R. E.

62nd DIVISION,

JULY, 1918.

ORIGINAL

VOLUME 19

Army Form C. 2118.

WAR DIARY
or
INTELLIGENCE SUMMARY.

HQ 62nd Divisional R.E.

(Erase heading not required.)

Instructions regarding War Diaries and Intelligence Summaries are contained in F. S. Regs., Part II. and the Staff Manual respectively. Title pages will be prepared in manuscript.

Place	Date	Hour	Summary of Events and Information	Remarks and references to Appendices
PAS	July 1st		CRE Chateau de la Haie Defences.	SBN
"	2nd-3rd		ditto.	PBN
"	4-5th		CRE with S.S.O.T. Chateau de la Haie Duets	PBN
"	6-10th		CRE (Sick)	PBH
"	11		CRE attended the inspection of 457 Field Coy. by Corps Commander.	PBN
"	12th		CRE modes and inspected Sto. Baths.	PBN
"	13th		Sto order received giving entraining orders & move n/o 22nd Corps Area	PBN
"	14th		NIL	PBN
PAS.	15th		Entrained 6.12 am at DOULLENS for 22nd Corps Area.	PBN
	16th		Train.	PBN
TOURS	17th-18th			PBN
ST IMOGES	19th			PBN
"	20th		CRE inspecting roads & water supplies	PBN
CHAMERY	21st-22nd		CRE up the Line.	PBN
"	23rd-25th		CRE Roads Bridges & water supplies	PBN
NANTEUIL	26-27		NIL.	PBN

Original

Army Form C. 2118.

WAR DIARY
or
INTELLIGENCE SUMMARY.
(Erase heading not required.)

VOL. 19.

H.Q. Char. Divl. R.E.

Place	Date	Hour	Summary of Events and Information	Remarks and references to Appendices
NANTEUIL	29.		C.R.E. inspects Roads and proposed line of advance to be held by Field Companies in case of counter attack.	F.P.N.
"	30.			I.B.N.
HAUTVILLERS	31.		Moved to HAUTVILLERS. — BISSEUIL.	P.N.

Arnott WEIRE

Maj. & Lieut.

CRE 62

3. 8. 18

W.D. 20

Original
Confidential.

War Diary
of
H.Q. 62nd Divisional R.E.

from
August 1st. 1918.
to
August 31st 1918.

VOLUME XX.

WAR DIARY
or
INTELLIGENCE SUMMARY.
(Erase heading not required.)

Army Form C. 2118.

HQ 62nd Divnl. R.E.
VOL XX   Original

Place	Date	Hour	Summary of Events and Information	Remarks and references to Appendices
	1918.			
BISSEUIL	4/8/18		Entrained at EPERNAY & moved to PAS. Detrained MONDICOURT.	SW
PAS.	15/8/18		Moved from PAS to AUTHIE.	SW
AUTHIE	19/8/18		Received orders to move to VI Corps area. Destination BAVINCOURT. Stayed night at GRENAS.	SW
GRENAS	20/8/18		Moved from GRENAS to BAVINCOURT.	SW
BAVINCOURT	21/8/18		Orders received to move back into IV Corps area. Moved from BAVINCOURT to DOULLENS.	SW
DOULLENS	22/8/18		Moved from DOULLENS to PAS.	SW
PAS.	23/8/18		Orders received to move back into VI Corps area. Moved to LA BRAZEQUE. 62nd. Divn. ordered to relieve 3rd. Divn. in Reserve 24.8.18.	SW
LA BRAZEQUE	24/8/18		Moved to LES QUESNOY FARM. Field Coys. marched to South of COURCELLES and sent for Reconnaissance of Roads forward of Railway.	SW
LES QUESNOY FARM →	25/8/18		Field Coys. and Pioneers worked on Roads and Water Supply from ERVILLERS to GOMIECOURT and COURCELLES all inclusive.	SW
	26/8/18		Work continued. Reconnaissance of dugouts for Mines and traps carried out by 457 Field Coy.	SW

Greenshield?
WE6 V1 9.15

WAR DIARY
or
INTELLIGENCE SUMMARY.
(Erase heading not required.)

Army Form C. 2118.

HQ 62nd Divnl R.E. Vol. XX. Original

Instructions regarding War Diaries and Intelligence Summaries are contained in F.S. Regs., Part II. and the Staff Manual respectively. Title pages will be prepared in manuscript.

Place	Date	Hour	Summary of Events and Information	Remarks and references to Appendices
LES QUESNOY FARM	27/8/18		As for 26.8.18.	SM
	28/8/18		Coys and OK.D.L.I. moved to GOMIECOURT and continued work on Roads and Water Supply. Roads in Northern half of Divnl. Sector allotted to D.L.I. and in Southern half to 460 Field Coy. Water Supply to 461 Field Coy to whom Water Lorries and Water Police were attached. Miscellaneous jobs to 457 Fd. Coy. All spare men of 457 Fd. Coy and 461 Field Coys work on roads under 460 Field Coy.	SM
	30/8/18		HQ. moved to GOMIECOURT.	
	31/8/18		Field Coys. and OK.D.L.I. continued work on Water Supply, Roads + dugouts.	SM

French Haire
CRE 62nd Divn
1.9.18

Vol 21.

Original
Confidential War Diary
of
Headquarters 62nd Divisional R.E.
from Septr. 1st 1918.
to Septr. 30th 1918.

VOL. XXI

Original

WAR DIARY
or
INTELLIGENCE SUMMARY.
(Erase heading not required.)

Army Form C. 2118.

H.Q. 62nd Divnl. R.E.
VOL. XXI

Place	Date	Hour	Summary of Events and Information	Remarks and references to Appendices
GOMIECOURT	SEPT 12th	—	C.R.E. inspected Roads in Divisional Area. All Companies employed on Roads, Wells, Water supplies, Camps etc in GOMIECOURT AREA	S.B.M.
"	12-10		C.R.E. on Roads, Water Supply, Baths etc	S.B.M.
MARICOURT WOOD	11th		Companies moved to VELU. C.R.E. moved to MARICOURT WOOD.	S.B.M.
	12th		C.R.E. inspected CANAL du NORD for possible crossings, proposed Ramps etc	S.B.M.
	13th		C.R.E. Road further Reconnaissance of CANAL du NORD.	S.B.M.
			Field Companies engaged in Clearing demolished Bridges, Ramps, Culverts etc	S.B.M.
	14-26th		Work on CANAL du NORD. Engineering:- Repair of Bed of Canal. Erecting Ramps.	S.B.M.
			Clearing debris in Road. Work from CANAL. Widening and Repair of Roads from CANAL to HAVRINCOURT. Construction of Infantry Landers. and footways across CANAL. DAM across CANAL etc.	
		J.35.c.0.0.		
	27th		C.R.E. moved to J.35.c.0.0.	S.B.M.
HERMIES	28th	6.A.M.	R.E. moved to HERMIES. Companies engaged in Bridges over CANAL de ST QUENTIN.	S.B.M.
FLESQUIERES		R.P.M.	C.R.E moved to "FLESQUIERES" Companies stacking Bridges over Canal at MARCOING	S.B.M.
	29-30		C.R.E. up the line, Tank Bridge erected over CANAL at St QUENTIN and several other Bridges to take Lorries and Horse Transport	S.B.M.

J. Bushell
Lt = 62nd Div R.E
3.10.18.

No. 22

ORIGINAL

Confidential

War Diary.

of

Headquarters - 62nd. Divisional R.E.

from:
October 1st 1918.
to
October 31st 1918.

Vol XXII

ORIGINAL H.Q. 62nd Divisional R.E.

Army Form C. 2118.

WAR DIARY
or
INTELLIGENCE SUMMARY.
Vol. XXII

(Erase heading not required.)

Instructions regarding War Diaries and Intelligence Summaries are contained in F. S. Regs., Part II. and the Staff Manual respectively. Title pages will be prepared in manuscript.

Place	Date	Hour	Summary of Events and Information	Remarks and references to Appendices
FLESQUIERES	Oct 1st	—	62nd Division relieved by 3rd Div. 62nd Div R.E. working on BRIDGES over CANAL d. ST QUENTIN	SBW
"	2nd		C.R.E. inspecting TANK and LORRY BRIDGES over CANAL ST QUENTIN	SBW
"	3–5		C.R.E. ——— BRIDGES and forward ROADS	SBW
"	6–9		C.R.E. Roads & Bridges	SBW
FLESQUIERES MESNIERES	10	10 AM	R.E. HQ moved to MESNIERES 457 Field Coy on R.S. 460 and 461st Field Coys. working on TANK BRIDGE over CANAL de ST QUENTIN under CE VI CORPS.	SBW SBW
MESNIERES	11			SBW
ESTOURMEL	12	10 AM	R.E. HQ. moved to ESTOURMEL	SBW
"	21		TANK BRIDGE completed. All field coys. rejoined Div. on Roads & water	SBW
"	14–16		Companies working on Roads, repair of wells and mopping BILLETS	SBW
"	17		C.R.E. at QUIEVY arranging solemn for crossing RIVER SELLE	SBW
"	17.		O.O. 71 issued	
"	18		C.R.E. amendment to O.O. 71 issued. R.E. HQ. moved to BEVILLERS	SBW
BEVILLERS	19.		C.R.E. on Bridge reconnaissances	SBW
"	20		All Companies engaged in Bridging the RIVER SELLE the attack over RIVER by Division	SBW

ORIGINAL

WAR DIARY
or
INTELLIGENCE SUMMARY.

H.Q. 62nd Divisional R.E.   Army Form C. 2118.

VOL. XXII.

No. 2

Place	Date	Hour	Summary of Events and Information	Remarks and references to Appendices
BEVILLERS	21st		C.R.E. reconnoitred forward Roads & Bridges.	SBN
	23rd		62nd DIV. Relieved by 3rd DIV. R.E. working on R.ds and Bridges	SBN
BEVILLERS	24th		R.E. H.Q. moved to SOLESMES. C.R.E. on forward Road Reconnaissance	SBN
SOLESMES			WARNING ORDER sent to Companies.	
	25th		All Companies moved to SOLESMES for work on Roads.	SBN
	26th		C.R.E. forward Road Reconnaissance in VERTAIN	SBN
	27th		" " " and BRIDGE widening in VERTAIN	SBN
	28.29-30th		" " "	
SOLESMES	31st	10 am	R.E. H.Q. moved from BEVILLERS to SOLESMES	SBN

Original

Confidential

War Diary

of

Headquarters - 62nd. Divisional R.E.

from

November 1st 1918 to November 30th 1918.

VOL. XXIII

Vol 23

ORIGINAL

WAR DIARY
or
INTELLIGENCE SUMMARY.

(Erase heading not required.)

Army Form C. 2118.

HEADQUARTERS,
62ND DIV. ENGINEERS.
A.G. ...... Rwal. R.E.
No. .... Vol. XXIII

Place	Date	Hour	Summary of Events and Information	Remarks and references to Appendices
SOLESMES	Nov. 1st - 2nd		C.R.E. Roads & Bridges	S.B.M
				S.B.M
ESCARMAIN	3		Preparations for attack.	S.B.M
"	4		62nd Div. attacked. R.E. on Bridges, Roads, Repairing Culverts &c.	S.B.M
			Div. H.Q. moved to RUESNES	S.B.M
RUESNES	5 Nov		Rpr. on Roads, Craters, Culvert Bridges &c. Moved to FRASNOY	S.B.M
FRASNOY	6th		Moved to LE TRIEHON Roads	S.B.M
FRASNOY	7th		Moved from FRASNOY to LE TRIEHON	S.B.M
LE TRIEHON	8th		Roads and Craters &c.	S.B.M
	9th		Moved to NEUF MESNIL	S.B.M
NEUF MESNIL	10th		Bridges over River SAMBRE (Pontoon Bridges) at SOUS LE BOIS.	S.B.M
	11th		Moved to SOUS LE BOIS (MAUBERGE)	S.B.M
MAUBERGE	12 - 15th		C.R.E. on Roads Bridges &c.	S.B.M
COLLERET	16th		March into Germany Commenced. Moved to COLLERET. RE and Pioneers	S.B.M
	17		Moved to LEERS FOSTEAU	found an Bivouac S.B.M
HAM SUR HEURE	18th		Moved to HAM SUR HEURE	General working on S.B.M
"	19th		HAM SUR HEURE	Roads &c. S.B.M

ORIGINAL

WAR DIARY
or
INTELLIGENCE SUMMARY.
(Erase heading not required.)

Army Form C. 2118.

HEADQUARTERS, 62ND DIVL. ENGINEERS.
No. VOL XXIII

Place	Date	Hour	Summary of Events and Information	Remarks and references to Appendices
	Nov.			
HAM SUR HEURE	20th		Moved to ACOZ — Companies & Pioneers working on Roads.	SBM
ACOZ	21st			SBM
METTET	22nd		Moved to METTET — Companies working on Roads.	SBM
do.	23		METTET	SBM
DENEE	24		Moved to DENEE	SBM
YVOIR	25th		Moved to YVOIR	SBM
CINEY	26th		CINEY	SBM
LIGNION	27th		Moved to LIGNION	SBM
	28–30th		CRE on Recce Reconnaissance Companies and Pioneers on Roads.	

James HORE
LtCol RE
3.12.18.

Report on work of 62nd Div:
R.Es from March to Nov: 1918.

(Rec: from R.E. Library 5ᵗʰ December 1934.)

REPORT BY C.R.E. 62nd. DIVISION OF ENGINEER WORK OF 62nd. DIVL. R.E.
during Operations - Period March 1918 to Nov.11th. 1918.

(a) MARCH, 1918.

1.   Owing to the 62nd. Division not being deeply involved in the retreat of March 1918, but little experience of use for guiding the conduct of R.E. operations in retreat was obtained.

2.   The Field Coys. were however grouped together, in an approximate approach to a Battalion organisation, not for fighting only but for R.E. work as well, and this was found to be of considerable advantage.

This was particularly the case with the grouping of the transport of all Coys. under the command of a Captain.

Although this quasi-battalion organisation was adopted largely through force of circumstances, the simplicity and certainty of command, administration and supply obtained thereby appears to me to be the evidence in support of the value of a permanent Battalion Organisation for Divisional R.E.

3.   No new technical experience was obtained.

(b) JULY, 1918. BATTLE OF THE MARNE.

1.   The 62nd. Division was one of two Divisions attached to 5th. French Army during the attacks of that Army on 19th. July between RHEIMS and EPERNAY.

2.   The operations assumed a semi-mobile nature, an advance of some 5 miles being made in 10 days.

3.   The conditions were as follows:-

(a) The country was hilly and very thickly wooded except in the valleys.

(b) Water supplies from natural sources were ample.

(c) The ground had been fiercely fought over for 3 days prior to the advance.

(d) There was no opportunity whatever for previous reconnaissance. Taking over from Italians and French Colonial troops and strange French maps did but little to remedy this.

It was found that roads were extraordinarily little damaged and by getting labour on to them very early, it was not difficult to make and keep them.

Two lorry loads of picks, shovels, sandbags, and tracing tapes and 8 of barbed wire, proved more than sufficient to meet all demands, and about half of these stores were returned to the French on withdrawal of the Division.

The Field Coys. were at first grouped together, with their transport also grouped together and held as a reserve to resist a possible counter attack. This did not materialise, but the grouping was retained and again worked very well as regards the employment of the Field Coys. in proper R.E. work.

(c) OPERATIONS COMMENCING AUGUST 21st. 1918.

The experience of the 62nd. Division did not include any

.... preparative

preparative work for the battle, but from the 23rd. August the Division took part in all the major operations and the following conclusions are arrived at:-

1. A reconnaissance officer, on a motor bicycle when possible, reporting direct to C.R.E. was very useful.

2. Valuable reports were obtained by use of intelligent N.C.O.s for reconnaissance, whenever they were set definite tasks.

3. Mounted Orderlies drawn from transport of Field Coys. were useful.

4. With the additional transport provided by a small size German G.S. wagon, R.E. Headquarters required no other transport from Division from the beginning to the end of the advance and left no equipment behind.

5. The loss, early in the advance, of the Box Car was severely felt.

6. The supply of the more essential and portable R.E. stores was assured to the end of the advance by taking every opportunity of staging the Dump forward on Coy. bridging wagons. This Dump consisted of picks, shovels, nails, hammers, sandbags, tracing tape, C.I. culverts.
Even in rapidly moving warfare there is a steady and legitimate demand for sandbags.
By leaving the bridging equipment to be brought forward at intervals by Corps lorries, it was possible to keep this Dump mobile without extra transport. It started with 10 pontoon wagon loads on 27th. August and after minor replenishments, 3 wagon loads were handed over to Corps on 5th. November, 10 miles west of MAUBEUGE.

7. Some arrangements are necessary for R.E. examination of enemy Pioneer prisoners.

8. In advancing through a district from which the civilians have not been evacuated, useful results can be obtained by ordering them early to work on roads. After a few days difficulties arise, but while they are still disorganised and perhaps frightened, they were found willing on receipt of orders from their local Mayors to turn out and work. They work well and require no supervision.

9. Parties following the attack closely, and repairing roads before unskilled hands start filling shell holes with earth, saved much subsequent work.

10. Constant mudscraping enabled indifferent roads to carry a surprising amount of traffic.

11. Each Battalion of the Division was supplied and maintained with 2000 yds. tracing tape from the beginning of May and this proved very useful on several occasions.

(sd) L.C.TRENCH.

Lt.-Col.,R.E.,
C.R.E., 62nd. Division.

PA IN BOX 3074

PUBLIC RECORD OFFICE.

CLOSED FOR 100 YEARS

One Document, being 62 DIVISION (a): Headquarters Branches and Services: Assistant Provost Marshal: W/O 95/3074 1917 JAN — 1919 MAR

has been removed to W/O 154/72

March 1965

G. H. Adams

P. McCaffrey P.P.

(12517) Wt. 10696/324 3,000 9/32 Hw. G.620

Original

Confidential War Diary

of

Headquarters - 22nd Divisional R.E.

from

December 1st. 1918.

to

December 31st 1918.

Vol. XXIV.

Original

Army Form C. 2118.

WAR DIARY
or
INTELLIGENCE SUMMARY.
(Erase heading not required.)

No. VOL. XXIV

Place	Date	Hour	Summary of Events and Information	Remarks and references to Appendices
LEGNION	DEC 1st–4th		CRE on Road Reconnaissance. Companies & Pioneers working on Roads.	SBM
	5th		Movrs to CHATEAU at BARVAUX CONDROZ.	SBM
	6–9		BARVAUX CONDROZ (on the 6th CRE visited GERMAN CAMP at ELSENBORN) with O.C. 6ns Division	SBM
BARVAUX	9th & 10th		Movrs to BONTHOZ	SBM
	11th		MARCHED to VILLE near FERRIERE	SBM
	12th		" " FORGE	SBM
	13th		" " GRAND HALLEUX	SBM
	14th		" " VILLE DU BOIS	SBM
	15th		VILLE DU BOIS	SBM
	16th		Moved to DIEDENBERG	SBM
	17		" " WERTSFELD	SBM
	18th–20		WERTSFELD	SBM
	21		Marched to HELLENTHAL	SBM
	22		" " REIFFERSCHEID	SBM
	23		" " SCHLEIDEN	SBM
	24–31st		SCHLEIDEN. All RE employed in erecting STABLES, LATRINES, COOK HOUSES and making Tables, Forms & Beds for Divisional Headquarters.	SBM

21.12.18
J.W. Brooks Lt Col
CRE 6th Div

Original.
Confidential.

War Diary.

of

Hd. Qrs. 62nd. Divisional R.E.

from

January 1st. 1919
to
January 31st 1919.

Vol. XXV

Original.

WAR DIARY JANUARY 1919
or
INTELLIGENCE SUMMARY. 62nd Div. R.E. H.Q.
Vol. XXV

Army Form C. 2118.

Instructions regarding War Diaries and Intelligence Summaries are contained in F. S. Regs., Part II. and the Staff Manual respectively. Title pages will be prepared in manuscript.

(Erase heading not required.)

Place	Date	Hour	Summary of Events and Information	Remarks and references to Appendices
SCHLEIDEN	1-1-19		C.R.E. and Chief Engineer 2nd Army at EUSKIRCHEN.	ZF13
"	2-6th		All Conferences on Stabling Cookhouses Ablution Benches Etc, in their respective Brigade Group Areas. R.A.R.E. sections similarly employed with R.A Group at GEMUND	ZF13 ZF13
"	7-1-19		C.R.E. with D.A.D.R. on roads.	ZF13
"	8-1-19		C.R.E. visits all conferences.	ZF13
"	9-1-19		All conferences + R.A.R.E. on Stabling Cookhouses Etc	ZF13
"	10-1-19		C.R.E. to BLANKENHEIM, as to reserves of place for R.E Material.	ZF13
"	11-1-19, 14-1-19		C.R.E. inspects work of R.A.R.E. sections in + around GEMUND	ZF13
"	15-1-19		C.E. IX Corps visits C.R.E. at SCHLEIDEN	ZF13
"	16-1-19		C.R.E. to 457 Field Coy at MECHERNICH.	ZF13
"	17-1-19, 20-1-19		All conferences + R.A.R.E. on Stabling Hutting Cookhouses Etc in their Group Areas	ZF13
"	21-1-19		C.R.E. visits all conferences + R.A.R.E.	ZF13
"	22-1-19		C.R.E. with G.S.O.1. inspecting H.Q. Area.	ZF13
"	23-1-19		C.R.E. to KOMMERN inspecting Rat. Supply.	ZF13
"	24-1-19, 25-1-19		Corps + R.A.R.E section on Stabling Rifle Ranges Hutting Etc. in Group Areas	ZF13
"	26-1-19		C.R.E visits all conferences + R.A.R.E. inspecting their work in respective Group Areas	ZF13
"	31-1-19		C.R.E to GEMUND inspecting work of R.A.R.E section.	ZF13

[signature] Major
A/C.R.E 62 2nd R.E.

WS 26.

Original
Confidential
War Diary
of
H.Q. 2nd. Divisional R.E.

From
February 1st 1919
to
February 28th 1919.

VOL. XXVI.

Original

Army Form C. 2118.

HEADQUARTERS.

Instructions regarding War Diaries and Intelligence Summaries are contained in F. S. Regs., Part II. and the Staff Manual respectively. Title pages will be prepared in manuscript.

WAR DIARY
or
INTELLIGENCE SUMMARY.

FEBRUARY 1919

62 Div R.E. H.Q.

VOL XXVI

(Erase heading not required.)

Place	Date	Hour	Summary of Events and Information	Remarks and references to Appendices
SCHLEIDEN	1-2-19		C.R.E. to 457 Field Coy NIECHERNICH inspecting work in Coy Group Area	ZZ913.
"	2-2-19		C.E. IX Corps visits CRE at SCHLEIDEN.	ZZ913
"	3-2-19 6-2-19		All Coys + RARE on Stabling, Hutting, Rifle Ranges + Schemes	ZZ913
"	7-2-19		CRE to conference at Div H.Q.	ZZ913
"	8-2-19 9-2-19		All Coys + RARE on Stabling, Hutting, Rifle Ranges + Schemes	ZZ913.
"	10-2-19		CRE to conference at 185. Bde H.Q. by IX Corps Commander.	ZZ913.
"	11-2-19 15-2-19		All Coys + RARE on Stabling, Hutting, Rifle Ranges + Schemes	ZZ913
"	16-2-19		CRE visits all Conferences + RARE (Inspection of work)	ZZ913
"	17-2-19 18-2-19		All Coys + RARE on Stabling, Hutting, Rifle Ranges + Schemes	ZZ913
"	19-2-19		CRE to KALL inspecting work on Stables etc.	ZZ913.
"	20-2-19		CRE visits C.E. IX Corps inspecting work on Divisional Area.	ZZ913
"	23-2-19 23-2-19		CRE inspecting work in Brigade Group Areas.	ZZ913.
"	24-2-19 28-2-19		All Coys + RARE return on Stabling, Hutting, Rifle Ranges Schemes etc. Lt Col French R.E. CRE 62 Div hands the Division to take up appointment at War Office. 23-2-19 Major Froggatt R.E. of 461 Field Coy. Acting C.R.E.	ZZ913

Froggatt
Major
A/CRE 62 Div. R.E.

Vol I

Original
Confidential
War Diary.
of
H.Q. Highland Divisional R.E.
from
March 1st 1919
to
March 31st 1919.

Vol. XXVII

ORIGINAL
VOL XXVII

Army Form C. 2118.

WAR DIARY
March 1919

INTELLIGENCE SUMMARY. 62nd Divisional R.E. H.Q.

(Erase heading not required.)

Instructions regarding War Diaries and Intelligence Summaries are contained in F.S. Regs., Part II. and the Staff Manual respectively. Title pages will be prepared in manuscript.

Place	Date	Hour	Summary of Events and Information	Remarks and references to Appendices
SCHLEIDEN	1-3-19		CRE round Field Coys & RARE section inspecting work	ZA713
"	2-3-19 & 4-3-19		All Coys on Ranges Balloon shooting etc	ZA713
"	5-3-19		461. Field Coy move to new area at FRAU WULLERSHEIM.	ZA713
"	6-3-19 & 9-3-19		Coys finishing off work in respective Bde Group Areas.	ZA713
"	10-3-19		45-Y Field Coy move to new area at WISSERSHEIM.	ZA713
"	11-3-19 & 12-3-19		RARE making & finishing guard hut for ration stand at OLEF	ZA713
DUREN	13-3-19		CRE & Headquarters move to new area at DUREN.	ZA713
"	14-3-19 & 19-3-19		CREs dump formed in DUREN BARRACKS CRE inspecting range at DROVE	ZA713
"	26-3-19		CE VI Corps visits DROVE range with CRE. From 15-3-19 the	ZA713
"			62nd Division will be known as the HIGHLAND DIVISION	ZA713
"	23-3-19 & 25-3-19		Coys on work in their respective Bde Group Areas. Baths Washhouses etc	ZA713
"	26-3-19 & 27-3-19		do " " " " "	Z
"	26-3-19		Commander in Chief pays goodbye to the Division	ZA713
"	29-3-19 & 31-3-19		Coys & RARE section on work in their respective Bde Group Areas	ZA713

D. Doyall
Major R.E.
A/CRE Highland Division

ORIGINAL

WAR DIARY

H.Q. HIGHLAND DIV

RE

VOL. XXIX

MAY 1919

Army Form C. 2118.

WAR DIARY
or
INTELLIGENCE SUMMARY.
(Erase heading not required.)

HEADQUARTERS R.E. HIGHLAND DIVISION

MAY 1919

Place	Date	Hour	Summary of Events and Information	Remarks and references to Appendices
KEUZAU	1-5-19 to 31-5-19		All Units were employed on R.E. Service in the Divisional Area	
	5-5-19		Colonel COUSSMAKER D.S.O. M.C. O.E. proceeded on leave to U.K.	
	5-5-19		Major SHARPE R.E. acts C.R.E. during absence of Col. COUSSMAKER	
	15-5-19		457 Field Coy paraded at DUNEN AERODROME with 2nd Brigade for inspection by the Army Commander, General ROBERTSON.	
	23-5-19		Colonel COUSSMAKER returns from leave	
	24-5-19		Major SHARPE returns to 460 Field Coy.	

J.J. Coussmaker
Lt Colonel
C.R.E. HIGHLAND DIVISION.

Confidential.

WAR DIARY

of

C.R.E. HIGHLAND Division.

(Volume XXX)

From 1.6.19.

To 30.6.19.

Army Form C. 2118.

WAR DIARY
or
INTELLIGENCE SUMMARY.

(Erase heading not required.)

Head quarters. R.E.
Highland Division
JUNE 1919.

Instructions regarding War Diaries and Intelligence Summaries are contained in F. S. Regs., Part II. and the Staff Manual respectively. Title pages will be prepared in manuscript.

Place	Date	Hour	Summary of Events and Information	Remarks and references to Appendices
KREUZAU	1st to 30th		H.Qrs. Section employed on general work for Headquarters; and moving R.E. dump to KREUZAU, building shed for small stores.	nil. nil.
	18th		Composite Field Coy under Major SHARPE proceeded to OPLADEN in case of hostilities recommencing should the Peace terms not be signed. Composite Coy moved to HILDEN.	nil.
	20th		PEACE SIGNED.	nil
	24th		Composite Coy returns to former billets.	nil
	29th		Captain W.E.LOYD proceeds to IV Corps to act S.O.R.E. returning on 28th	nil.
	10th		Lieut G.H.P. Wolfenden acts adjutant during the absence of Capt. Loyd	nil.
			DEPARTURES	
			ARRIVALS	
			HONOURS.	
	3rd		Major SHARPE awarded M.C. 18th Captain WALKER. 2nd i.c. 461 Coy 1st Major F.W. RICHARDS demobilised.	nil. nil.
	3rd		Lieut Underhill " M.C. 23rd Major OATES. O.C. 461 Coy	nil.
			30th Captain FOOTE O.C. 457 Coy 14th Captain I.F.W. demobilised.	nil.

F. ? ???
LIEUT. COLONEL
C.R.E. HIGLAND Div

(6414) Wt. W3906/P1607 2,500,000 7/18 McA & W Ltd (E 3591) Forms W3091/4. Army Form W.3091.

Cover for Documents.

Nature of Enclosures.

CONFIDENTIAL

WAR DIARY.
of
HEADQUARTERS R.E.

From JULY 1st to JULY 31st

VOL XXXI

Notes, or Letters written.

WAR DIARY or INTELLIGENCE SUMMARY.
(Erase heading not required.)

Army Form C. 2118.

JULY 1919

HEADQUARTERS ROYAL ENGINEERS HIGHLAND DIVISION

Place	Date	Hour	Summary of Events and Information	Remarks and references to Appendices
KREUZAU	1st to 31st		Headquarters Section employed throughout the month on R.E. Services for Division. Cook house and dining hall contracted for the Infantry party attended. Completing Store shed at the R.E. dump, and bridging stream for lorries.	ref. ref.
			Moving Prehistoric animals to take part in the IV Corps Tattoo	ref.
	22nd		Show taking place on August 16th. C.R.E. attended R.E. Sports and Peace Celebrations.	ref.
	30th		Capt. W.E. LOYD proceeds on 14 days leave to U.K.	ref.
	29th		Lieut. G.J. GRIFFIN joins H. Qrs. to act as Adjutant during absence of Capt. W.E. LOYD.	ref.

F.J. McMahon
Lieut.-Colonel, R.E.
C.R.E. 1st Highland Division

Confidential.

War Diary.

of

Highland Divisional Engineers.

From Aug. 1st 1919.
To Aug 31st 1919.

Army Form C. 2118.

WAR DIARY
or
INTELLIGENCE SUMMARY

(Erase heading not required.)

AUGUST 1919   H.Q.R.E.   Highland Division

Instructions regarding War Diaries and Intelligence
Summaries are contained in F. S. Regs., Part II.
and the Staff Manual respectively. Title pages
will be prepared in manuscript.

Place	Date	Hour	Summary of Events and Information	Remarks and references to Appendices
KREUZAU	1		C.R.E. meets C.E. IV Corps at NIDEGGEN Tattoo Camp. Adjutant visits BOGHIEM Range	
	2		C.R.E. and assistant adjutant R.E. visit German contract works in Area. Adjutant visits Boghiem Range	
	3		C.R.E. and Adjutant visit Boghiem Rifle Range. All Ranks informed of early move to U.K.	
	4		C.R.E. visits STOCKHEIM and NIDEGGEN Tattoo Camp.	
	5		Received administrative instructions of Division's move to U.K. Adjutant visits Boghiem & PUSSAU Ranges	
	6		C.R.E. visits Divisional Wagon Park, Gun Factory, Dūren. Adjutant closes work at Boghiem	
	7		Wagon Limber G.S. one and medical cart sent to Divisional Wagon Park Duren.	
	8		H.Q.R. 10 horses left for Duren Arundel Collecting Camp	
	9		H.Qrs. closed at 1400 hours & conveyed by lorry to Duren. Assistant Adjutant ill. 2 G.O.R. Sgt. & Corporal acquiring it.	
DUREN		16:30	H. Qrs. entrained	
CHARLEROI	10	07:00	By train 2 all Ranks	
TOURNAI		16:00	By train. All Ranks H.Y.	
LILLE		18:30	By train	
BETHUNE		20:30	By train	
CALAIS	11	07:00	By train. Breakfast at No.6 Camp. Embarked S.S. Prince Leopold & sailed at 11:40 hrs.	
FOLKESTONE		13:00	Proceed to SHORNCLIFFE Stn. entrained. Supper at PETERBORO 23:00 hrs	

(continued)

WAR DIARY
or
INTELLIGENCE SUMMARY.
(Erase heading not required.)

Army Form C. 2118.

H. Qrs. R.E. Highland Div.

Place	Date	Hour	Summary of Events and Information	Remarks and references to Appendices
CLIPSTONE	August 1916 12	0200	Detrained & marched to No. 3 lines	
	13-15		"marching in". Inspection of Barrack furniture & R.E. fixtures	
	16		Lieut. H.A. Underhill rejoins H.Qrs	
	17		Sunday	
	18-19		Continuation of Inspection	
	20		Fire Regulations etc. detailed from units stationed in No. 3 lines	
	21		Inspection by C.R.E. of Cook houses & Subsidiary Buildings	
	22		Lieut. H.A. Underhill leaves H.Qrs. to rejoin 1/1/1/7-1th Coy at CANNOCK CHASE	
	23		Capt. W.E. Loyd returned from leave & resumed duties as adjutant	
	24		All spare men on fatigue duties	
	31st		All men joining before July 1st 1916 to be demobilised forthwith.	

L.J. Snowman
C.R.E. Highland Division

www.ingramcontent.com/pod-product-compliance
Lightning Source LLC
Chambersburg PA
CBHW080914230426
43667CB00015B/2674